George Iles, R. R. (Richard Rogers) Bowker

Reader's Guide in economic, social and political Science

George Iles, R. R. (Richard Rogers) Bowker

Reader's Guide in economic, social and political Science

ISBN/EAN: 9783337130978

Printed in Europe, USA, Canada, Australia, Japan

Cover: Foto ©ninafisch / pixelio.de

More available books at **www.hansebooks.com**

THE READER'S GUIDE

IN

Economic, Social and Political Science

BEING

A CLASSIFIED BIBLIOGRAPHY, AMERICAN, ENGLISH, FRENCH AND
GERMAN, WITH DESCRIPTIVE NOTES, AUTHOR, TITLE
AND SUBJECT INDEX, COURSES OF READING,
COLLEGE COURSES, ETC.

EDITED BY

R. R. BOWKER AND GEORGE ILES

NEW YORK
THE SOCIETY FOR POLITICAL EDUCATION
G. P. PUTNAM'S SONS, Publishing Agents
New York and London
1891

Copyright, 1891,
By The Society for Political Education.

INTRODUCTION.

When the Society for Political Education was established in 1880, with that devoted apostle of progress, Richard L. Dugdale, as its first Secretary, its field was almost unworked. There seemed to be little interest in the subject in America; books on political economy and allied topics were few and slow of sale; the Society was a pioneer in the renascence which has since developed. One of its first tasks was to acquaint Americans with the literature of its subject, and one of its first publications therefore was the Bibliography (Tract No. 2) in the preparation of which Mr. Dugdale had the co-operation of W. G. Sumner, David A. Wells, W. E. Foster, Geo. Haven Putnam, and others. The progress of ten years is well shown in the present work, in which the bulk of the great editorial labor has been done by my indefatigable associate, George Iles, a worthy successor of Richard L. Dugdale, who has been Secretary of the Society during the past two years. The Guide has had the very helpful co-operation of a great number of specialists in most of the specific subjects, and is notably indebted to Professors E. R. A. Seligman, Richmond M. Smith, and F. J. Goodnow, of the University Faculty of Political Science of Columbia College, Worthington C. Ford, Rev. J. G. Brooks, of Cambridge, Mass., and Percival Chubb; to Professors Felix Adler and James Bryce; to Messrs. H. C. Baird, G. H. Baker, F. Bancroft, Geo. W. Cable, D. R. Dewey, D. B. Eaton, B. E. Fernow, David Dudley Field, Rev. R. J. Holaind, S.J., C. H. Kellogg, Gifford Pinchot, Wm. Potts, W. M. F. Round, W. W. Spooner, D. A. Wells, Andrew D. White, Horace White, F. W. Whitridge, and C. F. Wingate, for general or special revision.

The present Bibliography is planned on the general lines of cataloguing approved by the American Library Association, and provides in fact, though not in form of page, a department of the "A. L. A. Catalogue." The main features are a classification by specific subjects;

suggestions as to courses of reading at the head of each, when practicable and desirable; and descriptive notes, impartial in character, under the more important titles. The titles are given in full when so obtainable, with size, price, etc., when possible. The size is given in the A. L. A. letter designations when examination permitted, otherwise by publishers' designations. The A. L. A. colon initials, for the most usual Christian names (as J: for John) are also used. Each title is independently entered, so that it can be cut out and pasted on the usual catalogue card. Under each heading, the titles are arranged in alphabets, according to the country of origin—American, English, French, German, etc.

The general arrangement of subjects has been made by the editors, after careful comparison with the scheme of the Columbia Faculty of Political Science, and largely on its lines. There are of course many titles which belong under more than one subject; these are given under one heading only, but the very full index will give clue to them in the others. The index comprises the titles in the addenda.

To some extent the subjects of this Guide occupy common ground with History and Law. But few titles in these departments of literature are given, as excellent bibliographies for both are in the hands of the public, namely, Soule's "Lawyers' Reference Manual of Law-Books and Citations" [Boston Book Co., Boston, formerly Soule & Bugbee, 1883], and Adams' "Manual of Historical Literature" [Harper, 1889].

It is believed that the courses in political and economic science at the leading American colleges, which are given in summary, will be found of interest. The courses prescribed for reading, elementary, intermediate, and advanced, have been carefully selected. In cases where the Guide is used by debating clubs, Tract No. 28 of the Society's series, "Questions for Debate," can accompany it with advantage.

It is hoped by the editors that their "labor of love" may be requited by its promotion of thoughtful attention to the important subjects to which this pamphlet offers a key and finally of good citizenship in America.

R: R. B.

NEW YORK, March, 1891.

TABLE OF CONTENTS.

	PAGE
POLITICAL ECONOMY:	
Bibliography, Methods of Study and Works of Reference,	5
History,	7
General Works—American,	9
English,	11
French,	14
German,	14
Essays and Criticisms,	16
LAND AND RENT,	18
Public Lands,	24
CAPITAL AND LABOR,	24
Property, Capital,	24
Profit, Interest, Usury,	25
Labor, History and Relations to Capital,	25
Trades Organizations, Strikes,	29
Wages,	31
Co-operation,	32
Profit-sharing,	33
Arbitration, Conciliation,	34
MONEY, CURRENCY, BANKING:	
Money, Currency,	35
Gold, Silver, Bimetallism,	38
Banking, Exchange, Credit,	40
Savings-banks, Speculation, Crises, Panics,	43
COMMERCE AND TRADE,	45
History, Works of Reference,	45
Prices,	46
Railroad Management and Legislation,	47
Canals,	52
Competition, Monopoly, Trusts and Boycotts,	52
Fire Insurance,	53
Life Insurance,	53
INTERNATIONAL TRADE,	54
Tariffs and Foreign Commerce, Historical and General Works,	54
For Protection,	58
For Free Trade or Tariff Reform,	60
Commercial Union, Reciprocity,	65
PUBLIC FINANCE,	66
Revenue, Taxation, Single Tax,	66
Public Debts,	72

TABLE OF CONTENTS.

	PAGE
SOCIAL SCIENCE AND SOCIOLOGY,	73
Socialism, Communism, Anarchism,	76
Population, Census,	81
Colonies, Colonization,	82
IMMIGRATION AND RACE QUESTIONS,	83
The Negro,	84
The Indian,	85
PAUPERISM AND POOR LAWS,	86
CHARITIES AND CHARITY ORGANIZATION,	87
PUBLIC HEALTH AND SANITATION,	88
WORKINGMEN'S DWELLINGS,	89
CRIME AND PRISONS,	90
THE LIQUOR QUESTION,	91
POLITICAL SCIENCE:	
General Works,	91
History and Early Institutions,	95
AMERICAN GOVERNMENT:	
Elementary Works,	96
Advanced Works,	98
Essays and Criticisms,	99
AMERICAN POLITICAL AND CONSTITUTIONAL HISTORY,	101
ENGLISH CONSTITUTION AND GOVERNMENT,	103
CANADIAN CONSTITUTION AND GOVERNMENT,	105
OTHER FOREIGN GOVERNMENTS AND CONSTITUTIONS,	106
GOVERNMENT ADMINISTRATION: General Works,	107
THE SUFFRAGE,	108
Election System, Electoral Reform,	108
Minority Representation,	110
CIVIL SERVICE AND ITS REFORM,	110
POST-OFFICE—TELEGRAPH SERVICE,	112
WAR AND NAVY,	113
FORESTRY,	113
Irrigation,	115
PARTIES, PARTY HISTORY,	115
Caucus, Machine,	116
PARLIAMENTARY PRACTICE,	116
CHURCH AND STATE,	116
MUNICIPAL GOVERNMENT,	118
Police,	119
INTERNATIONAL LAW, TREATIES, ARBITRATIONS AND DIPLOMACY,	119
STATISTICS AND STATISTICAL SCIENCE,	123
U. S. Government Publications,	125
ADDENDA,	126
READING COURSES,	128
COURSES IN ECONOMIC AND POLITICAL SCIENCES, AMERICAN COLLEGES AND UNIVERSITIES,	129
INDEX,	139

POLITICAL ECONOMY: BIBLIOGRAPHY, METHODS OF STUDY, AND WORKS OF REFERENCE.

Cossa's Guide is the best bibliography and historical sketch. His historical part, p. 73-227, ch. 2, summarizes ancient writers treating political economy (as Plato, Xenophon, Aristotle, Cicero, Seneca, Pliny, Cato), and those of the middle ages (as Magnus, Duns Scotus, Thomas Aquinas), and the other chapters (in the English edition) come up to 1880. For brief views of the literature and history of political economy, see introductions to or chapters in Laughlin's edition of Mill, exceptionally valuable for its biographical and bibliographical notes, Bowker's Economics, Perry's Elements, Ely's Introduction, McCulloch's edition of Adam Smith, Courcelle-Seneuil and Rau. Bibliographical notes are appended to most articles in Lalor's Cyclopedia. For full contents of works, see department Political Economy (p. 911-25), in Brooklyn Library Catalogue, to be found in most large libraries. For analytic references to specific chapters in general works, see the valuable section headings of Andrews' "Institutes." G. P. Putnam's Sons, N. Y., R. Clarke & Co., Cincinnati, and other booksellers issue priced catalogues of economic books. The *Political Science Quarterly* (Columbia Coll.), New York, and *Quarterly Journal of Economics* (Harvard Univ.), Boston, register current bibliography. See also numerous articles in periodicals (consult Poole's Index, etc., and Brooklyn Lib. Cat., p. 911-25), especially Rossi's "Introduction à l'histoire des doctrines économiques" (preface to his historical lectures at the Collège de France), in *Journal des Economistes*, v. 2, 1842; Baudrillart's "De l'histoire de l'économie politique" in same, v. 5 (new series). 1867; W. Newmark's "Progress of Economic Science during the Last 30 Years," in *Jour. Statis. Soc.* of London, v. 24. 1861; T. E. Cliffe-Leslie's "Political Economy in Germany," in *Fortnightly Rev.*, July, 1875; C. F. Dunbar's "Economic Science in America, 1786-1876," in *North Amer. Review*, Jan., 1876; H. S. Foxwell's "The Economic Movement in England," in *Quar. Journal of Economics*, Oct., 1887; and C. Gide's "Political Economy in France," *Political Science Quarterly*, Dec., 1890. Prof. Boehm-Bawerk's "Capital and Interest," 1890, is a critical history of economical theory, valuable and suggestive.

Adams, H: C. **Outlines of Lectures on Political Economy.** Ann Arbor, Mich., Sheehan & Co., 1886. 8°, 85 p. 50 c.

Prepared for the use of students at Michigan and Cornell Universities, where the author lectures on political economy and finance. The author shows that political economy should seek not merely to explain the individual actions of men, but also to discover a scientific basis for the formation and government of industrial society.

Colange, LEO de, *ed.* **Dictionary of Commerce, Manufacture, etc.** Boston, Estes & Lauriat, 1880-1. 2 v. 8°, $13.50.

Includes also commercial law, banking, exchange, insurance, patents, canals, commercial geography of the world, customs regulations, docks, interest and annuities, licenses, maritime law, measures and weights, money, railroads, revenue regulations, shipping, tariff duties, taxation, etc.

Foster, W: E. References to Political and Economic Topics ; to accompany a series of lectures delivered in Providence, 1884-5. Providence, R. I., Providence Press Co., 1885. 27 p. D. pap., gratis.

Lalor, J: J., *ed.* **Cyclopædia of Political Science,** Political Economy, and the Political History of the United States, by the best American and European writers. Chicago, Melbert B. Cary & Co., 1883-4. 3 v., 847, 1055, 1136 p. O. $18.

An invaluable work of reference, well up to date, articles in alphabetical arrangement, from a few lines to elaborate special treatises. The foreign portion is mostly translated from Block's *Dict. de la Politique*, Coquelin and Guillaumin's *Dict. de l'Economie Politique*, Bluntschli's *Staatswörterbuch*, or original articles by Cliffe Leslie. U. S. political history, etc., are by Prof. Alex. Johnson. Nearly thirty leading American authorities are among the contributors in special subjects.

Laughlin, J. LAURENCE. Study of Political Economy. N. Y., Appleton, 1885. 153 p. S. $1.

Brings out the value of economics in discipline. Gives important hints to the teacher, minister, journalist, and lawyer. The ordinary student will find this manual of much directive service. It contains a brief bibliography.

Questions for debate in politics and economics, with subjects for essays and terms for definition. (Economic tract, no. 28.) N. Y., Society for Political Education, 1889. 40 p. O. pap., 25 c.

An enlarged and revised reissue of Economic tract, no. III.

Sumner, W: GRAHAM. Problems in Political Economy. N. Y., Holt, 1884. 125 p. S. flex. cl., $1.25.

A series of questions for students.

Bohn's Political Cyclopedia. Lond., Bohn, 1848. N. Y., Scribner & W. 4 v. D. $5.60.

"A dictionary of political, constitutional, statistical and forensic knowledge, covering civil administration, political economy, finance, commerce, laws and social relations." Not brought up to date.

Cumming, A. N. Value of Political Economy to Mankind. Glasgow, Maclehose.

The Oxford Cobden Club prize essay for 1880.

McCulloch, J: R. Dictionary of Commerce and Commercial Navigation. New ed., rev. by A. J. Wilson. Lond. and N. Y., Longmans, 1882. il. 8°, $21.

McCulloch, J: R. The Literature of Political Economy. Lond., 1845. 8°.

Contains a list of the most important works on the subject, published before 1845.

Macleod, H: D. Dictionary of Political Economy. V. 1. Lond., 1863. O. $12.

A work of great research, but colored by the author's peculiar views. A second edition of v. 1 is "preparing," and v. 2, completing this work, is "in progress."

Palgrave, R. H. INGLIS, *ed.* Dictionary of Political Economy. [*In prep.*] Lond. and N. Y., Macmillan.

In this work it is proposed to state the position of political economy at the present time, with references to history, law, and commerce. Short notices of deceased economists will be included, with mention of their principal writings. A list of leading living writers will be given. An eminent staff of contributors is engaged for this work, which is to be published in 12 to 14 parts of 128 p. each. Part I. ready January, 1891, others at intervals of about three months.

Sidgwick, H: Scope and Method of Economic Science. Lond. and N. Y., Macmillan, 1885. D. 60 c.

Cossa, LUIGI. **Guide to the Study of Political Economy,** with preface by W. S. Jevons ; tr. from 2d Italian ed. (1877). Lond. and N. Y., Macmillan, 1880. 237 p. S. $1.25.
The best manual of the kind. It sketches the history of economic theory, explains its leading methods, and gives sound criticisms of economic writers, with bibliography.

Coquelin, C:, and **Guillaumin,** U. G., *eds.* **Dictionnaire de l'économie politique.** Paris, 1851-3. 3d ed., 1864. 2 v., 970, 883 p. 8°.
A standard of great merit, its articles being written by the best French writers on economic science. An alphabetic cyclopedia of economic science—" a scientific monument," says Cossa, " such as no other nation can boast of." Needs re-writing to date. There is no English translation.

Say, LEON, and **Chailley,** Jos., *eds.* **Nouveau Dictionnaire de l'économie politique.** Livraisons 1-3. Paris, Guillaumin, 1890. 384 p. 8°.
A new work on the lines of the Coquelin dictionary. Excellent, but chiefly treats of French questions and refers but little to other than French authors.

Conrad, J., **Elster,** L., **Lexis,** W., **Loening,** EDGAR, *eds.* **Handwörterbuch der Staatswissenschaft.** V. 1, pts. 1-6, 1046 p. V. 2, pts. 7-9, 446 p. 8°. Jena, Fischer, 1890.
To be completed in 35 pts. by 1892. The most comprehensive dictionary of political economy ever published, with collaborators from all countries.

Schönberg, GUSTAV, *ed.* **Handbuch der Politischen Oekonomie.** Tübingen, 1890. 3d ed. 3 v. 8°, 1888.
Written in coöperation with 21 of the most eminent German authorities, chiefly of the historical school. The most comprehensive work for those desirous of studying modern views.

On the study and methods of political economy, see also Buckle's remarkable passage in his Hist. of Civilization, v. 1, p. 150-8; Mill on Method in Political Economy, in his Essays; Leslie Stephens' Hist. of English Thought, v. 2, p. 243-328, and, in present day, Science Economic Discussions, by Prof. R. M. Smith and others, and articles in the economic and general periodicals (consult Poole's Index and for latest issues, the quarterly Coöperative Index). Among them Henry George in *Popular Science Monthly*, v. 16, 1879.

POLITICAL ECONOMY : HISTORY.

Ely, R: T. **The Past and the Present of Political Economy.** Baltimore, Johns Hopkins University, 1884. 64 p. O. pap., 35 c.

Wells, DAVID A. **Recent Economic Changes,** and their effect on the production and distribution of wealth, and the well-being of society. N. Y., Appleton, 1889. 12+493 p. O. $2.
A graphic recital of the economic revolution effected by the progress of invention and enterprise. Tendencies now supreme in commerce and finance are traced to their origin, with incidental light on their probable course in the future. The work is a storehouse of fact admirably digested.

Ashley, W. J. **Introduction to English Economic History and Theory.** Part 1: The Middle Ages ; The Manor and Village Community; Merchant and Craft Guilds; Economic Theories and Legislation. N.Y., Putnam, 1889. 8°, $1.50.

Bagehot, WALTER. **Economic Studies.** Lond. and N. Y., Longmans, 1880. 8°, $3.50.
Contains some fresh and vigorous essays on the early economic condition of nations.

Ingram, J: K. **History of Political Economy.** Lond. and N. Y., Macmillan, 1888. 250 p. O. $1.50.
A history of economic theory, reprinted with additions from the ninth edition of the Encyclopædia Britannica, with a preface by Prof. E. J. James. " The best outline in the English language," says Ely.

Ingram, J: K. **The Present Position and Prospects of Political Economy.** London, 1878.

Marshall, A. **The Present Position of Economics.** Lond. and N. Y., Macmillan, 1885. 60 c.
Author Prof. of Pol. Econ. in Univ. of Cambridge.

Rogers, J. E. THOROLD. **The Economic Interpretation of [English] History.** N. Y., Putnam, 1888. 547 p. O. $3.
Instructive as showing the powerful influence economics have had in English history.

Twiss, TRAVERS. **View of the Progress of Political Economy in Europe since the 16th Century.** Lond., 1847. 8°. [Out of print and scarce.]
An excellent work, very concise, but covers only a limited period—the last four centuries.

Blanqui, J. A. 1798–1854. **History of Political Economy in Europe.** Tr. by Emily J. Leonard, with an introduction by David A. Wells. N. Y., Putnam, 1880. xii+575 p. O. $3.
Not always trustworthy in its statements and criticisms, and half a century old. " A brilliant but light writer," says Cossa. Succeeded J. B. Say as professor.

Block, MAURICE. **Le progres de la science economique depuis Adam Smith.** Paris, 1890. 2 v. 8°.
Written from the classical standpoint. For advanced students. "A work which in some respects compares with the best productions of recent times in any country. Of the first importance and of enduring value."—*E. R. A. Seligman.*

Laveleye, EMILE de. **New Tendencies of Political Economy;** tr. by G: Walker. N. Y., I. S. Homans, 1879. 12°, pap., 25 c.

Villeneuve-Bargemont, J. P. A. de. **Histoire de l'économie politique.** Paris, 1841. 2 v. 8°.
Of religious bias, aiming to oppose a "Christian political economy" to the "English" doctrine. "Now wholly forgotten," says Cossa.

Dühring, E. **Kritische Geschichte der National Oekonomie und des Socialismus.** 1871. 3d ed., Berlin, 1879. 8°.
The most recent history, but ill-balanced, specially emphasizing List and Carey.

Eisenhart, H. **Geschichte der Nationalökonomik.** Jena, 1881. 243 p. 8°.
The most philosophical sketch of the subject.

Kautz, JULIUS. **Die Geschichtliche Entwickelung der National Oekonomie und ihrer Literatur.** Vienna, 1860. 2 v. 8°.
The best book on the subject. It has never been translated.

Roscher, W: **Geschichte der National Oekonomie in Deutschland.** Munich, 1874. 2 v. 8°.
Cossa calls this "the most remarkable and satisfactory work on the history of political economy in one of the most cultivated nations of Europe."

Roscher, W: **Zur Geschichte der Englischen Volkswirthschaftslehre.** Leipzig, 1851–2.
"A learned and elegant exposition of the changes in English political economy, 16th–17th centuries."—*Cossa.*

POLITICAL ECONOMY. GENERAL WORKS.

As elementary works, *American*, see Mason and Lalor's Primer; for private reading, Bowker's or Perry's (smaller book); for school study, Perry's or Chapin's (free trade), Steele's (protection), or F. A. Walker's "Elementary Course." *English*, see Jevons' capital Primer; Marshall's, readable and illustrative, or Macleod's, rather analytic and abstruse, also Roger's bright lessons Americanized by G. H. Putnam ; see also translations of Bastiat and About. For high school and college use, the leading works are Perry's (best known, now in 18th ed.), F. A. Walker's (scientific and moderate), Laughlin's (with good diagrams), Ely's ("historical school"), Andrew's (very succinct and scientific), and Thompson's or Bowen's (protectionist). Gregory, Sturtevant, and other writers also cover this field. The great writers of the past are Adam Smith, Ricardo (on rent), Malthus (on population), Mill; the early French economists; and, in America, H. C. Carey, head of the protectionist school. Of living or recent writers, Wells, the free-trade leader, Sumner, extremely individualistic, Amasa and his son F. A. Walker, and for the protectionists, Greeley and Denslow, may be noted among Americans; Cairnes, Jevons, Bagehot, Fawcett, Thorold Rogers, among English; Cherbuliez and Chevalier among French; Roscher and Cohn among Germans.

AMERICAN WORKS.

Andrews, E. B. **Institutes of Economics.** Boston, Silver, Burdett & Co., 1889. 227 p. D. $1.30.

Author Pres. of Brown Univ. "A succinct text-book" for colleges, high schools, and academies. Extremely concise and thorough in analysis ; references to the best authorities on special themes preface each section, and foot-notes guiding to illustrative facts follow.

Bowen, Francis. **American Political Economy.** 1870. New ed. N. Y., Scribner, 1885. D. $2.50.

Author Prof. at Harvard Univ. A systematic treatise, with special reference to the U. S. Includes remarks on management of the currency and finances since the outbreak of the war. Reviews Ricardo's doctrine of rent, and favors protection.

Bowker, R: R. **Economics for the People.** 1886. 3d ed. N. Y., Harper, 1890. 279 p., S. 75 c.

Author a business man. "Plain talks on economics, especially for use in business, in schools, and in women's reading classes." Intended for popular reading, as well as for study. Includes chapters on economic history and literature, and supersedes same writer's brief summary "Of Work and Wealth." Adopted in the Chautauqua reading course.

Carey, H: C. 1793-1879. **Principles of Social Science.** 1837-40. 3 v. Phila., H. C. Baird & Co. 8°, $3.

The comprehensive work on political economy of the most original of American economists, who is not merely the chief American advocate of protection. His views concerning value (as the cost of reproduction) and rent (opposing Ricardo by a theory of increasing production from land) command even more attention from German than from American economists. For full contents, see Brooklyn Lib. Cat.

Carey, H: C. **Manual of Social Science.** Condensed from Carey's Principles of Social Science by Kate McKean. Phila., H. C. Baird & Co. D. $2.25.

Chapin, A. L. **First Principles of Political Economy.** N. Y., Sheldon, 1880. 213 p., S. 60 c.

Author Pres. of Beloit Coll., Wis. A systematic and comprehensive text-book, orthodox school, with questions after each chapter.

Clark, J. B. **The Philosophy of Wealth;** economic principles newly formulated. Boston, Ginn & Co., 1886. 235 p. D. $1.10.

Not a text-book nor an exhaustive treatise, yet may be used with advantage by classes instructed partly by lectures and partly by topical reading. A work thoroughly scientific in treatment, fully recognizing the influence of moral forces in the economic field.

Denslow, VAN BUREN. **Principles of the Economic Philosophy of Society, Government, and Industry.** N. Y., Cassell, 1888. 782 p. O. $3.50.

A clear and full exposition of economics from the standpoint of a protectionist. Useful for its quotations of definitions by leading writers, and for diagrams. Has excellent indexes, personal and general.

Ely, R: T. **Introduction to Political Economy.** N. Y., Chautauqua Press [Hunt & Eaton], 1889. 358 p. O. $1.

Author Prof. in Johns Hopkins Univ., Baltimore, Secy. of Amer. Economic Assoc., and a leader of the "new school" of national or historical economists, of which this text-book, prepared for Chautauqua students, is representative. Has a brief course of reading and bibliography.

Greeley, HORACE. 1811–72. **Essays on Political Economy.** New ed. Phila., Porter & Coates, 1877. 16°, $1.

"Serving to explain and defend the policy of protection to home industry as a system of national coöperation for the elevation of labor." The famous editor of the N. Y. *Tribune* was, next to Carey, the great American apostle of protectionism.

Gregory, J. M. **New Political Economy.** Cincinnati, Van Antwerp, Bragg & Co., 1883. 12°, $1.20.

Laughlin, J. LAURENCE. **Elements of Political Economy**, with some application to questions of the day. N. Y., Appleton, 1887. 363 p. D. $1.50.

A text-book explaining the elementary principles of political economy, with illustrative charts, and series of questions and problems. Intended for American youth whose education ends with the high school or academy. Clear and compact.

Macvane, S. M. **Working Principles of Political Economy.** N. Y., Effingham, Maynard & Co., 1890. 392 p. 8°, $1.50.

Mason, A. B., and **Lalor**, J. J. **Primer of Political Economy;** in sixteen Definitions and forty Propositions. Chicago, McClurg, 1876. 67 p. 16°, 60 c.

Newcomb, SIMON. **Principles of Political Economy.** N. Y., Harper, 1886. 548 p. O. $2.50.

An elaborate treatise, scientific in structure.

Perry, A. L. **Elements of Political Economy.** 1866. 18th ed. N. Y., Scribner, 1883. 608 p. O. $2.50.

Author Prof. in Williams Coll. A systematic treatise, long the leading text-book in Amer. colleges, with a historical introduction and a free-trade chapter on American tariffs.

Perry, A. L. **Introduction to Political Economy.** N. Y., Scribner, 1877. 348 p. D. $1.50.

A simpler re-working of this author's well-known "Elements," in six chapters on Value, Production, Commerce, Money, Credit, Taxation.

Richmond, WILFRID. **Christian Economics.** N. Y., E. P. Dutton & Co., 1888. 278 p. D. $2.

A volume chiefly of sermons intended to enforce the ethical relations in economics.

Steele, GEO. M. **Outline Study of Political Economy.** N. Y., Chautauqua Press, 1885. 195 p. D. 60 c.

Author Principal of Wesleyan Acad., Wilbraham, Mass. Follows Carey, sums up in favor of protection and of taxation on expenditure, *e.g.*, rent. A Chautauqua text-book.

Sturtevant, J. M. Economics; or, The Science of Wealth. N. Y., Putnam, 1879. 343 p. D. $1.75.

Thompson, R. E. Political Economy, with special reference to the industrial history of nations. 1875. 3d rev. ed. Phila., Porter & Coates, 1882. 419 p. D. $1.50.
> An exposition by a teacher favorable to protection, Prof. in the Univ. of Pa. A third and revised edition of his work of 1875, "Social Science and National Economy."

Walker, AMASA. 1799-1875. **The Science of Wealth;** a Manual of Political Economy. 1866. Student's ed. Phila., Lippincott. 12°, $1.50.

Walker, FRANCIS A. **Political Economy.** (American Science Series—Advanced Course.) N. Y., Holt, 1887. 537 p., O. $2.
> Specially valuable in its elucidations of the questions of land and wages.

Walker, FRANCIS A. **Political Economy.** (American Science Series—Briefer Course.) N. Y., Holt, 1883. 490 p. O. $1.20.
> Specially valuable for "some applications of economical principles" (to questions of the day) which form the last part.

Walker, FRANCIS A. **First Lessons in Political Economy.** (American Science Series—Elementary Course.) N. Y., Holt, 1889. 323 p. D. $1.00.
> For use in high schools and academies. Suitable for youths of from 16 to 18.

Wayland, F. 1796-1865. **Elements of Political Economy.** 1852. Recast by A. L. Chapin. N. Y., Sheldon, 1878. 12°, $1.75.
> For many years a standard text-book.

Note.—The important "Systematic Political Science," by the Faculty of Political Science of Columbia College, 9 vols., 8°, now in preparation, will include a volume on "Historical and Practical Political Economy," by R. M. Smith, and another on the "Historical and Comparative Science of Finance" (a subject hitherto generally included in the English text-books on Political Economy), by Edwin R. A. Seligman.

ENGLISH WORKS.

Bagehot, WALTER. 1826-77. **Postulates of English Political Economy.** N. Y., Putnam, 1885. 114 p. D. $1.
> An examination of two leading postulates—the transferability of labor and of capital—masterly and suggestive. Points out to opposite parties the common ground on which they can be reconciled. Part of a comprehensive survey which the author did not live to complete. Author editor of *The Economist*, London.

Cairnes, J. E. 1824-75. **Character and Logical Method of Political Economy.** 1857. 2d ed. N. Y., Harper, 1875. 229 p. 12°, $1.50.
> Includes valuable chapters on the Malthusian doctrine of population and on Ricardo's theory of rent. Cossa declares Cairnes "foremost among contemporary English economists."

Cairnes, J. E. **Some Leading Principles in Political Economy Newly Expounded.** N. Y., Harper, 1874. 506 p. O. $2.50.
> This is specially valuable for the subject of wages, in regard to which it establishes the standard of sound doctrine, and for some points in international trade. It contributes also to a re-analysis of cost and supply and demand. For full contents, see Brooklyn Lib. Cat.

Fawcett, H: 1833-88. **Manual of Political Economy.** 1863. 6th ed. Lond. and N. Y., Macmillan, 1886. D. $2.60.
> Readers who have not the time or the preliminary training required by the more comprehensive works, will find in this volume a briefer and simpler statement of the doctrine taught by Mill. This edition contains a chapter on State Socialism and Land Nationalization, with additions on the precious metals, slavery, coöperation, local taxation, etc.

Fawcett, *Mrs.* M. G. **Political Economy for Beginners,** with questions. 1869. 7th ed. Lond. and N. Y., Macmillan, 1889. 227 p. S. 75 c.

Fawcett, *Mrs.* M. G. **Tales in Political Economy.** Lond., 1874. 104 p., 16°, 90 c.
Author wife of Prof. Fawcett, and a clear and clever writer.

Jevons, W. STANLEY. 1835–82. **The Theory of Political Economy.** 1871. 2d ed. Lond. and N. Y., Macmillan, 1879. 315 p. 8°, $3.
Less available for general readers, because it employs the methods and nomenclature of pure mathematics, but, partly for this reason, it is one of the recent works which have contributed most to the progress of the science. His view is that value depends entirely upon utility.

Jevons, W. STANLEY. **Primer of Political Economy.** N. Y., Appleton. 134 p. S. 45 c.

McCulloch, J: R. 1789–1864. **Principles of Political Economy.** New ed. N. Y., Scribner & Welford, 1883. 517 p. O. $2.50.
A leading writer of the English free-trade school and its encyclopedist. Includes sketch of the rise and progress of the science (60 pages).

McCulloch, J: R. **Political Economy,** together with an Essay on the Interest and Value of Money, by JOHN LOCKE. New ed. Lond., 1878. 8°, $1.60.

Macleod, H. DUNNING. **The Principles of Economical Philosophy.** Lond., 1872–75. 2 v. 8°, $12.
"A learned and acute, but paradoxical writer, combining good observations on special questions, with dangerous errors and old sophisms," says Cossa. This comprehensive work opposes Say and Mill on credit and Ricardo on rent. For full analysis, see Brooklyn Lib. Cat.

Macleod, H. DUNNING. **Elements of Economics.** V. 1, 1881. N. Y., Appleton, 1886. D. $1.75.

Macleod, H. DUNNING. **Economics for Beginners.** Lond. and N. Y., Longmans, 1886. 171 p., S. $1.

Marshall, ALFRED. **Principles of Economics.** Lond. and N. Y., Macmillan, 1890. V. 1, 28+754 p. 8°, $4.
The most important work in English since J. S. Mill. To be completed in a 2d v.

Marshall, ALFRED and MARY PALEY. **Economics of Industry.** Lond. and N. Y., Macmillan, 1881. 231 p. S. $1.

Malthus, T: R. 1766–1834. **Principles of Political Economy.** Lond., 1821. **Definitions of Political Economy.** Lond., 1827.
Now chiefly of historical interest and not comparable with his Essay on Population. He supported the taxation of imported corn and the theory of over-production.

Martineau, HARRIET. 1802–76. **Illustrations of Political Economy.** Lond., 1859.
Excellent short stories illustrating economic principles. For full contents, see Brooklyn Lib. Cat., p. 742.

Mill, JAMES. 1773–1836. **Elements of Political Economy.** 1821. 3d ed. Lond., 1826.
Chiefly notable as the father and instructor of J. S. Mill. A résumé of Smith, Malthus, and Ricardo.

Mill, J: STUART. 1806-73. **Principles of Political Economy.** 1848. Lond. and N. Y., Longmans. Library ed., 2 v. O. $10. People's ed., 1 v. O. $1.75.

——— Same. N. Y., Appleton. 2 v. 616, 603 p. O. $4.

All his works demand attention, particularly also "Essays on some unsettled principles of political economy," written 1829-30, publ. 1844, which made his reputation as an economist. Of his great work Cossa says, "Even now the best English treatise on economics." For full analysis, see Brooklyn Lib. Cat.

Mill, J: STUART. **Principles of Political Economy**, abridged, with critical, bibliographical, and explanatory notes, and a sketch of the history of political economy, by J. LAURENCE LAUGHLIN. N. Y., Appleton, 1884. 658 p. O., with maps and diagrams, $3.50.

The best abridgment of the chief modern English economist. Its ample notes, incorporated in the text, bring it down to 1834, and adapt it for the use of American students who have mastered the rudiments of economics. It contains a prefatory sketch of the history of political economy and a comprehensive series of questions for review or examination.

Ricardo, DAVID. 1772-1823. **Principles of Political Economy and Taxation.** 1817. In his WORKS. N. Y., Scribner & W., 1881. $8.

R. was a retired banker, who devoted himself to study. "His fame rests on the theory of rent, already expounded by Anderson (1777), West (1815), and Malthus, but with less profundity and fulness."—*Cossa*. His doctrine of "comparative cost" is at the basis of international trade.

Rogers, J. E. THOROLD. 1824-90. **Manual of Political Economy.** N. Y., Macmillan, 1878. xxiii+324 p. D. $1.25.

A brief manual, by the eminent historian of prices. Differs from English school in some details. For full analysis, see Brooklyn Lib. Cat.

Rogers, J. E. THOROLD. **Social Economy.** Rev. for Amer. readers. N. Y., Putnam, 1872. 167 p. D. 75 c.

Senior, NASSAU W. 1790-1864. **Four Introductory Lectures on Political Economy.** 1852. Lond.

Twice Prof. at Oxford, 1826-47. Author of Political Economy (1836) in Encyc. Metropolitana. Author of the nearly discarded wage-fund theory and of the first complete analysis of cost of production. "Wealth, not happiness" is his dictum. See Cossa, p. 72, 178.

Sidgwick, H: **Principles of Political Economy.** 1883. N. Y., Macmillan. $4.

Shadwell, J. L. **A System of Political Economy.** Lond., 1877. 8°, $3.

A complete treatise on the subject, in which the author takes issue with some of the positions of Prof. Cairnes.

Smith, ADAM. 1723-90. **An Inquiry into the Nature and Causes of the Wealth of Nations.** 1776. Oxford, 1880. 2 v. 423, 594 p. O. 21s.

——— Same, cheap edition. N. Y., Putnam, 1878. xvi-780 p. D. $1.25.

This is the only book to which has ever been awarded the honor of a centenary commemoration. "Probably the most important book that has ever been written," says Buckle. "Caused more money to be made, and prevented more money from being lost, than the writings of any other author," says the London *Economist*, 1876. It remains standard, and can always be read with profit and interest. It has been called "the inner atom of political economy." The best edition is the first mentioned, which is edited by Thorold Rogers. McCulloch's edition is also a standard one.

A connected and comprehensive grasp of principles was the great achievement of Adam Smith; for though not without faults (for summary of which see Laughlin's Mill, p. 14, and Cossa, p. 168). "The Wealth of Nations" has been the basis of all subsequent discussion and advance in political economy. "The new period begins with Adam Smith." "Undoubtedly the greatest economist the world has ever seen," says Cossa. "Adam Smith stands in the centre of economic history," says Roscher; "what came before was preparation for, and after him, completion of his work."

Whately, R: 1787-1863. **Introductory Lectures in Political Economy.** Lond., 1831.

FRENCH WORKS.

About, EDMOND. **Handbook of Social Economy;** or, The Worker's A, B, C. N. Y., Appleton, 1873. 20+284 p. D. $2.

Trans. by W. F. Rae. A complete, readable book, which grew out of discussions with French workingmen.

Cherbuliez, ANTOINE ELISE. 1797-1869. **Précis de la science économique.** 2 v. O. Paris, 1862.

Admirable for its exactness of method, profundity of investigation, order and clearness of exposition. Cossa declares it to be certainly the best treatise on economic science in the French language.

Chévalier, MICHEL. 1806-79. **Cours d'économie politique.** 1842-50. 2d ed. Paris, 1855. 3 v. 8°.

Stands first among recent French economists. Prof. in Collège de France, and negotiated Franco-English treaty of 1860. "This work expounds admirably money and the means of transport," says Cossa.

Courcelle-Séneuil, J. G. b. 1813. **Traité théorique et pratique d'économie politique.** 1858-9. 2d ed. Paris, 1867. 2 v. $5.25.

One of the best treatises on the subject in the French language. There is as yet no English translation.

Cournot, M. **Principes de la théorie des richesses.** Paris, 1863. 527 p. 8°.

Has attained a high reputation in late years. The founder of the mathematical school in economics. Much quoted by Jevons and Marshall.

Gide, C. **Principes d'économie politique.** Paris, L. Larose & Forcel, 1884. 588 p. D.

Noteworthy as parting company in some respects with the classic French economists.

Laveleye, EMILÉ DE. b. 1822. **Elements of Political Economy.** 1882. N. Y., G. P. Putnam's Sons, 1883. 288 p. D. $1.50.

Prof. at Liege. "Ethical political economy."

Rossi, P. **Cours d'économie politique.** 1843-'51.

"This work naturalized the doctrines of Malthus and Ricardo on French soil," says Laughlin.

Say, J. B. 1767-1832. **Treatise on Political Economy,** 1803. 6th ed. 1841. New Amer. ed. Phila., Claxton, 1869. $2.50.

"To Say we must ascribe the merit of having developed in a clear, orderly, and attractive manner the truth contained in Adam Smith's work." See Cossa, p. 171. He developed a theory of "gluts."

Sismondi, J. C. L. de. 1773-1842. **Nouveaux principes d'économie politique.** 1819. 2d ed. 2 v. Paris, 1827.

"The earliest and most distinguished of the humanitarian economists," says Laughlin.

GERMAN WORKS.

Cohn, GUSTAV. **System der National Oekonomie.** Stuttgart, F. Enke, 1886. 2 v., 649, 796 p. O., 32 marks.

Professor Cohn, of Göttingen, is one of the foremost economists of Germany. His chapters on coöperation, the normal labor day, and the fundamental right to freedom of industry are of special value. V. 1 treats principles; v. 2, science of finance.

Hermann, F. B. W. v. d. 1869. **Staatswirthschaftliche Untersuchungen.** 1832. 2d ed. 8°, Munich, 1870.

These researches determine the more general conceptions of the science, and much influence later economists. A follower of Adam Smith. See Cossa, p. 50.

Hildebrand, BRUNO. d. 1878. **Die Nationalökonomie der Gegenwart und Zukunft.** V. 1. Frankfort, 1848.

The unfinished work of the founder of the nationalist historical school of German economists.

Knies, KARL. **Die politische Oekonomie vom Standpunkte der geschichtlichen Methode.** 1853. 2d ed. Brunswick, 1883.

This work formulates with great precision the canons of the historical school, complementing Hildebrand and Roscher. "Knies challenged absolutism of theory," says Ely, "and substituted the doctrine of relativism," i.e., that economic politics should vary with times and countries.

Kautz, JULIUS. **Die National Oekonomik als Wissenschaft.** O. Vienna, 1858.

List, F. 1789-1846. **National System of Political Economy.** Tr. by G. A. Matile, with notes by Richelot and Cotwell. Phila., Lippincott, 1856. 8°, $2.

An unfinished work. The first of German protectionists. "List's system proclaimed the temporary necessity of protectionism to help the growth of important industries in Germany, and thus to educate the nation at the cost of a momentary loss to consumers," says Cossa. The ruling idea is nationality, to which protection is ancillary. The parts treat of history of pol. econ., theory, various systems, public (international) policy.

Rau, K. H. d. 1870. **Lehrbuch der Politischen Oekonomie.** 1826-32. 5th ed. Leipsic, 1864. 3 v. O.

Prof. at Heidelberg, an expounder of Adam Smith. The 3 vols. cover national economy, economic politics, finance. "An encyclopædia of economic doctrines, rich in statistical and bibliographical illustrations, and practical applications. Till 1854 unchallenged as *the* textbook in German universities."

Roscher, W. b. 1817. **Principles of Political Economy.** 1854 (13th ed., 1877). N. Y., Holt, 1878. 2 v. 464, 452 p. O. $7.50.

This translation covers V. 1, "Grundlagen der Nationalökonomie," of the German complete "System der Volkswirthschaft;" v. 2, "Ackerbau," v. 3, "Handel und Gewerbe," v. 4, "Finanzwissenschaft," are not translated. Represents the so-called historical school of the Germans, which differs from that of Mill. The uninformed reader would not, however, be likely to find any important difference of doctrine or method between Roscher and Mill. This work is a vast storehouse of learning, but its utility is somewhat impaired by the lack of an index. Author Prof. of Pol. Econ. at Univ. of Leipzig. "In the history of economics and in economic history the most learned man living," says Andrews. The Amer. translation by J. J. Lalor, from 13th German ed. has additional chapters by author on paper money, international trade and the protection system, and trans. of essay on the historical method in political economy of L. Wolowski. The German work is now in its 16th ed., Stuttgart, 1883, 4 v. For full analysis, see Brooklyn Lib. Cat.; for list of R.'s works, see Laughlin's Mill, p. 34.

Schäffle, A. E. F. **Das gesellschaftliche System der menschlichen Wirthschaft.** 3d ed. Tübingen, 1873. 2 v. S°.

Remarkable for richness and variety of observations; author holds to the essential unity of ethics and economics.

Stein, LORENZ VON. **Lehrbuch der Nationalökonomie.** Vienna, 1887. 8°, 457 p., 10 marks.

A philosophical work, substantially in harmony with Schäffle's Socialism.

POLITICAL ECONOMY: ESSAYS AND CRITICISMS.

Bolles, A. S. Chapters in Political Economy. N. Y., Appleton, 1874. 206 p. D. $1.50.

Sixteen papers, chiefly on importance of pol. econ., on labor, on value, money and banking, on taxation. For full analysis, see Brooklyn Lib. Cat.

Carey, H: C. The Past, the Present and the Future. 1848. Phila., Baird. 174 p., 8°, $2.50.

Developes his views on land, food, etc., as against Malthusianism. For full contents, see Brooklyn Lib. Cat.

Elder, W: Conversations on the Principal Subjects of Political Economy. Phila., Baird, 1882. $2.50.

Elder, W: Questions of the Day, economic and social. 1871. Phila., Baird, 1871. $3.

A follower of H. C. Carey.

Franklin, B: 1706–90. **Essay on Political Economy.** In his WORKS. N. Y., T. MacCoun, 1882. 10 v., 4°, $20.

Lunt, E. CLARK. Present Condition of Political Economy and the demand for a radical change in its methods and aims. N. Y., Putnam, 1888. 114 p. O. 75 c.

Patten, SIMON N. The Premises of Political Economy. A re-examination of certain fundamental principles of economic science. Phila., J. B. Lippincott & Co., 1885. 244 p. D. $1.50.

A radical and suggestive piece of criticism. Emphasizes social causes.

Sumner, W. GRAHAM. Collected Essays in Political and Social Science. N. Y., H. Holt & Co., 1885. 173 p. O. $1.50.

Contents: Bimetallism; Wages; The argument against protective taxes; Sociology; Theory and practice of elections; Presidential elections and civil service reform; Our colleges before the country. Vigorous essays by the foremost American representative of the individualistic school of economists.

Wells, D. A. Practical Economics. A collection of essays respecting certain of the recent economic experiences of the United States. N. Y., Putnam, 1885. 59 p. O. $1.50.

Contains among other chapters The Silver Question; The Foreign Competitive Pauper-Labor Argument for Protection; Our Experience in Taxing Distilled Spirits.

Cairnes, J. E. Essays on Political Economy, Theoretical and Practical. 1873. Lond., 1878. 8°, $3.50.

Can be read to advantage as a supplement to his larger work. For full contents, see Brooklyn Lib. Cat.

Leslie, Th. E: CLIFFE-. d. 1882. **Essays in Political and Moral Philosophy.** 1879. Dublin.

Represents in England the historical school and the "professorial socialists" of Germany.

Price, BONAMY. Chapters on Practical Political Economy. 8°, London, 1878. $4.80.

Author Prof. of Pol. Econ. at Oxford. Includes a chapter on tariff revision in U. S. For full analysis, see Brooklyn Lib. Cat.

Ruskin, J: b. 1819. **Munera Pulveris.** 1863. Rev. ed. N. Y., Wiley, 1872. xxvii+164 p. 12°, 50 c.

"Six essays on the elements of political economy." *Contents:* Preface, Definitions, Store-keeping, Coin-keeping. Commerce, Government, Mastership. "The first accurate analysis," claims preface, "of the Laws of Political Economy which has been published in England, because no exhaustive examination is possible except to one acquainted with the Fine Arts."

Ruskin, J: "**Unto this Last**": four essays on the first principles of political economy. 1862. N. Y., Wiley. 12°, 50 c.

A glowing attack on orthodox political economy, culminating in more or less socialistic teachings. "The Crown of Wild Olive," "Political Economy of Art" and others of Ruskin's books also touch on economics, and should be read for their inspiring criticism on non-ethical economics.

Torrens, Robert. 1784-1864. **Essay on the Production of Wealth.** 1821.

Bastiat, M. F. 1801-50. **Essays on Political Economy.** N. Y., Putnam, 1877. xi+291 p. D. $1.25.

Contents: Capital and Interest (The Sack of Corn, the House, the Plane). That which is seen and that which is not seen (The Broken Window, etc.). Government. What is Money. The Law. Of this last the N. Y. *Nation* says: "The laws of an abstruse science have never been made more clear or expressed more forcibly." Translation revised, with notes, by D. A. Wells. This is a selection from and adaptation of his essays, and "Harmonies économiques," publ. 1850. "A less profound but popular and effective writer, an economic optimist," says Cossa. For list of B.'s works, see Laughlin's Mill, p. 28.

Schäffle, A. E. F. Gesammelte Aufsaetze. Tubingen, 1886. 2 v., 29S, 311 p. 12 marks.

Essays written during thirty years on political, economical and social topics of the time. The author is a social philosopher of the first rank; he holds to the essential unity of ethics and economics.

Wagner, Ad. **Rede über die sociale Frage.** 1872. Berlin.

Wagner represents the "professorial socialists" (Katheder-Socialisten), who belittle universal or natural laws, and emphasize the modifying action of the social power. Wagner's edition of Rau's "Course," and his large original work, "Lehrbuch der Oekonomie," in course of publication, are authoritative works of this school.

The American Economic Association, Professor R. T. Ely, Johns Hopkins Univ., Baltimore, Secretary, issues six pamphlets yearly, from leading economist of America (v. 1, 1886). membership subscription, $3, other, $4, yearly. The series is indispensable to an economic library.

The American Academy of Political and Social Science. Prof. E. J. James, Univ. of Penn., Philadelphia, Secretary, issues its *Annals* quarterly (v. 1, 1890-1)., membership subscription, $5 yearly.

The American Statistical Association, Prof. D. R. Dewey, Inst. of Technology, Boston, Secretary, issues four publications yearly (new series, v. 1, 1889). membership subscription, $2 yearly.

The American Social Science Association, F. B. Sanborn, Concord, Mass., Secretary, which includes an economic section. issues the *Journal of Social Science*, containing its transactions, in occasional parts (v. 1, 1866), membership subscription, $5 yearly.

The *Political Science Quarterly*, edited by the University Faculty of Political Science of Columbia College (v. 1, 1886), is published by Ginn & Co., 743 B'way, New York, $3 per annum.

The *Quarterly Journal of Economics* (v. 1, 1886-7), is published for Harvard University, by G. H. Ellis, 141 Franklin St., Boston, $3 per annum.

See also the *Economic Monographs* and *Questions of the Day*, of G. P. Putnam's Sons, and similar series of other publishers.

The *Economist* (London) founded 1843, by James Wilson, and afterward edited by W. Bagehot, is the first authority of its kind. The Statistical Society, founded 1839, issues a quarterly *Journal*. The famous Political Economy Club, organized in London by nineteen economists in 1821, issues no publications, but a list of questions debated at its monthly dinners is given in " Questions for Debate " (Economic tract, no. 28.)

The *Journal des Economistes*, Paris, founded 1842, is the leading French authority. The *Revue d'Economie Politique*, Paris, ed. by Professors of Economics at the Law-schools, represents the newer ideas in economics. Paris has a Société d' Economie Politique, publishing its proceedings in a bulletin, for questions discussed by which since 1865 see " Questions for Debate " (Economic tract, no. 28.)

The *Vierteljahrschrift für Volkswirthschaft und Culturgeschichte*, Berlin, founded 1863, originated with the liberal economists of the Manchester school who organized the Society of Political Economy in Berlin. See also the *Jahrbücher für Nationalökonomie und Statistik*, which were begun in 1863 by Hildebrand, and are now conducted by Prof. Conrad. They contain the fullest bibliography on the subject. See also Schmoller's *Jahrbücher für Gesetzgebung, Verwaltung und Volkswirthschaft*, which emphasize the social views. This and Conrad's are on the whole the best reviews of economics.

The *Giornale degli Economisti* is the leading Italian review.

LAND AND RENT.

Kinnear and Laveleye give a general view of the development of property in land. Maine is for advanced students. Pollock's sketch of British land laws is brief and clear. Leslie's account of British and Irish land systems is fuller. The Cobden Club essays, edited by Probyn, serve as a good introduction to modern systems of land tenure. Meyer's official report and Roscher's treatise are valuable. Prothero describes British agriculture. Ricardo is the chief expounder of the doctrine of rent [see note on his works, Political Economy, English]; Walker is his principal American disciple. The criticisms of Carey [see note on his works, Political Economy, American] have been adopted by the so-called "American" school of financial writers. Brooklyn Lib. Catalogue, p. 919, contains important entries. See, also, various chapters in Buckle. Green, Escott, and other standard historians bearing on land systems. Thorold Rogers in his " Cobden and Modern Political Opinion," 1873, p. 73-108, discusses the land question. Donaldson's History is indispensable to students of the Public Lands question in the United States.

Allinson, E: P., and **Penrose, Boies. Ground Rents in Philadelphia**, Phila., Wharton School of Finance and Economy, 1889. 19 p. O. pap., 25 c.

Cheyney, E. P. Anti-Rent Agitation in the State of New York, 1839-46. Phila., Wharton School of Finance and Economy, 1889. O. pap., 50 c.

Cox, S. S. Free Land and Free Trade. N. Y., Putnam, 1880. D. $1.

A clearly written little treatise on the application to the United States of the principles that governed the repeal of the British corn laws.

Dixwell, G: B. **Progress and Poverty**: a review of the doctrines of H: George. Cambridge, Mass., 1882. 46 p. O.

Egleston, MELVILLE. **Land System of the New England Colonies.** Baltimore, Johns Hopkins Univ., 1886. 66 p. O. pap., 50 c.

Elliott, J. R. **American Farms**: their condition and future. N. Y., Putnam, 1890. 6+262 p. D. $1.25.

George, H: **Irish Land Question**; an appeal to the land leagues. N. Y., Appleton, 1884. 85 p. D. pap., 25 c.

George, H: **Progress and Poverty.** An inquiry into causes of industrial depressions, and of the increase of want with increase of wealth. The remedy. 1879. N. Y., Henry George & Co., 1888. 250 p. O. cl., $1; pap., 35 c.

No recent economic work has excited more popular interest, or has received a wider circulation. The author's proposal that a "single tax" be imposed to equal ground-rent has called forth world-wide discussion. In addition to criticisms included under Land and Rent may be mentioned that found in last chapter, J: Rae's Contemporary Socialism [see Socialism]; and in G: Gunton's Wealth and Progress [see Capital and Labor.] R. Giffen in his Growth of Capital [see Capital]. states that British wealth in land is diminishing proportionately, and is now one-sixth of the whole.

In advocacy of the doctrines of Progress and Poverty [also of Tariff Reform and Ballot Reform], *The Standard* is published at 42 University Place, New York. $3 per annum. From the same office is issued a variety of tracts and leaflets similar in purpose.

George, H: **The Land Question**, what it involves and how alone it can be settled. N. Y., H: George & Co., 1888. 87 p. D. pap., 20 c.

Harris, W. T. **The Right of Property and the Ownership of Land.** Bost., Cupples & Hurd, 1887. 40 p. O. pap., 25 c.

Against H: George's theories.

Mayer, LOUIS. **Ground-rents in Maryland.** Baltimore, 1883. Cushings & Bailey. 158 p. O. $1.50.

Miller, J. BLEECKER. **Progress and Robbery**: Two American answers to H: George, the Demi-communist. N. Y., 1886. 40 p. O.

Moody, W: G. **Land and Labor in the United States.** N. Y., Scribner, 1883. 360 p. D. $1.50.

Nott, C: C. **A Good Farm for Nothing**: reasons for the decline of agriculture and farm values in New England. N. Y., *Evening Post*, 1889. 16 p. S. pap., 1 c.

Olmstead, DWIGHT H. **Land Transfer Reform**, or, the Free Transfer of Land. N. Y., Baker, Voorhis & Co., 1887. 116 p. O. pap., 25 c.

By one of the Land Commissioners appointed by Legislature of New York, 1884. Gives detailed information for the scientific registration and indexing of land records, including explanation of proposed legislative bills for block and lot indexing.

Phillips, W. A. **Labor, Land and Law**: a search for the missing wealth of the working classes. N. Y., Scribner, 1886. 471 p. D. $2.50.

An historical review of the shares of production taken by landlord, capitalist and employer, concluding with proposed remedies.

Ross, DENMAN W. **Early History of Land-Holding among the Germans.** Boston, Soule & Bugbee, 1883. 6+273 p. D.

Contains a bibliography of the general subject.

Sato, Shosuke. History of the Land Question in the United States. Baltimore, Johns Hopkins Univ., 1886. $1.25.

Walker, Francis A. Land and Its Rent. Bost., Little, Brown & Co., 1883. 220 p. S. 75 c.
Reviews the doctrines of Carey, Bastiat, Mill, Leroy-Beaulieu, and H: Geerge as to rent. Shows how economists have discriminated between land and other forms of property. Objects to Mill's proposal that the State should appropriate future unearned increment on grounds of political expediency, not on grounds of political equity. The best American book on the subject from the conservative standpoint.

Winn, H. Property in Land: an essay on the new crusade. N. Y., Putnam, 1888. 73 p. D. pap., 25 c.
An adverse criticism of H: George's propositions.

Argyll, Duke of, and George, H: Property in Land: a passage-at-arms. N. Y., J. W. Lovell Co., 1886. 77 p. S. pap., 15 c.

Arnold, Arthur. Free Land. Lond., Kegan Paul, 1880. 371 p. D.
Presents the British land question.

Bateman, J: Acre-ocracy of England, a list of the owners of 3000 acres and upwards, with their possessions and incomes arranged under their various counties. Lond., Pickering, 1876. 220 p. D.

Birkbeck, W. Lloyd. Historical Sketch of the Distribution of Land in England; with suggestions for some improvement in the law. Lond. and N. Y., Macmillan, 1885. D. $1.50.

Broderick, Geo. C. English Land and English Landlords. An inquiry into the origin and character of the English land system, with proposals for its reform. Lond. and N. Y., Cassell, 1881. 515 p. D.

Caird, James, *M.P.* Prairie Farming in America. N. Y., Appleton, 1859.

Elliott, T. J. The Land Question. Lond. and N. Y., Cassell & Co. 3s. 6d.
Treats of certain phases of the English land question.

Fisher, Joseph. History of Land-Holding in England. Lond., 1876. O.

Gomme, G. L. The Village Community, with special reference to the origin and form of its survivals in Britain. Contemporary Science Series. N. Y., Scribner, 1890. 299 p. D. $1.25.
Adds to the researches of Nasse, Maine, and Seebohm much new information.

Hill, Octavia. Our Common Land, and other short essays. Lond., Macmillan, 1877. 206 p. S.
A plea for preservation of commons and public parks.

Kay, Joseph. Free Trade in Land. With Preface by John Bright. Lond., Kegan Paul, 1879. O. 5s.

—— **Same.** 9th ed. With review of recent changes in the land laws of England, by G. O. Morgan. Omitting statistical appendix. Lond., Kegan Paul, 1885. 12+180 p. D. pap., 1s.
Gives a clear statement of the position in 1879 of the land question in Great Britain and Ireland, together with a summary of the systems of land tenure throughout Europe, with some of the results traceable to them.

Kinnear, J. B. Principles of Property in Land. Lond., Smith, Elder & Co. 8°. 5s.
Regards land-owning as one of the social and conventional rights which for the general good communities accord to individuals.

Leslie, T. E. Cliffe. Land Systems and Industrial Economy of Ireland, England, and Continental Countries. Lond., 1870. O.
A comprehensive survey.

Levy, J. H., *ed.* Symposium on the Land Question. Lond., Fisher Unwin, 1890. 74 p. 8°, 1s.

Low, David. Landed Property and the Economy of Estates. Lond., Longman, 1844. 12+680 p. D.
Though intended as a landlord's manual gives much information of general interest on landed property.

Macdonell, J. The Land Question, with particular reference to England and Scotland. Lond., Macmillan. 8°, 10s. 6d.

Maine, *Sir* H: J. Sumner. 1822-1888. Early History of Institutions. N. Y., Holt, 1880. 8°, $3.50.
Traces property in land to the period when bodies of men held together by the land they tilled replaced the earliest cultivating groups formed of kinsmen. A work of the first rank.

Maine, *Sir* H: J. Sumner. Village Communities in the East and West. N. Y., Holt, 8°, $3.50.
Compares the development of Indian and Teutonic village communities. Traces the process of feudalisation, and the early history of price and rent. A classic.

Mallock, W. H. Property and Progress; or, a brief inquiry into contemporary social agitation in England. N. Y., Putnam, 1884. 248 p. D. $1.
Chiefly a reply to George's "Progress and Poverty," and Hyndman's "England for All."

Montgomery, W. E. History of Land Tenure in Ireland. Cambridge Univ. Press, 1889. 191 p. 10s. 6d.
Valuable and suggestive.

Nicholson, J. S. Tenants Gain not Landlord's Loss. Edinburgh, D. Douglas, 1883. 11+173 p. D.

Ogilby, J: Essay on the Right of Property in Land with respect to the foundation in the law of nature and the rights of the people. Lond., 1780. O.

Ouvry, H. A. Stein and His Reforms in Prussia, with reference to the land question in England. Lond., 1873.
Appendix contains views of R: Cobden and J: Stuart Mill.

Pollock, F. The Land Laws. Lond. and N. Y., Macmillan, 1886. 224 p. D. $1.
Gives the British land laws concisely and clearly.

Probyn, J. W., *ed.* Systems of Land Tenure in various countries. Cobden Club Essays. New and rev. ed. Lond. and N. Y., Cassell, 1881. 6+534 p. D.
Contains Tenure of Land in Ireland, by Rt. Hon. M. Longfield; Law and Custom of Primogeniture, by Hon. G. C. Brodrick; Land Laws of England, by G. W. Hoskyns; Tenure of Land in India, by Sir G: Campbell; Land System of France, by T. E. Cliffe Leslie; Russian Agrarian Legislation of 1861, by Dr. J. Faucher; Agrarian Legislation of Prussia during Present Century, by R. B. D. Morier; Land System of Belgium and Holland, by E. de Laveleye; Farm Land and Land Laws of the U. S., by C. M. Fisher.

Prothero, Rowland E. Pioneers and Progress of English Farming. Lond., Longmans, 1888. 14+390 p. D. 5s.

Richey, ALEX. G. **Irish Land Laws.** 2d ed. Lond., Macmillan, 1881. 6+129 p. D. 3s. 6d.

Rogers, J. E. THOROLD. **History of Agriculture and Prices in England** from the year after the Oxford Parliament to the commencement of the Continental War. 6 v. Lond. and N. Y., Macmillan, 1888. O. $35.50.

> The most important contribution yet made to the economical and industrial history of England. Vol. 6 ends with 1702, in preface thereto, Sept., 1887, author expressed his intention of writing two concluding volumes, which would bring the record down to 1793, where Thomas Tooke's work begins, which with Mr. Newmarch's comes to 1856.

Seebohm, F: **The English Village Community,** examined in its relations to the manorial and tribal systems, and to the common or open field system of husbandry. 2d ed. Lond., Longmans, 1883. 21+464 p. D. 16s.

Sigurson, G. **History of the Land Tenures and Land Classes of Ireland,** with account of secret agrarian confederacies. Lond., 1871. 8°.

Torrens, Sir ROBERT. **Transfer of Land by Registration** under the duplicate method operative in British colonies. Cobden Club tract. Lond. and N. Y., Cassell. pap., 25 c.

Thornton, W. T. **Plea for Peasant Proprietors,** with outline for their establishment in Ireland. Lond., Macmillan, 1874. 268 p. D.

Wallace, ALFRED R. **Land Nationalization,** its necessity and its aims. Lond., W. Reeves, 1882. 14+244 p. D. 1s. 6d.

Young, ARTHUR. **Farmer's Tour through the East of England.** Lond., 1771. 4 v. 8°.

Young, ARTHUR. **Six Weeks' Tour through the Southern Counties of England and Wales.** Lond., 1976. 8°.

Young, ARTHUR. **Tour in Ireland.** Lond., 1780. 2 v. 8°.

Young, ARTHUR. **Travels in France** during the years 1787-89. Lond., 1793. 2 v. 8°. New ed. with introd. and notes by M. Betham-Edwards. N. Y., Scribner & Welford, 1889. 59+366 p. D. $1.40.

> Young's works contain the best contemporaneous account of the land-holding classes, and are replete with valuable economic object-lessons.

Foville, ALFRED de. **Le Morcellement.** Paris, Guillaumin, 1885. 283 p. D.

Laboulaye, EDOUARD. **Histoire du droit de propriété foncière en occident.** Paris, A. Durand, 1839. 12+532 p. D.

Laveleye, EMILE de. **De la propriété et de ses formes primitives.** 2me ed. Paris, Germer Bailliere & Cie., 1877. 24+395 p. D.

—— **Primitive Property.** Same, 'tr. by G. R. L. Marriott. With introd. by T. E. Cliffe Leslie. Lond., 1878. xliv+364 p.

> Describes methods of land-owning which prevailed in primitive times in Europe and Asia, and still prevail in Servia, parts of Holland, Switzerland, Russia and India. Traces the historical development of property.

Lavergne, LEONCE de. **Economie rurale de la France depuis 1789.** Paris, 1860. 485 p. D.

Lavergne, LEONCE de. **Rural Economy of England, Scotland, and Ireland.** Tr. with notes by a Scotch farmer. Edinburgh, 1855. 400 p. O.

Bernhardi, Theodor. Versuch einer Kritik der Gründe die für grosses und kleines Grundeigenthum angeführt werden. St. Petersburg, 1849. 668 p. D.
The best early theoretical investigation.

Eheberg, K. T. Agrarische Zustände in Italien. Leipzig, Düncker & Humblot, 1886. 9+158 p. D.

Meyer, Rudolf. Heimstätten und andere Wirthschaftsgesetze der Vereinigten Staaten von America, von Canada, Russland, China, Indien, Rumänien, Serbien und England. Berlin, H. Bahr, 1883. 32+632 p. D.

Reitzenstein, F. F. v., und Nasse, E. Agrarische Zustände in Frankreich und England. Leipzig, Duncker & Humblot, 1884. 16+222 p. D.

Roscher, W. Nationalökonomik des Ackerbaues. Stuttgart, J. G. Cotta, 1878. 10+668 p. O.
V. 2 of his System. A French tr. is pub. by Guillaumin, Paris.

Wagner, Adolph. Die Abschaffung des privaten Grundeigenthums. Leipzig, Düncker & Humblot, 1870. 84 p. D.
One of the most valuable discussions on the legitimacy of private property in land.

Loria, Achille. La Rendita Fondiaria e la sua Elisione Natural. Milan, 1880. 15+713 p. O.
The best book on rent as influencing methods of cultivation.

Mortgages in Foreign Countries, are treated fully in U. S. Consular Reports, nos. 110 and 111. (Washington Department of Senate, 1890.) Mortgage Statistics are discussed by G: K. Holmes in Pubs. of Am. Statis. Assoc., Boston, no. 9, March, 1890. An Investigation on Mortgage Indebtedness for the Eleventh Census is being conducted under the direction of G: K. Holmes. Statistics of Mortgages are given in Bureaus of Labor Reports: Illinois, 1888; Michigan, 1888; Nebraska, 1887-88.

The Financial Reform Almanac gives very full statistical and other information on the Land Question of the United Kingdom. Lond., Simpkin, Marshall & Co. 1s.

Canadian Chapter in Agrarian Agitation. G: Iles. *Popular Science Monthly*, Aug., 1886.

Farm Mortgages and the Small Farmer. W. F. Mappin. *Political Science Quarterly*, Sept., 1889.

The Mortgage Evil (with special reference to Indiana). J. P. Dunn. *Political Science Quarterly*, March, 1890.

Western Mortgages. J. W. Gleed. *Forum*, March, 1890.
Western Farm Mortgages. D. R. Goodloe. *Forum*, Nov., 1890.
Property in Land. Sir George Campbell. *Westm. Review*, Feb., 1890.
Why the Farmer is not Prosperous. C. W. Davis. *Forum*, April, 1890.
When the Farmer will be Prosperous. C. W. Davis. *Forum*, May, 1890.
Exhaustion of the Arable Lands. C. W. Davis. *Forum*, June, 1890.
Probabilities of Agriculture. C. W. Davis. *Forum*, Nov., 1890.
The Nationalization of Land. 1. How to nationalize the land. F. L. Soper. *Westm. Review*, Sept., 1889. 2. The national administration of the ladd. F. L. Soper. *Westm. Review*, Oct., 1889. 3. The nationalization of the land: a reply. *Westm. Review*, Jan., 1890.
Ethics of Land Tenure. J. B. Clark. *International Journal of Ethics*, Philadelphia, Oct., 1890.

PUBLIC LANDS.

Atkinson, E: Our National Domain. [Folded chart.] 2d ed. Bost., A. Williams & Co., 1880. 50 c.
<small>A graphical presentation of comparative areas of the States of the Union and of countries of Europe, also of principal crops of U. S.</small>

Decisions of the Department of the Interior and General Land Office in cases relating to the Public Lands. Washington, 1882. 5 v., 8°.
<small>The Department publishes subsequent decisions from time to time.</small>

Donaldson, T. The Public Domain, its history, with statistics. House Exec. Doc. 47, part 4, 46th Cong., 3d Session. Washington, Gov. Pr. Office, 1884. 1343 p. D.
<small>A comprehensive work.</small>

Knight, G: N. History and Management of Federal Land Grants for Education in the Northwest Territory. N. Y., Am. Historical Assoc., 1886. 175 p. 8°.

Public Land Commission. Existing Laws Relating to Survey and Disposition of the Public Domain. 1 v. General and permanent. 2 v. Local and temporary. 3 v. Washington, Gov. Pr. Office, 1884.

Shinn, C: H. Land laws of mining districts. Baltimore, Johns Hopkins Univ.: 1884. D. pap., 50 c.

The Land Commissioner of the U. S., Washington, publishes an annual report as part of the report of the Secretary of the Interior. It contains much practical information. The General Land Office also issues circulars showing the manner of proceeding to obtain title to public lands, etc., and other synopses of decisions, circulars, instructions, etc., for list of which see Appendix on U. S. Government Publications, in American Catalogue.

Disposition of our Public Lands. A. B. Hart. *Quarterly Journal of Economics*, Jan., 1887.

Railroad Indemnity Lands. F: Perry Powers. *Political Science Quarterly*, Sept., 1889.

CAPITAL AND LABOR.

Property as now existing is attacked as respects land by many writers [see Land and Rent], and otherwise by socialists and others [see Socialism]. The best historians of the Labor movement are Ely, for America, Thornton and Howell for Great Britain, and Le Play for Europe. Walker, for America, has written the best work on Wages, Rogers and Brassey are the leading English authorities. Barnard, Hughes, and Neale have treated Coöperation with much ability. Gilman's is the leading work on Profit-Sharing. The official reports of Wright on various phases of the Labor Question are very valuable.

PROPERTY, CAPITAL.

Clark, J: B. Capital and Its Earnings. Baltimore, American Economic Assoc., 1888. 69 p. O. pap., 75 c.

Giffen, R. The Growth of Capital. Lond., Bell & Sons, 1890. 162 p. 8°, 7s. 6d.
<small>A statistical review of the recent growth of British capital.</small>

Comte, F. C. L. De la propriété. Paris, 1834. 2 v. O.

Thiers, M. A. De la propriété. Paris, Paulin, L'Heureux & Cie., 1848. 439 p. D.

Böhm-Bawerk, E. v. **Capital and Interest:** a critical history of economical theory; tr. with a preface and analysis by W. Smart. Lond. and N. Y., Macmillan, 1890. 45+431 p. S°. $4.
A critical work of great ability, covering not only Capital and Interest, but other important questions of political economy. For advanced students.

Marx, KARL. **Das Kapital,** Kritik der politischen Oekonomie. Hamburg, 1873. 8°. V. 2. Nach seinem tode herausgegeben von F. Engels, Hamburg, 1885, 8°.

—— Same. **Capital:** a critical analysis of capitalistic production, from 3d German ed. N. Y., Appleton, 1889. 816 p. O. $3.
Expounds the theory of surplus value. For criticisms, see Socialism.

Constitutional Guarantees of the Right of Property. George Hoadley. *Journal of Social Science* (Saratoga papers of 1889). N. Y., Putnam, 1890.

Theory of Capital. F. H. Giddings. *Quarterly Journal of Economics,* Jan., 1890.

PROFIT, INTEREST, USURY.

Atkinson, E: **The Margin of Profits;** how it is now divided, what part of present hours of labor can now be spared. N. Y., Putnam, 1887. 123 p. D. cl., 75 c.; pap., 40 c.
Includes reply of E. M. Chamberlain, representing the labor unions, and Mr. Atkinson's rejoinder.

Kelly, J. B. **Summary of the History and Law of Usury.** Lond., R. J. Kennett, 1835. 275 p. O.

Murray, J. B. C. **History of Usury Laws from the Earliest Period.** Phila., 1866. O. $2.

The Usury Question, by Calvin, Bentham, Dana, and Wells, with bibliography. Economic tract, No. 4. N. Y., Soc. for Political Education, 1881. pap., 25 c.

Profits under Modern Conditions. J: B. Clark. *Political Science Quarterly,* Dec., 1887.

Rate of Interest, and Laws of Distribution. Sidney Webb. *Quarterly Journal of Economics,* Jan., 1888.

LABOR, HISTORY, AND RELATIONS TO CAPITAL.

Atkinson, E. **Labor and Capital Allies, not Enemies.** N. Y., Harper. S. 25 c.
Can be heartily recommended for the general reader.

Barns, W. E. **The Labor Problem;** plain questions and practical answers; with an introduction by R: T. Ely, and contributions by Jas. A. Waterworth and Fred. Woodrow. N. Y., Harper, 1886. 330 p. S. $1.
Mr. Ely discourses upon "Coöperation in Literature and the State;" Mr. Waterworth on "The Conflict Historically Considered;" and Mr. Woodrow on "Side-Lights on the Labor Problem." A symposium is added in which prominent political economists, manufacturers, workingmen, and others give their views.

Bilgram, HUGO. **Involuntary Idleness.** An exposition of the discrepancy existing between the supply of, and the demand for, labor and its products. Phila., Lippincott, 1889. 119 p. S. $1.
Holds that an expansion of the volume of money, by extending the issue of credit-money, will prevent business stagnation and involuntary idleness. Disputes the claim that interest naturally accrues to capital.

Ely, R. T. **The Labor Movement in America.** N. Y., T. Y. Crowell & Co., 1886. 373 p. D. $1.50.
A history which includes the platforms of the principal labor organizations.

Fall, C. G. **Employers' Liability** for Personal Injury to their Employees. Boston, Mass. Bureau of Statistics of Labor, 1889.
<small>Prepared under the direction of Carroll D. Wright. Reprinted from Bureau's 14th Annual Report, for 1883.</small>

Gladden, *Rev.* W. **Working-People and Their Employers.** N. Y., Funk & Wagnalls, 1887. 241 p. D. cl., $1; pap., 25 c.
<small>Outspoken, sympathetic, and sensible.</small>

McNeill, G. E., **George,** H., and others. **The Labor Movement.** Bost., A. M. Bridgman & Co., 1886. 650 p. O. $3.75.
<small>Chiefly descriptive of the history of organizations of labor, written by representatives of the leading trades. Professor E. J. James contributes three excellent chapters on the history of labor and recent labor legislation in Europe.</small>

Meriwether, Lee. **A Tramp's Trip:** how to see Europe on fifty cents a day. N. Y., Harper, 1887. 5+276 p. D. $1.25.

Meriwether, Lee. **Tramp at Home.** N. Y. Harper, 1889. 10+296 p. D. $1.25.
<small>Both the foregoing give valuable pictures of workingmen as they are.</small>

Newcomb, Simon. **A Plain Man's Talk on the Labor Question.** N. Y., Harper, 1886. 195 p. S. 60 c.
<small>This work discusses "Society and Its Wants," "Capital and Its Uses," and "The Laborer and His Wages," in a candid and conciliatory spirit.</small>

Porter, R. P. **Bread-Winners Abroad.** N. Y., J. S. Ogilvie & Co., 1885. 420 p. $1.50.

Thompson, Phillips. **The Politics of Labor.** N. Y., Belford, Clarke & Co., 1887. D. $1.25.

Trumbull, M. M. **"Wheelbarrow's"** articles and discussions on the Labor Question, including controversy with Lyman J. Gage on the ethics of the Board of Trade, and controversy with Hugh O. Pentecost and others on the Single Tax Question. Chicago, Open Court Pub. Co., 1890. 303 p. D. $1.

Ward, C. Osborne. **History of the ancient working people** from the earliest known period to the adoption of Christianity by Constantine. Washington, W. H. Lowdermilk & Co., 1889. 519 p. D. $2.00.

Williams, Talcott. **Labor a Hundred Years Ago.** Economic tract, No. 24. N. Y., Soc. for Political Education, 1888, pap., 15 c.

Willoughby, W. F., and **Graffenried,** *Miss* Clare de. **Child-Labor.** Baltimore, American Economic Assoc., 1890. 75 c.
<small>Two prize essays.</small>

Wright, Carroll D. **Growth and Purposes of Bureaus of Statistics of Labor.** Boston, Wright & Potter, 1888.

Wright, Carroll D. **Present Actual Condition of the Workingman.** Boston, G: H. Ellis, 1887.

Wright, Carroll D. **Relation of Political Economy to the Labor Question.** Boston, A. Williams & Co., 1882. 53 p. S. 60 c.
<small>Considers phases of the Labor Question from the ethical standpoint.</small>

Wright, Carroll D. **The Factory System.** Washington, Gov. Pr. Office, 1884. 78 p.
<small>Reprinted from v. 2, Tenth Census Reports, Washington, 1882.</small>

Wright, Carroll D. Uniform Hours of Labor. Boston, Mass., Bureau of Statistics of Labor, 1889.
<small>Reprinted from Bureau's 12th Annual Report, for 1881. Proves that mills working ten hours were as profitable as mills working eleven to twelve hours.</small>

Wright, Carroll D. Working Girls of Boston. Boston, Mass. Bureau of Statistics of Labor, 1889. 133 p. O.
<small>Reprinted from Bureau's 15th Annual Report, for 1884.</small>

Young, E. Labor in Europe and America. A special report on the rate of wages, the cost of subsistence, and the condition of the working classes in the countries of Europe, and also in the United States and British America. Wash., Gov. Pr. Office, 1875; *also*, Phila., S. A George & Co., 1875. 864 p. O. $3.50.
<small>Contains elaborate historical introduction on ancient labor. Author was chief of U. S. Bureau of Statistics.</small>

Giffen, R. The Progress of the Working Classes in the Last Half Century. Economic tract, No. 16. N. Y., Soc. for Political Education, 1884, pap., 25 c.
<small>A later word on this subject is included in Essays on Finance, 2d series [see Public Finance.]</small>

Howell, G. Conflicts of Capital and Labor, historically and economically considered. New and rev. ed. Lond. and N. Y., Macmillan, 1890. 6+536 p. 12°, $2.50.
<small>Treats of British trades-unions from the standpoint of a trades-unionist. A most important work.</small>

Kay, Joseph. Social Condition and Education of the People in England—1848. N. Y., Harper, 1864. 323 p. D. $1.50.

Ludlow, J. M., *and* Jones, Lloyd. Progress of the Working Classes, 1832-1867. Lond., A. Strahan, 1867. 304 p. D.

Morrison, C. Essay on the Relations between Capital and Labor. Lond., Longmans, 1854. 328 p. O.

Pidgeon, D. Old World Questions and New World Answers. N. Y., Harper, 1885. 193 p. S. pap. 25 c.
<small>An Englishman's appreciative description of leading factory towns of New England, with chapters on The Factory System, Labor, Wages, and the Tariff, etc.</small>

Ruskin, J: Fors Clavigera; letters to the workmen of Great Britain. 3 v. N. Y., J. Wiley & Sons, 1871-78. O.

Stubbs, *Rev.* Chas. W. Village Politics. Addresses on the Labor Question. Lond., 1878. 193 p. S. $1.25.
<small>Interesting in its suggestions concerning English agricultural laborers.</small>

Taylor, E. W. C. Introduction to a History of the Factory System. London, R. Bentley & Sons, 1886. 441 p. demy O. 16s.
<small>A faithfully prepared volume. Only English authorities are cited.</small>

Thornton, W. T. On Labor: its claims and dues. 3d ed. rev. Lond., Macmillan, 1888. O.
<small>Chiefly valuable for its positive information about trades-unions, their organization, laws, purposes, abuses, etc.</small>

Toynbee, Arnold. Industrial Revolution in England. Lond., Rivington, 1884. 37+263 p. O. Also, N. Y., Humboldt Pub. Co., 1890. pap. 60c.; cl. $1.
<small>The best book on the subject. Inspired with the highest moral feeling.</small>

Tuckett, J. A. **History of the Past and Present State of the Laboring Population.** Lond., Longmans, 1846. 2 v. 878 p. O.

About, E. **Handbook of Social Economy**; or, the worker's A, B, C. N. Y., 1873. xx+284 p. D. $2.

A popular exposition of elementary economic notions, with especial reference to the fallacies most widely accepted by the wages class.

Cassagnac, A. GRANIER de. **Histoire des classes ouvrières et des classes bourgeoises.** Paris, Desrez, 1838. 574 p. D.

Chevalier, MICHEL. **Sur l'organisation du travail, les principales causes de la misère et les moyens proposes pour y remedier.** Paris, Capelle, 1848. 516 p. D.

De la Chavanne, C. DARESTE. **Histoire des classes agricoles en France.** Paris, Guillaumin, 1858. 7+556 p. O.

Fougerousse, A. **Patrons et ouvriers de Paris.** Reformes introduites dans l'organisation du travail par divers chefs d'industrie. Paris, Guillaumin, 1880. 288 p. O.

Jannet, C. **L'organisation du travail d'apres F. Le Play, et le mouvement social contemporain.** Paris, Société d'Economie Sociale. 33 p. 8°.

Lavergne, LÉONCE DE. **Economie rurale de la France depuis 1789.** Paris, Guillaumin, 1860. 3+487 p. D.

Le Play, P. G. F. **Les ouvriers Européens.** 2me ed. 6 v. 8°. Tours. Alfred Mame et fils., 1878-9. Paris, Dentu.

Le Play, P. G. F. **L'organisation du travail.** 4me ed. Tours, Mame, 1877. 600 p. D.

——— Same. **The Organization of Labor.** 2d ed., tr. by G. Emerson, Phila., Claxton, 1872. 417 p. D.

Leroy-Beaulieu, PAUL. **De l'etat moral et intellectuel des populations ouvrieres et de son influence sur le taux des salaires.** Paris, Guillaumin, 1868. 28+303 p. D.

Leroy-Beaulieu, PAUL. **La question ouvrière au xixe siècle.** Paris, G. Charpentier, 1881. 339 p. D.

Leroy-Beaulieu, PAUL. **Le travail des femmes au xixe siécle.** Paris, Charpentier & Cie., 1873.

Levasseur, E. **Histoire des classes ouvrières en France, depuis la conquete de Jules César jusqu'a la révolution.** Paris, Guillaumin, 1859. 2 v. O.

Levasseur, E. **Histoire des classes ouvrières en France, depuis 1789 jusqu'a nos jours.** Paris, L. Hachette & Cie., 1867. 2 v. O.

Proudhon, P. J. **System of Economical Contradictions, or the Philosophy of Misery.** Tr. by B. R. Tucker. Boston, B. R. Tucker, 1888. 469 p. O. $3.50.

V. 4 of Works. The greater part of this vol. is devoted to questions of labor, machinery, competition and monopoly. Based on denial of God.

Simon, JULES. **L'ouvrière.** Paris, L. Hachette & Cie., 1861. 8+383 p. O.

Thierry, AUGUSTIN. **Essai sur l'histoire du tiers état.** Bruxelles, Meline, Cans & Cie., 1855. 427 p. D.

Engels, F: Condition of the Working-Class in England in 1844, with appendix written 1886, and preface 1887. Tr. by Florence K. Wischnewetsky. N. Y., J. W. Lovell Co., 1887. 211 p. D. $1.25.

Hasbach, W: Das Englische Arbeiterversicherungswesen. Geschichte seiner Entwickelung und Gesetzgebung. Leipzig, Düncker & Humblot, 1883. 447 p. D.
<small>Gives details of insurance methods adopted by the working population of England.</small>

Ketteler, *Bishop* F. von. Die Arbeiterfrage und das Christenthum. Mainz, F. Kirchheim, 1864. 212 p. O.

Lange, F. A. Die Arbeiterfrage. 3d ed. Wintherthur, 1875.
<small>"Abounds in acute and important discussions."—*Cossa*.</small>

Meyer, R. Die Emancipationskampf des vierten Standes. Berlin, H. Bahr, 1882. 532p. O.

Tait, W. Cave. Arbeiter-Schutzgesetzgebung in den Vereinigten Staaten. Tübingen, 1884. 178 p. O.

The Commissioner of Labor, Washington, began March, 1886, to issue annual reports. 1st Report, 1885, Industrial Depressions. 496 p. 2d, 1886, Convict Labor in the U. S., 612 p. 3d. 1887, Strikes and Lockouts, 1172 p. 4th, 1888, Working Women in Large Cities. 631 p. 5th, 1889, Railroad Labor, 888 p. And in 1889, special report on Marriage and Divorce, 1074 p.

The Department of State, Washington, has issued two series of consular reports on labor in Europe and other parts of the world (1878, 1 v., 1885, 3 v.), which are exhaustive on rates of wages, cost of living, housing, clothing, and general social condition of laborers.

Many of the States of the Union have Bureaus of Statistics of Labor, which publish reports. Of these Bureaus that of Massachusetts is much the best organized and most important. Those of New Jersey and Connecticut are excellent. Within a recent period that of New York has done commendable work.

TRADES ORGANIZATIONS, STRIKES.

Brisbane, Albert. Concise Exposition of the Doctrine of Association. N. Y., J. S. Redfield, 1847. 80 p. D.

Carr, E. S. Patrons of Husbandry of the Pacific Coast. San Francisco, A. L. Bancroft & Co., 1875. 461 p. O.

Chamberlin, E. M. Sovereigns of Industry. Boston, Lee & Shepard, 1875. 165+21 p. D.

Dacus, J. A. Annals of the Great Strikes in the United States, 1877. Chicago, J. S. Goodman, 1877. 480 p.

Goodwin, T. S. The Grange: a study in the science of society. N. Y. Putnam, 1874. 245 p. D.

Grosvenor, W. M. Trades-Unions: investigated in the light of common-sense. N. Y., Commercial Bulletin Print, 1885. 39 p. O. pap., 15 c.
<small>An adverse criticism.</small>

Lloyd, H: D. Strike of Millionaires against Miners, the story of Spring Valley. N. Y., Belford, Clarke & Co., 1890. 264 p. D. cl. $1; pap. 50 c.

Martin, E. W. History of the Grange Movement. Phila., National Pub. Co., 1873. 535 p. O.

Miller, J. BLEECKER. **Trade Organizations in Politics;** *also,* **Progress and Robbery,** an answer to Henry George. N. Y., Baker & Taylor Co., 1887 218 p. O. $1.25.

Missouri, Labor Statistics Bureau. **Official history of the great strike of 1886** on the Southwestern Railway System. Jefferson City, Mo., 1887. 117 p. O.

National Grange of the patrons of husbandry. Digest of laws and enactments. Phila., 1882. 104 p. D.

Seligman, E. R. A. **Two Chapters on the Mediæval Guilds of England.** Baltimore, American Economic Assoc., 1887. pap., 75 c.

Smith, H. L., and **Nash,** VAUGHAN. **Story of the Dockers' Strike,** told by two East Londoners. Lond., 1889. 180 p. D.

Strikes and Lockouts. 3d Annual Report Commissioner of Labor, Washington, 1888.
This most important report gives full statistics.

Trade Guilds of Europe. U. S. Consular Reports. Washington, Department of State, 1885. 332 p. O.

Wright, CARROLL D. **Historical Sketch of the Knights of Labor.** Boston, G: H. Ellis, 1887.

Levi, LEONE. **Work and Pay.** London, 1877. O.
A series of popular lectures on topics connected with industrial organization.

Trant, W. **Trades-Unions.** N. Y., Scribner & Welford, 1884. 60 c.
A good account of trades-unions in England.

Crousel, A. **Etude historique économique et juridique sur les coalitions et les grèves dans l'industrie.** Paris, A. Rousseau, 1887. 6+543 p. O.

Dauby, J. **Des grèves ouvrières.** Nouvelle ed. Bruxelles, G. Mayolez, 1883. 19+211 p. D.

Hubert-Valleroux, P. **Les corporations d'arts et métiers,** et les Syndicats professionels en France et a l'étranger. Paris, Guillaumin 1885. 21+423 p. O.

Le droit au travail. A discussion by leading French economists and publicists. Guillaumin, Paris, 1848.

Paris, *Comte* de. **Les associations ouvrières en Angleterre.** Paris, Germer Baillière, 1869. 8+334 p. D.

―――― Same. **Trades Unions of England.** Tr. by N. J. Senior, and ed. by T: Hughes, M. P. Lond., Smith, Elder & Co., 1869. 14+246 p. D. 7s. 6d.

Reinaud, EMILE. **Les syndicats professionels,** leur rôle historique et économique. Paris, Guillaumin, 1886. 8+267 p. D.

Smith, L. **Les coalitions et les grèves,** d'apres l'histoire et l'économie politique. Paris, Guillaumin, 1886. 288 p. O.

Barnreither, J. M. **English Associations of Workingmen.** Tr. by Alice Taylor. Lond., Swan Sonnenschein, 1889. 473 p. O.
The latest and best survey.

Brentano, LUJO. **On the History and Development of Guilds,** and the Origin of Trades-Unions. Lond., Trübner, 1870. viii+278+16+135 p. O.
This is not a satisfactory work, and is quoted here only because there happens to be now in print no other book covering the same ground.

Brentano, Lujo. **Zur Geschichte der Englischen Gewerkvereine.** Leipzig, Duncker & Humblot, 1871. 288 p. O.

Brentano, Lujo. **Zur Kritik der Englischen Gewerkvereine.** Leipzig, Duncker & Humblot, 1872. 369 p. O.
Best work next to Barnreither.

Studnitz, Arthur von. **Nordamericanische Arbeiterverhältnesse.** Leipzig, Dünker & Humblot, 1879. 426+119 p. D.

Farmers' Movement in the United States. *Journal Social Science Assoc.*, 1873. v. 6. p. 100-115.

The New Trades-Unionism. F. Harrison. *Nineteenth Century*, Nov., 1889.

WAGES.

Atkinson, E: **The Distribution of Products,** or, the Mechanism and the Metaphysics of Exchange. N. Y., Putnam, 1885. 303 p. D. $1.25.
Contains What Makes the Rate of Wages? What is a bank? The Railway, the Farmer and the Public.

Atkinson, E: **The Industrial Progress of the Nation: Consumption Limited, Production Unlimited.** N. Y., Putnam, 1890. 395 p. O. $2.50.
Contains "The Distribution of Products," (not book above); chapters on the Food Question; The Relative Strength and Weakness of Nations; What Shall be Taxed; What Shall be Exempt; A Single Tax on Land; Slow-Burning Construction.

Gunton, G: **Wealth and Progress;** the economic philosophy of the eight-hour movement. N. Y., Appleton, 1887. 382 p. D. $1.
The author holds that a reduction of the working day to eight hours will solve the problem of unemployed labor. He emphasizes the statement that wages when high increase consuming power, and so tend to enlarge the market for product and labor.

Schoenhof, J. **The Industrial Situation and the Question of Wages.** N. Y., Putnam, 1885. 157 p. D. $1.
Aims to prove that low wages mean low efficiency of labor, and the converse.

Scudder, M. L., Jr. **The Labor-Value Fallacy.** Chicago, Patriots' League, 1886. 95 p. D. pap., 10 c.

Walker, Francis A. **The Wages Question:** a treatise on wages and the wage-receiving class. N. Y., Holt, 1876. 428 p. O. $3.50.
Holds that wages are paid out of production—in opposition to the wages-fund theory. Describes causes which render competition between capital and labor imperfect to the disadvantage of labor. Brings out the importance of the entrepreneur, or captain of industry, who stands between capital and labor. Discriminates real from nominal wages.
A work which takes account of sentiment as affecting economic forces.

Weeks, Joseph D. **Report on statistics of wages in manufacturing industries,** with reports on average retail prices of necessaries of life; and on trades-societies, strikes and lock-outs. V. 20 of Census for 1880. H. R. Misc. Document, no. 42, pt. 20, 47th Congress, 2d Session. Washington, 1886, 4°.

Wood, Stuart. **Theory of Wages.** Balt., American Economic Assoc., 1889. 69 p. O. pap., 75 c.

Wright, Carroll D. **Wages and Prices in Massachusetts:** an historical review, 1752-1860; 1860-1883. Boston, Mass. Bureau of Statistics of Labor, 1885. 370 p. O.
A comparison of wages and prices, together with other important circumstances of living—as the comparative cleanliness and order of homes. Reprinted from the Bureau's 16th Annual Report, for 1885.

Brassey, T: **Foreign Work and English Wages,** considered with reference to depression of trade. Lond., Longmans, 1879. 417 p. O.
Contains some useful data and criticisms of trades-unions.

Brassey, T: **On Work and Wages.** N. Y., Putnam, 1886. 296 p. S. $1.
Contains much information about the wage-receiving class, and the experience of an employer in dealing with that class; treats also of the rights of wage-receivers.

Fawcett, H: **The Economic Position of the British Laborer.** Lond., 865. D. $1.50.

Industrial Remuneration Conference. Report of proceedings and papers read, Jan. 28-30, 1885. Lond., Cassell & Co., 1885. 24+528 p. O.

Levi, LEONE. **Wages and Earnings of the Working-Classes in 1883-4.** With some facts illustrative of their economic conditions: drawn from authentic and official sources. London, Murray, 1885. 3s. 6d.
Full of valuable information.

McDonnell, W. D. **History and criticism of the various theories of wages.** Lond., Simpkin, Marshall & Co., 1888. 5+72 p. D.
The Whately prize essay.

Rogers, J. E. THOROLD. **Six Centuries of Work and Wages:** the history of English labor. Lond., Swan Sonnenschein, 2d ed. rev., 15s. N. Y., Putnam. 591 p. O. $3.
Based on his "History of Agriculture and Prices," see note thereon [Land and Rent.]

Rogers, J. E. THOROLD. **Work and Wages.** Abridged ed. Lond., Swan Sonnenschein & Co., 1890. 206 p., 8°, 2s. 6d.

Chevallier, EMILE. **Les salaires au XIXme siècle.** Paris, Arthur Rousseau, 1887. 303 p. O. 8 francs.
An able work.

Villey, EDMOND. **La question des salaires.** Paris, L. Larose & Forcel, 1887. 299 p. D.

Roesler, C. F. H. **Zur Kritik der Lehre vom Arbeitslohn.** Erlangen, F. Encke, 1861. 245 p. O.
An excellent history of theories of wages.

Wages and Cost of Production are treated in the Report for 1889 of Mass. Bureau of Statistics of Labor.

Wages is treated among the Collected Essays of Prof. W. G. Sumner. N. Y., Holt, 1885.

Law of Wages and Interest. J. B. Clark. *Annals Am. Acad. Pol. and Soc. Science*, Phila., July, 1890.

Natural Rate of Wages. F. H. Giddings. *Political Science Quarterly*, Dec., 1887.

The Eight-Hours Law Agitation. F. A. Walker. *Atlantic Monthly*, June, 1890.

CO-OPERATION.

Barnard, C: **Coöperation as a Business.** Comprising a summary of the results of coöperative work in the United States and in Europe, in manufacturing, trade, house-building, etc.; with some consideration of the causes of the success or failure of different enterprises, and also of the probable increase in this country of the application of methods of coöperation to various branches of practical business. N. Y., Putnam, 1881. $1.

Dexter, SEYMOUR. **Treatise on Coöperative Savings and Loan Associations.** N. Y., Appleton, 1889. 299 p. D. $1.25.
A thoroughly practical manual; gives the New York statutes governing these associations.

History of Coöperation in the United States. Baltimore, American Economic Assoc., 1888. 540 p. D. $3.50.
<small>Contains Coöperation in New England, by E. W. Bemis; in the Middle States, by E. W. Bemis; in the Northwest, by Albert Shaw; on the Pacific Coast, by C. H. Shinn; in Maryland and the South, by D. R. Randall; and Three Phases of Coöperation in the West, by Amos G. Warner.</small>

Rosenthal, H. S. Manual for Building and Loan Associations. Cincinnati, S. Rosenthal & Co. 255 p. D. $1.50.

Wright, Carroll D. Coöperative Distribution in Great Britain, with a brief account of coöperative progress in other countries. Boston, Mass. Bureau of Statistics of Labor, 1886. 110 p. O. pap.
<small>Reprinted from the Bureau's 17th Annual Report, for 1886.</small>

Wright, Carroll D. Manual of Distributive Coöperation. Boston, Mass. Bureau of Statistics of Labor, 1885. 111 p. O. pap.

Ackland, Arthur H. D., *and* Jones, B. Workingmen Coöperators; what they have done, and what they are doing: an account of the artisans' coöperative movement in Great Britain. N. Y., Cassell, 1884. 136 p. S. 40 c.
<small>The best brief account of coöperative practice in Great Britain.</small>

Holyoake, G: J. History of Coöperation in England; its literature and its advocates. xi-420 p. D. 2 v., v. 1, 1812-44; v. 2., 1845-78. Phila., Lippincott, 1875. $4.50.
<small>The author has been a worker in behalf of coöperation, and writes as a zealous advocate, but he bitterly criticises certain forms of coöperation. He gives a mass of valuable information, but his literary method is defective and his political economy questionable.</small>

Holyoake, G: J. Manual of Coöperation; an epitome of "Holyoake's History of Coöperation." N. Y., J. B. Alden, 1885. 78 p. D. 35 c.

Hughes, T: *and* Neale, E. V., *edrs*. Manual for Coöperators. Manchester, Eng., Central Coöperative Board, 1881. 265 p. D.
<small>The standard English authority, by two life-long leaders in coöperation.</small>

Coöperative Building Associations. Report of Special Committee Am. Social Science Assoc. *Journal of Social Science*, 1888. Also same *Journal*, Saratoga papers of 1889, published 1890.

Coöperative Production in France and England. E: Cummings. *Quarterly Journal of Economics*, July, 1890.

PROFIT-SHARING.

Dolge, Alfred. Just Distribution of Earnings. N. Y., Alfred Dolge 1889. 93 p. pap.
<small>Gives an account of the participation in earnings between Mr. Dolge and his employees at Dolgeville, N. Y.</small>

Gilman, Nicholas Paine. Profit-Sharing between Employer and Employé; a study in the evolution of the wages system. Boston, Houghton, Mifflin & Co., 1889. 460 p. O. $1.75.
<small>The one comprehensive book on this subject.</small>

Wright, Carroll D. Profit-Sharing. Boston, Mass. Bureau of Statistics of Labor, 1886. 86 p. pap., O.
<small>Reprinted from the Bureau's 17th Annual Report, for 1886.</small>

Taylor, SEDLEY. Profit-Sharing between Capital and Labor. Lond., Kegan Paul, 1884. 13+170 p. D. N. Y., J. Fitzgerald, 1886. 47 p. O. pap., 15 c.

Godin, JEAN B. A. The Association of Capital with Labor. Being the Laws and Regulations of Mutual Assurance, regulating the Social Palace at Guise. N. Y. Social Science Association, 1881. 50 c.

Böhmert, V. Gewinnbetheiligung: Untersuchungen über Arbeitslohn und Unternehmergewinn. Leipzig, Brockhaus, 1878. 484 p. D.

Profit-Sharing. J. S. Nicholson. *Contemporary Review*, Jan., 1890.

ARBITRATION, CONCILIATION.

Bayles, J. C. The Shop Council. N. Y. Soc. for Political Education, 1887, pap., 15 c.

Ryan, DAN. J. Arbitration between Capital and Labor: a history and an argument. Columbus, O., A. H. Smythe, 1885. 127 p. O. $1.

Weeks, JOSEPH D. Arbitration and Conciliation (Industrial) in France and England. Address before the manufacturers and workingmen of Pittsburgh, January, 1879. Pittsburgh, Pa., Am. Iron and Steel Pub. Co., 1879. 16 p. D. pap., 25 c.

Weeks, JOSEPH. Arbitration and Conciliation; their Practical Operation in the Settlement of Differences between Employers and Employees in England. Pittsburgh, Pa., Am. Iron and Steel Pub. Co., 1879. 45 p. D. pap., 25 c.

Weeks, JOSEPH D. Industrial Conciliation and Arbitration in New York, Ohio, and Pennsylvania. Pittsburgh, Pa., 1881. Also included in the 12th (1880) Annual Report of the Massachusetts Bureau of Statistics of Labor, with comments by Carroll D. Wright, Chief. Boston, 1881.

Weeks, JOSEPH D. Labor Differences and Their Settlement. Economic tract, No. 20, N. Y., Soc. for Political Education, 1885, pap., 25 c.

Wright, CARROLL D., *comp.* **Industrial Conciliation and Arbitration in** England, Massachusetts, Ohio, Pennsylvania, and New York. Boston, 1881. pap., 173 p. O.

Compiled from material in the possession of the Mass. Bureau of Statistics of Labor.

Crompton, H. Industrial Conciliation. Lond., H. S. King & Co., 1876. 4+181 p. D.

Price, L. L. F. R. Industrial Peace; its advantages, methods, and difficulties: a report of an inquiry made for the Toynbee trustees. N. Y., Macmillan, 1887. 127 p. O. $1.50.

A study of arbitration and conciliation, chiefly as worked out in the iron and coal industries of Northumberland.

The Relations of Industrial Conciliation and Social Reform. *Journal Statistical Soc.*, June, 1890.

MONEY, CURRENCY, BANKING.

Walker's is the best American treatise on Money ; Bagehot and Jevons are the leading English authorities. Horton is the chief American bimetallist ; Seyd and Cernuschi are the principal foreign bimetallists. Gold as the standard of value has been ably discussed by Laughlin among American writers, by Knies among those of Germany. Atkinson's report on bimetallism to the U. S. Government is very valuable. On Banking Gilbart's is the best English treatise ; the chief American work is Bolles'. Wirth's book on Crises is most able. Horton, Jevons, and Laughlin give extensive bibliographies. Subjects under this heading are in part also treated in works under Public Finance ; for example, Adams' Public Debts contains much information about U. S. currency not obtainable elsewhere, and Bourne's History of the Surplus Revenue of 1837 is an important chapter of monetary history.

MONEY, CURRENCY.

Andrews, E. B. An Honest Dollar. Baltimore, American Economic Assoc., 1889. 50 p. O. pap. 75 c.

Holds it wrong to identify a fall of prices with cheapening of commodities, and that scarcity of money is one of the chief causes for fall in prices. So extremely hurtful are fluctuations in value of money held to be, that to prevent them a Government non-partisan commission is suggested, with power to inflate the currency when prices tend to fall, and contract it when they tend to rise. Commends double standard, with relation between gold and silver fixed by law. Discusses composite standards of value. An able, suggestive essay.

Bancroft, G: Plea for the Constitution of the United States of America wounded in the house of its guardians. N. Y., Harper, 1886. 95 p. S. pap. 25 c.

A protest against the legal-tender decision of the Supreme Court, March 3, 1884. Criticised by H. H. Neill, The Legal Tender Decision, *Political Science Quarterly*, June, 1886. The decision of the court with statement of the case is published in v. 110, U. S. Reports, Cases adjudged in the Supreme Court, Oct. Term, 1883.

Clarke, F. W., comp. Weights, Measures, and Money of all Nations. N. Y., Appleton, 1888. 117 p. D. $1.50.

Dunbar, C. F. Laws of the United States relating to Currency and Finance, from 1789 to 1890. Cambridge, Mass., C. W. Sever, 1891. 300 p. D. $2.50.

Presents the exact texts of the more important acts and parts of acts.

Gallatin, ALBERT. Considerations on the Currency and Banking System of the United States. Phila., 1831. 108 p. O.

Gouge, W: M. Short History of Paper Money and Banking in the United States. Phila., 1833. 12+140+240 p. D.

The best early history. A work on which Sumner, Walker, and other authorities have in part based their labors. Pt. 2 was reprinted in London, 1833, with an introd. by W. Cobbett, who entitles the book "The Curse of Paper Money and Banking."

Horton, S. D. Partial List of Modern Publications on Money. In Report of International Monetary Conference, Paris, 1878. Senate Exec. Document no. 58, 45th Congress, 3d Session. Washington, Gov. Pr. Office.

King, CLARENCE. Statistics of the Production of the Precious Metals in the United States. U. S. Interior Dept., Census Office, 10th Census, 1880. V. 13. Washington, Gov. Pr. Office, 1881. 541 p. Q.

Knox, J. Jay. **United States Notes;** a history of the various issues of paper money by the Government of the U. S. 3d ed. rev. N. Y., Scribner, 1888. 12+247 p. D. $1.50.

Mr. Knox was Comptroller of the Currency. Chap. XII is an historical sketch of the Distribution of the Surplus among the States. An appendix contains the Decision of the Supreme Court, with the dissenting opinion, upon the Legal Tender Case.

Legal Tender Decision, United States Supreme Court, 1884. In U. S. Reports, v. 110.

Prof. E. J. James, in pubs. of American Economic Assoc., March, 1888, discusses the Decision, and in a concluding note names the principal comments on the Decision published in law magazines. See also notes under Bancroft, G., and Knox, J. Jay.

Linderman, H. R. **Money and Legal Tender in the United States.** N. Y., Putnam, 1879. 173 p. D. $1.25.

"The various legislative provisions with regard to the coinage of money and the regulation of currency in the United States are treated in this essay with brevity, but with precision and clearness." Mr. Linderman was Director of the Mint.

McAdam, Graham. **An Alphabet in Finance.** A simple statement of permanent principles and their application to questions of the day. N. Y., Putnam, 1877. xiii+210 p. D. $1.25.

Simple, popular, and effective, but now rather out of date. Introd. by R. R. Bowker.

Newcomb, Simon. **The A B C of Finance;** or, money and labor questions explained to common people in short and easy lessons. N. Y., Harper, 1879. 115 p. Tt. 40 c.

A popular exposition of elementary economic notions, with especial reference to the fallacies most widely accepted by the wage-receiving class.

Phillips, H: jr. **Historical Sketches of the Paper Currency** of the American Colonies prior to 1789. 2 v. Roxbury, Mass., W. E. Woodward, 1866. 233, 264 p. O.

Poor, H. V. **Money and Its Laws;** embracing a history of monetary theories and of the currencies of the United States. N. Y., H. V. & H. W. Poor, 1877. 623 p. O. $5.

Raguet, Condy. **Currency and Banking.** Phila. and Lond., 1839. 262 p. O.

One of the most important financial works ever written.

Richardson, W. A. **Practical Information Concerning the Public Debt of the United States,** with the National Banking Laws. Washington, W. H. & O. H. Morrison, 1872. 186 p. O.

An excellent summary of information.

Schurz, Carl. **Honest Money and Labor.** (Economic Monographs, no. 11.) N. Y., Putnam, 1879. O. pap. 25 c.

Spaulding, E. G. **History of the Legal-Tender Act.** Buffalo, N. Y., 1869. 6+213+40 p. O.

Shows how the Act came to be passed; what views controlled Congress at the time; the limitations then considered essential, etc.

Sumner, W: G. **History of American Currency.** With chapters on the English Bank Restrictions and Austrian Paper Money. N. Y., Holt, 1878. 390 p. D. $3.

Deals with facts more than with theories. The historical information which it contains has never been brought together before within the compass of a single work. The English "Bullion Report" of 1810 is given in full in an appendix.

Walker, FRANCIS A. Money. N. Y., Holt, 1878. 550 p. O. $4.

The standard American treatise. Author rejects the word *Currency* and extends the term *Money* to include bank-notes. Substitutes the definition "common denominator in exchange" for "measure of value." Holds that paper money, nominally or really convertible into coin, is liable to over issue. States and impartially examines the various theories of money.

Walker, FRANCIS A. Money in Its Relations to Trade and Industry. N. Y., Holt, 1879. 339 p. D. $1.25.

In part an abridgment of "Money," with chapters on the relations of money to trade and industry.

Wells, DAVID A. Robinson Crusoe's Money. N. Y., Harper, 1876. O. cl. $1; pap. 50 c.

An exposition, in the form of a facetious and satirical story, of the principles of money and currency. Illustrated by Nast.

White, A. D. Paper-Money Inflation in France: a history and its application. Economic tract, no. 7. N. Y., Soc. for Political Education, 1882. 46 p. D. pap. 25 c.

White, HORACE. Money and Its Substitutes. Economic tract., no. 6. N. Y., Society for Political Education, 1882. 31 p. D. pap. 25 c.

Out of print as a tract. Published v. 2, Lalor's Cyclopædia.

Bagehot, W. International Coinage. A practical plan of assimilating English and American money, as a step toward a universal money. 2d enl. ed. Lond. and N. Y., Longmans, 1889. 93 p. O. 75 c.

Fullarton, J. Regulation of Currencies. 2d ed. enl. and rev. Lond., Murray, 1845. 253 p. O.

An examination of the proposals to restrict the future issues on credit of the Bank of England and other banks.

Hamilton, R. Money and Value. Lond., Macmillan, 1878. O.

An enquiry into the means and end of economic production, with an appendix on the depreciation of silver and on Indian currency.

Jevons, W. STANLEY. Investigations in Currency and Finance. Lond. and N. Y., Macmillan, 1884. 428 p. with 20 diagrams, O. $7.50.

Contains a bibliography of finance of 50 pages.

Jevons, W. STANLEY. Money and the Mechanism of Exchange. N. Y., Appleton, 1879. xxiii+350 p. D. $1.75.

Very simple and elementary. It contains descriptions of the Clearing-House and the check bank. It is the best popular book for laying a basis of sound doctrines.

Nicholson, J. S. Treatise on Money and Essays on Present Monetary Problems. Lond., Blackwood, 1888. 14+375 p. D. 10s. 6d.

Overstone, *Lord* [Samuel Jones Loyd before being created Lord Overstone.] **Metallic and Paper Currency.** Ed. and in part abridged by J: R. McCulloch. Lond., 1857. 647 p. D.

Contains acute and sagacious remarks on the administration of the Bank of England, its circulation, and charter; with evidence before Select Committees of the House of Commons on Banks of Issue, in 1840; on Commercial Distress, in 1848.

Wilson, JAMES. Capital, Currency, and Banking. 2d ed. Lond., D. M. Aird, *Economist* office, 1859. 203+100 p. D. 7s. 6d.

Articles reprinted from the *Economist* on the principles of the Bank Act of 1844, and on the crisis of 1847.

Chevalier, MICHEL. **La monnaie.** 2me ed. Aug. Paris, Capelle, 1866. 8+779 p. O.

Wolowski, L. 1810–1876. **De la monnaie.** Paris, 1868. 72 p. S.

Hertzka, H. **Währung und Handel.** Wien, 1876. 8+416 p. O.
The best book in the three languages on the operation of depreciation in the currency, whether by inconvertible paper or by the attempt to use two metals, one of which falls in value.

Hildebrand, R: **Theorie des Geldes.** Jena, G. Fischer, 1883. 147 p. O.

Magliani, AG. **La questione monetaria.** Firenze, 1874.

T. Tooke in History of Prices [see Prices] gives a brief sketch of the state of the coinage in the last two centuries.

GOLD, SILVER, BIMETALLISM.

Atkinson, E: **Bimetallism in Europe.** 50th Congress, 1st Session. Ex. Doc. 34. Washington, Gov. Pr. Office, 1887. 280 p. O. Also published as U. S. Consular Report, no. 87, Dec., 1887.
Report to the President of the United States. It contains tr. of A. Soetbeer's "Materials toward the Elucidation of the Economic Conditions affecting the Precious Metals," by F. W. Taussig. A. Soetbeer is the first authority on Production of Gold and Silver.

Fawcett, W. L. **Gold and Debt, an American Handbook of Finance.** With 80 tables and diagrams, together with a digest of the monetary laws of the United States. Chicago, S. C. Griggs & Co., 1876. 270 p. D. $1.75.
Contains statistics of paper money, gold and silver in circulation in the U. S. and Europe at various periods since 1825; some account of the increase of public debts; and a compilation of the monetary laws of the U. S.

Ford, W. C. **The Standard Silver Dollar and the Coinage Law of 1878.** Economic tract, no. 13. N. Y., Soc. for Political Education, 1884. 31 p. D. pap. 20 c.

Horton, S. DANA. **Silver in Europe.** Lond. and N. Y., Macmillan, 1890. 290 p. 12°. $1.50.
By a leading bimetallist. Includes review of Paris Monetary Congress (September, 1889); and Questions of the Royal [British] Commission on Gold and Silver (1870), and answers.

Laughlin, J. LAURENCE. **History of Bimetallism in the United States.** N. Y., Appleton, 1885. 258 p. O. with charts and tables, $2.25.
An exhaustive work. Holds that gold has not appreciated, that silver has declined in value owing to decreased demand for it as coin, civilized nations preferring gold. These views are deduced from an extensive array of facts and figures. Author maintains that the coinage of silver dollars should cease. Includes a bibliography.

McCulloch, HUGH. **Bimetallism.** (Economic Monographs, no. 17.) N. Y., Putnam, 1879. O. pap. 25 c.

Richardson, H. W. **The Standard Dollar.** Economic tract, no. 15. N. Y., Soc. for Political Education, 1884. 40 p. D. pap. 25 c.

Wells, DAVID A. **Silver Question, The,** the Dollar of the Fathers vs. the Dollar of the Sons. (Economic Monograph, no. 2.) N. Y., Putnam, 1878. D. pap. 25 c.

Bagehot, W. **The Depreciation of Silver.** Lond., H. S. King & Co., 1877. 136 p. O. 5s.

Barbour, D. **Theory of Bimetallism,** and the effects of the partial demonetisation of silver on England and India. Lond. and N. Y., Cassell, 1886. 158 p. O. 6s.

Crump, Arthur. An Investigation into the Great Fall in Prices which took place coincidentally with the Demonetization of Silver in Germany. Lond. and N. Y., Longmans, 1889. 198 p. O. $2.

Fowler, W: Appreciation of Gold. Cobden Club tract. Lond. and N. Y., Cassell, 1886. pap. 25 c.

Gibbs, H. H., Grenfell, H. R., and others. Bimetallic controversy; a collection of papers, etc. Lond., E. Wilson, 1885. 7 + 404 p. O.

_{Earl Grey, Lord Sherbrooke, Lord Bramwell, Bonamy Price, W. Stanley Jevons, Sir T: H. Farrer, R. Giffen, C. Daniell, H. A. Macleod and H. Cernuschi, are contributors.}

Gold and Silver Commission. Final report of the Royal [British] Commission to inquire into the recent changes of the relative values of the precious metals. Senate Mis. Doc. 34. 50th Congress, 2d Session. Washington, Gov. Pr. Office, 1889. 199 p. O.

_{Reprint of final report presented to Parliament, 1888. The report in full was published Lond., 1887-88, 4 v. O.}

Huskisson, W. The Question Concerning the Depreciation of our Currency, stated and examined. Lond., Murray, 1810. 154 p. D.

Jacob, W. Historical Inquiry into the Production and Consumption of the Precious Metals. Lond., 1831. 2 v. O. Phila., 1832. 12 + 427 p. O.

_{Of historical value. Now superseded by Soetbeer and other authorities.}

Price, Bonamy. Principles of Currency and Banking. N. Y., Appleton, 1876. 176 p. D. $1.50.

Report on the High Price of Bullion, Select Committee, House of Commons, 1810. Lond., J. Johnson & Co., 1810. 237 + 115 p. O.

Seyd, Ernest. Bimetallism in 1886, and the further fall in silver. Lond., E. Wilson & Co., 1887, pap. 1s.

Seyd, Ernest. Bullion and the Foreign Exchanges, Theoretically and Practically Considered. Lond., E. Wilson & Co., 1868. 699 p. O.

_{Followed by a defence of Double Valuation with special reference to the proposed system of Universal Coinage. Treats the subject from the standpoint of a bullion broker. Contains essays in favor of the so-called "double standard."}

Cernuschi, H: Nomisma; or "Legal Tender." N. Y., Appleton, 1877. 157 p. D. $1.25.

_{Evidence before U. S. Monetary Commission, Washington, Feb., 1877; "Monetary Pacification by Rehabilitation of Silver," and " he Bimetallic Future," from the Paris *Siecle*; " Silver Vindicated," and three letters on the Silver Question.}

Chevalier, Michel. On the Probable Fall in the Value of Gold, the commercial and social consequences which may ensue, and the measures which it invites. Tr. by R: Cobden. N. Y., Appleton, 1859. O. $1.25.

Congrès monétaire international, compte rendu et documents. Paris, 1890.

_{Proceedings of congress held during Paris Exposition, 1889.}

Wolowski, L. L'or et l'argent. Paris, 1870. 40 + 440 + 134 p.

Knies, Karl. Geld und Kredit. Berlin, 1873-79. 2 v. O.

_{Knies is superior to Roscher in legal knowledge among German economists, though inferior to him in historic learning. This work has become classical.}

Soetbeer, AD. **Precious Metals,** Materials toward the Elucidation of the Economic Conditions affecting.

Tr. by F. W. Taussig, included in E: Atkinson's report on Bimetallism in Europe, which see.

In the proceedings of the International Monetary Conferences held in Paris, August, 1878, April–July, 1881, and during the Exposition of 1889, and in the report of the U. S. Silver Commission organized under a joint resolution of Congress, August, 1876, all being public documents published for distribution, will be found a large amount of information pertaining to the use of the two metals, gold and silver, as standards of value.

An annual report on the state of the Finances is issued by the Secretary of the Treasury, Washington. An annual report of the Director of the Mint on the production of precious metals in the United States is published by the Treasury Department, Washington.

For bibliographies of bimetallism see Laughlin's History of Bimetallism, and Laughlin's abridgment of Mill's Political Economy.

Bimetallism is treated among the Collected Essays of Prof. W. G. Sumner. N. Y., Holt, 1885.

Our Gold Coinage. J. B. Martin. *Journal of Institute of Bankers*, Lond., June, 1882.

Silver or legal-tender notes. Worthington C. Ford. *Political Science Quarterly*, Dec., 1889.

Silver Question in the United States, with diagrams showing silver certificates and silver in circulation, net gold in treasury, and silver dollars coined 1878–90. F. W. Taussig. *Quarterly Journal of Economics*, April, 1890.

The Silver Situation. Horace White. *Quarterly Journal of Economics*, July, 1890.

The American Silver Bubble. Robert Giffen. *Nineteenth Century*, Aug., 1890.

How the Silver Act Will Work. F. W. Taussig. *Forum*, Oct., 1890.

BANKING, EXCHANGE, CREDIT.

Atkinson, E: **What Is a Bank?** What service does a bank perform? Economic tracts, no. 1. N. Y., Society for Political Education, 1882. 36 p. D.

Now out of print as a tract. Forms a chapter in "The Distribution of Products," N. Y., Putnam, 1887.

Bolles, A. S. **Practical Banking and Bankers' Commonplace Book.** N. Y., Homans Pub. Co., 1884. 300 p. O. $3.

Bolles, A. S. **The National Bank Act and Its Judicial Meaning.** N. Y., Homans Pub. Co., 1888. 400 p. O. $3.

Clarke, M. ST. CLAIR, *and* **Hall,** D. A., *comp.* **Legislative and Documentary History of the Bank of the United States,** including the original Bank of North America. Washington, 1832. 808 p. O.

Cleaveland, J: **Banking System of New York.** Together with an account of the New York Clearing-House. 2d ed. by G. S. Hutchinson. N. Y., 1864. O. $5.50.

Goddard, T: H. General History of the most Prominent Banks in Europe and the United States; with Alex. Hamilton's report to Congress on currency. N. Y., H. C. Sleight, 1831. 254 p. O.

Hotchkiss, PHILO P. **Banks and Banking, 1771-1888,** an historical sketch based upon official records. N. Y., Putnam, 1888. 51 p. O. pap. 75 c.

Morse, J. T. **Treatise on the Law Relating to Banks and Banking.** 2d ed. Boston, Little, Brown & Co., 1879. O. $6.

A very complete and thorough presentation of positive law on this subject in the United States at the time of writing.

Richardson, H. W. The National Banks. N. Y., Harper, 1880. S. cl. 40 c.; pap. 25 c.

Royall, W: L. **Andrew Jackson and the Bank of the United States,** including a history of Paper Money in the United States. (Economic Monographs, no. 19.) N. Y., Putnam, 1880. O. pap. 25 c.

Scudder, M. L., JR. **National Banking.** (Economic Monographs, no. 12.) N. Y., Putnam, 1879. O. pap. 25 c.

Bagehot, W. **Lombard Street.** A description of the money market. N. Y., Scribner, 1874. viii+359 p. D. $1.25.

Interesting descriptions of the mechanism of the English credit institutions, with able discussions of many points of theory.

Crump, ARTHUR. **Banking, Currency, and the Exchanges.** Lond., Longmans, 1866. D. 6s.

Crump, ARTHUR. **English Manual of Banking.** Lond., E. Wilson & Co., 1886. D. 15s.

A compendium of valuable information about banking institutions, banking methods, phraseology, devices, etc.; also about laws of banking in Great Britain, with much information about methods, etc., on the continent.

Francis, J: **History of the Bank of England** from 1694 to 1844, continued to 1862 by I. S. Homans. N. Y., 1862. O. $4.

Gilbert, J. W. **History, Principles, and Practice of Banking.** Rev. to 1881 by A. S. Michie. 2 v. Lond., G. Bell & Sons, 1882. O. 10s. 6d.

A standard work. The most exhaustive on the subject.

Goschen, G: J. **Theory of the Foreign Exchanges.** Lond., E. Wilson & Co., 1886. O. 6s.

The standard work on the subject.

Hankey, T. Principles of Banking. Its utility and economy, with remarks on the Bank of England. 4th ed. Lond., E. Wilson & Co., 1884. O. 2s. 6d.

Treats of the organization and working of the Bank of England, with discussions on some disputed points in the management of the Bank.

Kerr, A: W. **History of Banking in Scotland.** Glasgow, D. Bryce & Son, 1884. 245 p. O.

Lawson, W: J. **History of Banking,** with account of the origin, use, and progress of the Banks of England, Ireland, and Scotland. Lond., R: Bentley, 1850. 525 p. O.

Macleod, H: DUNNING. **Elements of Banking.** Lond. and N. Y., Longmans. D. $1.75.

Macleod, H: Dunning. **Theory and Practice of Banking.** 2d ed. 2 v. Lond. and N. Y., Longmans. O. $9.50.

Works which are full of suggestion, and also very rich in historical material and economic discussion ; but they contain matters of doctrine in which the author is at issue with the recognized authorities, and that, too, on points of the first importance.

Macleod, H: Dunning. **Theory of Credit.** Lond. and N. Y., Longmans, v. 1, 1889, 366 p. O. $2.50. V. 2, pt. 1, 1890, 180 p. O. $1.50.

"Confuses capital and credit. Is right in holding that value depends not on cost of production, but on supply and demand."—*Horace White.*

Price, Bonamy. **Currency and Banking.** N. Y., 1876. 176 p. D. $1.50.

Rae, G: **The Country Banker;** his clients, cares and work; with an American preface by Brayton Ives. N. Y., Scribner, 1886. 14+320 p. D. $1.50.

One of the best popular accounts of the banking business.

Rogers, J. E. Thorold. **First Nine Years of the Bank of England.** Lond. and N. Y., Macmillan, 1887. 31+183 p. O.

Seyd, Ernest. **Reform of the Bank of England Note-Issue.** Lond., 1873. 181 p. O.

Statistical critique on the operation of the Bank Charter Act of 1844, with the Bank of England's weekly statements from 1844 to 1871.

Somers, R: **Scotch Banks and System of Issue;** including tr. of "Les banques d'Ecosse," by L. Wolowski. Edinburgh, A. & C. Black, 1873. 12+244 p. O.

Tennant, C: **Bank of England and the Organization of Credit in England.** 2d ed, enl. Lond., Longmans, 1866. 16+869 p. D.

With the evidence of Isaac and Emile Périere before the French commission of inquiry into the Bank of France ; also abstract of the American free banking act.

Torrens, R. **Sir Robert Peel's Act of 1844** explained and defended. Lond., 1857. 16+216 p. O.

With examination of the principles of currency propounded by Mr. Tooke and Mr. Wilson, and of the chapter on the regulation of the currency in J: S. Mill's "Principles of Political Economy."

Wilson, A. J. **Banking Reform;** an essay on prominent banking dangers and the remedies they demand. Lond., 1879. 6+190 p. O.

Courcelle-Seneuil, J. G. Traité théorique et pratique des opérations de banque. 1853. 6me ed. Paris, 1876.

Courtois, Alph., *fils.* Histoire des Banques en France. 2me ed. Paris, Guillaumin, 1881. 7+375 p. O.

Horn, J. E. La liberté des banques. Paris, Guillaumin, 1866. 464 p. D.

Péreire, Isaac. Principes de la constitution des banques et de l'organisation du credits. 2me ed. Paris, Guillaumin, 1865. 324 p. O.

Walras, L. Théorie mathématique du billet de banque. Lausanne, 1880.

Wolowski, M. L. La question des banques. Paris, Guillaumin, 1864. 592 p. D.

Hübner, Otto. Die Banken. Leipzig, H. Hübner, 1854. 9+476 p. O.

Schulze-Delitsch, H. Vorschuss- und Creditvereine als Volksbanken 1855. 15th ed. Leipzig, 1876.

Ferraris, C. F. **Moneta e corso forzoso.** Milano, 1879.

Rota, P. **Principii de scienza bancaria.** 2da ed. Milano, 1873.

Report of Comptroller of the Currency, for 1876 (Gov. Pr. Office, Washington) contains excellent history of State banking in the U. S.

R. Giffen, in Essays in Finance, 2d series, N. Y., Putnam, 1886, has a chapter on Gold Supply; the Rate of Discount and Prices. State Tamperings with Money and Banks is one of the Essays, Moral, Political, and Æsthetic, of Herbert Spencer. N. Y., Appleton.

Bank Notes. J. B. Martin. *Journal of Institute of Bankers*, Lond, March, 1880.

Future of Banking in the United States. Horace White. *Political Science Quarterly*, Dec., 1886.

The Note Circulation. R. H. Inglis Palgrave. *Journal of Institute of Bankers*, Lond., Jan., 1890.
Exhaustive discussion of present British system, with advocacy of local note circulation.

SAVINGS BANKS.

Keyes, EMERSON W. **History of Savings Banks in the U. S.** N. Y., Bradford Rhodes, 1876. 2 v. O.
" Singles out in an admirable way the best provisions in the laws pertaining to savings banks, such as those regulating the investment of their funds and their supervision.—*Herbert B. Adams.*

Lewins, W: **History of Savings Banks in Great Britain and Ireland.** Lond., C. E. Layton, 1882. 945 p. O. 7s. 6d.
Includes a full account of the origin and progress of Mr. Gladstone's financial measures for Post-Office Banks, Government Annuities, and Government Life Insurance.

Postal Savings Banks for the United States. N. Y., State Charities Aid Assoc., 1885. 23 p. O.
Describes their operation in foreign countries, and advocates their establishment in the U. S. State Charities Aid Assoc. also publishes Report of Special Committee on Postal Savings Banks, Jan., 1887. 13 p. O.

The British Post-Office issues several pamphlets on Postal Savings Banks; the little pamphlet on "Thrift" is said to have been prepared by Prof. H: Fawcett, while Postmaster-General.

Early History of School Savings Banks in the U. S. J. H. Thiry. *Journal of Social Science*, 1888.

Savings Banks in the U. S. John P. Townsend. *Journal of Social Science*, 1888.

SPECULATION, CRISES, PANICS.

Carey, H. C. **Financial Crises,** their causes and effects. Phila., H. C. Baird & Co., 1863. 8°, pap. 25c.

Gibson, G. RUTLEDGE. **Stock Exchanges of London, Paris, and New York:** a comparison. N. Y., Putnam, 1889. 125 p. D. $1.

Scudder, M. L., *Jr.* **Congested Prices.** Chicago, Jansen, McClurg & Co., 1883. 52 p. D. 50 c.
On financial panics, disputing the theory that they must recur periodically. Incidentally describes how prices are made in grain and stock exchanges.

Baxter, ROBERT. Panic of 1866, with its lessons on the Currency Act Lond., Longmans, 1866. 100 p. D.

Crump, ARTHUR. Theory of Stock Exchange Speculation, with preface and notes by H. W. Rosenbaum. N. Y., H. W. Rosenbaum, 1887. 14+136 p. O.

Evans, D. M. Commercial Crisis, 1847-8. 2d ed. enl. Lond., Letts, Son & Steer, 1849. 155+103 p. O.

Evans, D. M. Commercial Crisis, 1857-8, and the Stock Exchange panic of 1859. Lond., Groombridge & Sons, 1859. 200 p. O. 15s.

Evans, D. M. Speculative Notes and Notes on Speculation, Ideal and Real. Lond., Groombridge & Sons, 1864. 10+340 p. O. 10s. 6d.

Giffen, R. Stock Exchange Securities: an essay on the general causes of fluctuations in their prices. Lond., G. Bell & Sons, 1879. 8°, 8s. 6d.

Goadby, EDWIN, *and* Watt, W. Present [1885] Depression in Trade. With preface by Leone Levi. Lond., Chatto & Windus, 1885. 99 p. pap. 1s.

Medley, G. W. The Trade Depression; its causes and remedies. Cobden Club tract. Lond. and N. Y., Cassell, 1885. pap. 20 c.

Moffat, R. S. Economy of Consumption. An omitted chapter in political Economy, with special reference to commercial crises and trades-unions. Lond., Kegan Paul, 1878. 663 p. O. 18s.

Mongredien, A. Trade Depression, recent and present. Cobden Club tract. Lond. and N. Y., Cassell, 1885. pap. 10 c.

Wallace, A. R. Bad Times. Lond. and N. Y., Macmillan, 1885. 118 p. D. 75 c.

An essay on the depression of British trade 1874-85, attributing it to enormous foreign loans, excessive war expenditure, increase of speculation and of millionaires, and the depopulation of the rural districts. Land reform is specially advocated as a remedy.

Juglar, CLEMENT. Des Crises Commerciales et de leur retour périodique en France, en Angleterre, et aux Etats Unis. 2me ed. Paris, Guillaumin, 1889. 20+560 p. O.

Laveleye, E. de. Le Marché Monetaire et ses Crises depuis 50 ans. Paris, Guillaumin, 1865. 314 p. O.

Wirth, MAX, Geschichte der Handelskrisen. Frankfort am Main, Sauerländer, 1883. 660 p. D.

The best work on the subject.

Carl Schurz in life of Henry Clay, and E. M. Shepard in life of Martin Van Buren [American Statesman Series], give sketches of the panic of 1837. David A. Wells, in Recent Economic Changes, N. Y., Appleton, 1889 reviews the business depression which began in 1873. R. Giffen, in Essays on Finance, 2d series, N. Y., Putnam, 1886, has a chapter on Trade Depression and Low Prices. Horace White, in Lalor's Cyclopædia of Political Science, treats Commercial Crises.

COMMERCE AND TRADE.

Works of Reference for Commerce and Trade will also be found under Political Economy, General, also under International Trade, and Statistics. The official reports of the Treasury Department, Washington, and of the British Board of Trade, as noted, are most valuable. Tooke's History of Prices is a classic; Rogers' work [Land and Rent] worthily extends it. The Railroad Question in its American phase has been treated from a manager's standpoint with most ability by Fink. Sterne is his principal critic. Of official reports on railroads those to the N. Y. State Legislature and of the Inter-State Commerce Commission are the most informing. Among foreign writers on railroads and their problems, the principal are Jeans, Picard, Cohn, and von Weber. For a general survey Hadley (American) is best. James' essay on The Canal and Railway is suggestive.

HISTORY, WORKS OF REFERENCE.

Bristed, J: Resources of the United States, agricultural, commercial, financial, political, and literary. N. Y., J. Eastburn & Co., 1818. 506 p. O.

Homans, I. S. *and* I. S., Jr., *eds.* Cyclopædia of Commerce and Commercial Navigation. N. Y., 1858. 6+2007 p. Q.

Pitkin, TIMOTHY. Statistical View of the Commerce of the United States, including account of banks, manufactures, internal trade, revenues and expenditures. New Haven, Conn., Durrie & Peck, 1835. 600 p. O.
A reliable work.

Weeden, W. B. Economic and Social History of New England, 1620-1789. Boston, Houghton, Mifflin & Co., 1890. 2 v. 964 p. D. $4.50.
Full of interesting detail.

Cunningham, W. Growth of English Industry and Commerce during the early and middle ages. 2d ed. enl. Lond. and N. Y., Macmillan, 1890. 15+626 p. O. $5.
A capital book. Contains a list of authorities.

Gilbart, J. W. Ancient Commerce. Lond., 1847. Also in his Lectures and Essays, Lond., Bell & Daldy, 1885. 5 v.

Levi, LEONE. History of British Commerce and of the Economic Progress of the Nation from 1763 to 1878. Lond., Murray, 1879. 8°, 18s.
An excellent commercial and industrial history, with illustrations of economic doctrine.

Lindsay, W. S. History of Merchant Shipping and Ancient Commerce. Lond., Sampson Low, 1876. 4 v. O. 90s.

McCullagh, W: T. Industrial History of Free Nations considered in Relation to their Domestic Institutions and External Policy. Lond., 1846. 2 v. 8°.
A work of interest. The second volume, treating of the commercial history of Holland and Flanders, is of special value. It is unfortunately out of print.

Macgregor, J: Commercial and Financial Legislation of Europe and America, with a pro-forma revision of the taxation and customs tariff of the United Kingdom. Lond., H: Hooper, 1841. 320 p. O.

Wilson, A. J. Resources of Modern Countries. Essays toward an estimate of the economic position of nations, and British trade prospects. Lond., Longman, 1878. 2 v. 8°.
<small>Full of information not otherwise readily accessible, respecting the wealth, debts and resources of the different commercial countries.</small>

Yeats, J: Growth and Vicissitudes of Commerce from 1500 to 1789. An historical narrative of the industry and intercourse of civilized nations. 2d ed. Lond., Virtue, 1872. 8°, 5s.

Yeats, J: Technical History of Commerce. New ed. Lond., Virtue 1872. 8°, 5s.

Yeats, J: Manual of Recent and Existing Commerce from 1789 to 1872. Showing the development of industry at home and abroad during the continental system, the protectionist policy, and the era of free trade. Lond., Virtue, 1872. 8°, 21s.
<small>The three foregoing works are mediocre in quality.</small>

Pigeonneau, H. Histoire du commerce de la France. 2 v. Paris, L. Cerf, 1885-89. 468, 486 p. D.
<small>From its origin to the time of Richelieu. An admirable work.</small>

Murhard, CARL. Theorie des Handels. Göttingen, 1831. 396 p. D.

Neumann-Spallart, F. X. von. Uebersichten der Weltwirthschaft. Stuttgart, J. Maier, 1879-84. 1880-84.

Roscher, W: Nationalökonomie des Handels und Gewerbefleisses. Stuttgart, Cotta, 1881. 823 p. D.
<small>V. 3 of his System.</small>

McCulloch's Dictionary of Commerce and Commercial Navigation contains important information [see Works of Reference, under Political Economy, General].

The Treasury Department, Washington, publishes an annual Report of the Chief of the Bureau of Statistics, on the Foreign Commerce, navigation, immigration, and tonnage of the United States, also a quarterly report covering the same field. Also, an annual report on Domestic Commerce of the U. S.

The Boards of Trade in the principal cities publish annual statements of local commerce.

The British Board of Trade, London, publishes annual Statistical Abstracts of Commerce of the United Kingdom with Foreign Countries and with the Colonies and India.

Nature and Significance of Corporations. R: T. Ely. *Harper's Magazine*, May, 1887.

Growth of Corporations. R: T. Ely. *Harper's Magazine*, June, 1887.

Future of Corporations. R: T. Ely. *Harper's Magazine*, July, 1887.

PRICES.

Patten, SIMON N. The Stability of Prices. Baltimore, American Economic Assoc., 1888. 64 p. O. pap. 75 c.
<small>Discusses, among other topics, the Ricardian theory of rent.</small>

Tables of Prices of commodities, and immigration for a series of years. Bureau of Statistics, Treasury Department. Washington, Gov. Pr. Office, 1886. 2 v. 528, 598 p. O.

Mulhall, M. G. History of Prices Since 1850. Lond., Longmans, 1885. 204 p. D. 6s.

Of little value.

Tooke, T: History of Prices and of the state of the circulation, 1793-1837, preceded by a brief sketch of the state of the coinage in the last two centuries. Lond., 1838. 2 v. 8°. Continuation, 1838-9. Lond., 1850. 1839-47. Lond., 1848.

Tooke, T: *and* **Newmarch, W.** Same, 1848-56. Lond., 1867. 2 v. 8°.

This work forms a series with Rogers' History of Agriculture and Prices [see Land]. The series deservedly occupies a very high rank in economic literature.

Tooke, T: High and Low Prices of the last thirty years, from 1793 to 1822. Lond., Murray, 1824.

Gives tabular details, with observations thereon.

A. Soetbeer's Precious Metals, tr. by F. W. Taussig [see Atkinson's report, Gold, Silver, Bimetallism] pt. vii, treats of Changes in General Prices. Appendix II. gives prices in 1886.

Valuable schedules of prices will be found in Evans' "Imports and Duties" [see International Trade]; also in annual issues of the "American Almanac." The catalogues of the English coöperative stores and of the American dry-goods or bazar houses are useful for comparison of prices.

Index Numbers. R. Giffen. *Bulletin de l'Institut internationalýde Statistique.* Paris, 1887.

The *Economist*, London, publishes monthly a Commercial Supplement, with prices computed on an Index number.

RAILROAD MANAGEMENT AND LEGISLATION.

Adams, C: F., Jr. 1835. **Notes on Railroad Accidents.** N. Y., Putnam, 1879. 6+280 p. D. $1.50.

Adams, C: F., Jr. Railroads: their Origins and Problems. Rev. ed· N. Y., Putnam, 1878. 230 p. D. $1.25.

Adams, C: F., Jr., *and* **H. Chapters of Erie,** and other essays. Boston, J. R. Osgood & Co., 1871. $2.

Contains A Chapter of Erie, An Erie Raid, The Railroad System, by C. F. Adams, Jr. The New York Gold Conspiracy, Captaine John Smith, The Bank of England Restriction, British Finance in 1816, by H: Adams. The Legal-Tender Act, by Francis A. Walker and H: Adams.

Alexander, E. Porter. Railway Practice: its principles and suggested reforms reviewed. N. Y., Putnam, 1887. 60 p. D. 75 c.

A criticism from a railway manager's standpoint of proposed solutions of the railway problem, especially those of Mr. J. F. Hudson in his work "The Railways and the Republic," and Professor R. T. Ely in *Harper's Magazine*, July, August, and September, 1887.

Amendment to the Inter-State Commerce Act, approved March 2, 1889; with a summary of its provisions. Phila., T. & J. W. Johnson & Co., 1889. 15 p. O. pap. 10 c.

American Railway, The, its construction, management, and appliances. With an introd. by Hon. T: M. Cooley, Chairman Interstate Commerce Commission. N. Y., Scribner, 1889. xxviii+456 p. Q. $6.

Each chapter is written by a specialist. For the general reader. Abundantly illustrated.

Ashley, Ossian D. **Anti-Railway Legislation.** N. Y., 1889. 24 p. pap. 5 c.
By the President of the Wabash Western Railway Co. Written to show that legislation hostile to railways is war upon the great industrial interests connected therewith.

Atkinson, E: **The Railway, the Farmer, and the Public.** Economic tract, no. 19. N. Y., Soc. for Political Education, 1885. 68 p. pap. 15 c.
Also contained in the author's "Distribution of Products," N. Y., Putnam, 1887.

Cooley, T: M. **Popular and Legal Views of Traffic Pooling.** Chicago, *Railway Review*, 1884. 15 p. O.
Reprinted from *Railway Review* of April 26, 1884. Writer is now Chairman Inter-State Commerce Commission.

Crawford, J. B. **Credit Mobilier of America,** its origin and history. Boston, C. W. Calkins & Co., 1880. 229 p. D.
The Credit Mobilier was established to construct the Union Pacific Railroad.

Dabney, Wm. D. **Public Regulation of Railways.** N. Y., Putnam, 1889. 12°, $1.25.
An able discussion. Intended to be suggestive only, not exhaustive.

Dos Passos, J. R. **Inter-State Commerce Act:** an analysis of its provisions. N. Y., Putnam, 1887. 125 p. D. $1.25.

Fink, Albert. **Cost of Railroad Transportation,** railroad accounts, and governmental regulations of railroad tariffs. Louisville, Ky., 1875. 48 p. O.
Extract from the annual report of the Louisville & Nashville R. R. Co., 1874.

Fink, Albert. **Argument Before the Committee of Commerce** of the U. S. Senate on the Reagan bill for the regulation of Inter-State Commerce, Washington, Feb. 11, 1879. N. Y., 1879. 28 p. O.

Fink, Albert. **Railroad Problem and its Solution,** argument before the Committee on Commerce of the U. S. House of Representatives, in opposition to the bill to regulate Inter-State Commerce, Washington, Jan. 14, 1880. N. Y., 1882. 84 p. O.

Fink, Albert. **Argument Before the Committee on Commerce** of the U. S. House of Representatives on Inter-State Commerce, Washington, March 17 and 18, 1882. Washington, Gov. Pr. Office, 1882. 38 p. O.

Fink, Albert. **Testimony Regarding Inter-State Commerce** before U. S. Senate Committee on Labor and Education, N. Y., Sept. 17, 1883. N. Y., 1883. 62 p. O.

Fink, Albert. **Argument Before the Committee on Commerce** of the U. S. House of Representatives, Washington, Jan. 26, 1884. Washington, Gov. Pr. Office, 1884. 32 p. O.

Fink, Albert. **Regulation of Inter-State Commerce by Congress,** testimony before the select committee on Inter-State Commerce of the U. S. Senate, N. Y., May 21, 1885. Washington, Gov. Pr. Office, 1885. 40 p. O.

Fink, Albert. **Report upon the Adjustment of Railroad Transportation Rates to the Sea-board,** N. Y., Dec. 1, 1881. N. Y., 1882. 59 p. O.
Mr. Fink is regarded as the leading railroad authority of America; he was for some years Commissioner of the Trunk Line Association. The documents of his above mentioned present his experience of railroad affairs, and show the failure of competition to do justice to either shipper or investor. His views as to the best methods of legislating on railroad questions are given, and the limitations and difficulties of such legislation are presented. He holds that railway federation, whether by pools or otherwise, would remedy the principal evils of railroad practice. The pamphlets of Mr. Fink not issued at Washington were privately printed; they are to be found in the principal public libraries.

Flint, H. M. Railroads of the United States, their history and statistics, with a synopsis of the railroad laws of the United States. Phila., J. E. Potter & Co., 1868. 452 p. D.

Hadley, A. T. Railroad Transportation, its history and its laws. N. Y., Putnam, 1885. 269 p. D. $1.50.

The best book on the subject.

Hamilton, Adelbert. The Inter-State Commerce Law, with annotations. Northport, N. Y., E. Thompson, 1887. 219 p. O. pap. $2.50; hf. shp. $3.

Harper, J. C. Law of Inter-State Commerce; with notes of decisions. Cincinnati, R. Clarke & Co., 1887. 225 p. O. $2.

Hudson, J. F. The Railways and the Republic. N. Y., Harper, 1886. 489 p. O. $2.

A statement of the railroad problem, with a suggestion that railroads be made public highways, rolling-stock to be supplied by private enterprise. The author would prohibit pools.

Intercontinental Railway Line. Report of the International American Conference. Washington, Gov. Pr. Office, 1890. 215 p. O.

Intercontinental Railway Line. Report of the Committee on Foreign Affairs, House of Representatives. Washington, Gov. Pr. Office, 1890. 5 p. O.

Inter-State Commerce. Report and Testimony Senate Select Committee, Washington, Jan., 1886. 49th Congress, 1st Session, Report 46. 1st pt., Report, 216+258 p. O. 2d pt., Testimony, 1478 p. O. Washington, Gov. Pr. Office, 1886.

New York [State] Legislature. Report of the Special Committee appointed Feb. 28, 1879, to investigate alleged abuses in the management of railroads chartered by the State of New York. 5 v. Albany, 1880.

Contains information of importance.

Pierce, E. L. A Treatise on the Law of Railroads. A compendious and complete digest of the American and English law in the various relations of railroads to the public, to 1881. Boston, Little, Brown & Co., 1881. 8°, $6.

Poor's Manual (annual) of the Railroads of the United States. N. Y., H. V. and W. H. Poor.

A standard for reference. Publication began 1867.

Railway Question, The, report of the committee on transportation of the American Economic Assoc.; *also*, "The Agitation for Federal Regulation of Railways," by Edmund J. James. Baltimore, American Economic Assoc., 1887. 68 p. O. pap. 75 c.

Seligman, E. R. A. Railway Tariffs and the Inter-State Commerce Law. N. Y., Ginn & Co., 1887. 5+87 p. O. 75 c.

Reprinted from the *Political Science Quarterly*, 1887. Explains the theory of rates. Defends pools. Refers to all the foreign literature.

State Railroad Commissions. Ten years' working of the Mass. Railroad Commission, with Railroad Commission laws of the States having Commissions. N. Y., *Railroad Gazette*, 1883. 72 p. D. pap. 50 c.

State Railroad Ownership. Tr. of the document submitted to the Prussian Parliament by the Cabinet in 1879, containing argument therefor. N. Y., *Railroad Gazette,* 1880. 64 p. D. pap. 25 c.

Sterne, SIMON. **Argument on Bill to Create a Board of Railroad Commissioners,** delivered at Albany, N. Y., March 7, 1878, before State Committee on Railroads. N. Y., 1878. 40 p. O. pap.

Sterne, SIMON. **The Railway in its Relation to Public and Private Interests.** Address to merchants and business men of New York, April 19, 1878. N. Y., 1878. 88 p. O. pap.

Sterne, SIMON. **Closing Argument before Special Assembly Committee on Railroads,** on behalf of the Chamber of Commerce and Board of Trade and Transportation of New York, delivered at Albany, N. Y., Dec., 1879. N. Y., 1880. 156 p. O. pap.

Mr. Sterne is a leading member of the New York bar. The address and arguments of his above mentioned give an able exposition of the railroad situation from the New York shippers' point of view. They contain a plea for a State Commission and national regulation Mr. Fink's recommendations are criticised. The pamphlets were privately printed, and are now only to be had at the chief public libraries.

Acworth, W. M. **Railways of England.** 2d ed. Lond., Murray, 1890. 16+427 p. O.

A popular description, illustrated.

Francis, J: **History of the English Railway,** 1820-1845. Lond., Longmans, 1851.

Grierson, J. **Railway Rates, English and Foreign.** Lond., Stanford, 1886. 280 p. 8°, 5s.

From the standpoint of a railroad officer: the author is general manager of the Great Western Railway of England.

Jeans, J. S. **Railway Problems,** an inquiry into the economic conditions of railway working in different countries. Lond. and N. Y., Longmans, 1887. 28+560 p. O. 12s. 6d.

Waring, C: **State Purchase of Railways.** Lond., Chapman & Hall, 1887. 204 p. 8°, 5s.

Advocates the assimilation of railway tariffs to the uniformity of postal rates.

Noel, OCTAVE. **Les chemins de fer en France et à l'étranger,** étude financiere et statistique. Paris, Berger, Levrault & Cie., 1887. 14+444 p. D.

Foville, ALFRED de. **La transformation des moyens de transport,** et ses consequences économiques et sociales. Paris, Guillaumin, 1880. 460 p. D.

Picard, ALF. **Les chemins de fer Francais,** étude historique sur la constitution et le régime du reseau, débats parlementaires, actes législatifs, reglementaires administratifs. 6 v. V. 1, Periode anterieure 1851. V. 2, 1851-70. V. 3, 1870-79. V. 4, Documents annexes. V. 5, 1879-83. Conventions. V. 6, 1879-83. Documents annexes. Paris, J. Rothschild, 1884-85.

Picard, ALF. **Traité des chemins de fer.** Economie politique, Commerce, Finances, Administration, Droit, Etudes comparees sur les chemins de fer etrangers. 4 v. Paris, J. Rothschild, 1889. Large 8°, 100 francs.

An excellent encyclopedia on railroads and all subjects related thereto.

Cohn, Gustav. Untersuchungen über die Englische Eisenbahnpolitik.
2 v. O. V. 1. Die Entwickelung der Eisenbahngesetzgebung in England.
V. 2, Zur Beurtheilung der Englischen Eisenbahnpolitik. Leipzig. Duncker
& Humblot, 1874-75.

**Cohn, Gustav. Die Englische Eisenbahnpolitik der letzen 10 Jahre
(1873-83).** Neue folge. Mit einem register über das ganzewerk. Leipzig.
Duncker & Humblot, 1883. 8+196 p. O.
Best scientific view of the subject.

Engel, E. v. Eisenbahnreform. Jena, H. Costenoble, 1888. 219 p. S°.
Advocates zone tariffs for passenger service.

Kupka, P. F. Die Verkehrsmittel in den Vereinigten Staaten. Leipzig,
Duncker & Humblot, 1883. 413 p. O.

Ulrich, Franz. Das Eisenbahntarifwesen und nach seiner besonderen
Entwickelung in Deutschland, Oesterreich-Ungarn, der Schweiz, Italien,
Frankreich, Belgien, den Niederlanden und England. Berlin, J. Guttentag,
1886. 504 p. S°, 10 marks.
A comprehensive history of railroad development in Europe, with an instructive discussion of the problems of railway rates.

—— Same. **Traité général des tarifs de chemins de fer.** Paris, 1890.
10+555 p. O.

Weber, Max von. Nationalität und Eisenbahnpolitik. Wein, A. Hartleben, 1876. 111 p. O. 3 marks.

Weber, Max von. Privat-Staats-und Reichs-Bahnen. Wein, A. Hartleben, 1876. 95 p. O.
These are two excellent works on the question of State control.

Railway Morals and Railway Policies is one of the Essays, Moral, Political,
and Æsthetic, of Herbert Spencer. N. Y., Appleton.

The Inter-State Commerce Commission, Washington, issues an annual report, v. 1, 1887 (its Statistician's annual reports began 1889); the State Commissioners of Railroads in many of the States of the Union issue annual
reports (those of Conn., Ill., Ia., Kan., Mass., Mich., N. Y., and Pa., are the
most valuable); the monthly bulletins, Agricultural Department, Washington,
contain rates of transportation.

Nature of the Railway Problem. R: T. Ely. *Harper's Magazine*, July, 1886.

Economic Evils in American Railway Methods. R: T. Ely. *Harper's Magazine*, Aug., 1886.

Reform of Railway Abuses. R: T. Ely. *Harper's Magazine*, Sept., 1886.

Changes in the Form of Railway Capital. T. L. Greene. *Quarterly Journal
of Economics*, July, 1890.

Prohibition of Railway Pools. Arthur T. Hadley. *Quarterly Journal of
Economics*, Jan., 1890.

Railroad Business under the Interstate Commerce Act. A. T. Hadley. *Quarterly Journal of Economics*, Jan., 1889.

Railroad Passenger Fares in Hungary. Jane J. Wetherell. *Annals Am.
Acad. Pol. and Soc. Science*, Phila., July, 1890.
Describes zone tariff and gives its results.

Railway Reorganization. Simon Sterne. *Forum*, Sept., 1890.

Workings of the Interstate Commerce Law. A. T. Hadley. *Quarterly Journal of Economics*, Oct., 1887.

CANALS.

Chapman, G: W., *comp.* **Manual of Canal Laws Relating to the New York State Canals,** with the regulations established by the Canal Board. Albany, N. Y., 1873. 473 p. O.

Haupt, L. M. **Canals and Their Economic Relation to Transportation.**

James, E. J. **Canal and Railway,** with a note on the development of railway passenger traffic.

<small>The two foregoing essays are bound together in series of American Economic Assoc., Baltimore, 1890. 85 p. $1.00.</small>

Jeans, J. S. **Water-ways and Water Transportation** in different countries, with a description of the Panama, Suez, Manchester, and other canals. Lond., Spon, 1890. 514 p. O. 14s.

Weber, MAX von. **Die Wasserstraasen Nord-Europa's.** Ergebnisse von im auftrage des Herrn Königl Preuss. Ministers für Offentliche Arbeiten unternommenen Studienreisen. Leipzig, W: Engelmann, 1881. 397 p. O.

Statistics of Canals in U. S. are contained in v. 4, Census Report of 1880.

The Commissioner of Navigation makes an annual report to the Secretary of the Treasury, first report, 1886. The Canals of Canada are described in U. S. Consular Reports, Nos. 20 and 42. (Washington, Gov. Pr. Office.) The Canal Commissioner of New York, Albany, issues an annual report.

The Department of Railways and Canals at Ottawa publishes an annual, descriptive and statistical report of the railways operated or subsidized by the Canadian Government, and of its canals. Supplement No. 1 to the report for 1889 gives comparisons of traffic through Erie Canal since 1869.

COMPETITION, MONOPOLY, TRUSTS, AND BOYCOTTS.

Baker, C: WHITING. **Monopolies and the People.** N. Y., Putnam, 1889. 263 p. D. $1.25.

<small>Discusses natural and artificial monopolies, competition, etc.</small>

Clark, J: B., *and* **Giddings,** FRANKLIN H. **The Modern Distributive Process;** studies of competition and its limits, of the nature and amount of profits, and of the determination of wages, in the industrial society of to-day. Boston, Ginn & Co., 1888. 69 p. O. 75 c.

<small>Reprinted from *Political Science Quarterly*.</small>

Cook, W. W. **Trusts;** the recent combinations in trade, their character, legality, and mode of organization, and the rights, duties, and liabilities of their managers and certificate holders. N. Y., L. K. Strouse & Co., 1888. 63 p. S. pap., 50 c.

Dodd, S. C. T. **Combinations: Their Uses and Abuses.** With a history of the Standard Oil Trust. N. Y., G. F. Nesbitt & Co., 1888. 46 p. D. pap.

<small>An argument by the Solicitor of the Standard Oil Trust relative to bills pending before the N. Y. Legislature, based upon testimony given before the Senate Committee on General Laws.</small>

Investigation Relative to Trusts. Report of Committee on General Laws transmitted to Legislature of the State of New York, March, 1888. Albany, 1888. 692 p. O.

Proceedings of the Committee on Manufactures, House of Representatives of the United States, in relation to Trusts, March, 1888. 50th Congress

1st Session, Report No. 3112. Washington, Gov. Pr. Office, 1888. 956 p. O.
Contains testimony of great importance by organizers of trusts, especially the Standard Oil Trust, and testimony of their opponents.

Report of the Select Committee, appointed Feb. 29, 1888, to investigate and report upon alleged combinations in manufactures, trade, and insurance in Canada. 2d Session, 6th Parliament, Ottawa, 1888.

Kleinwächter, J. F. Die Kartelle, ein Beitrag zur Frage der Organization der Volkswirthschaft. Innsbruck, 1883. 246 p. D.

Competition and the Trusts. G: Iles. *Popular Science Monthly,* March, 1889.

Development of Monopolies in Their Relation to the State. H. S. Foxwell. An essay read before British Assoc. for Adv. Science, Sept., 1888. Tr. *Revue d'Economie Politique,* Paris, Oct., 1889.

Economic and Social Aspects of Trusts. G: Gunton. *Political Science Quarterly,* Sept., 1888.

Economic Law of Monopoly. E. B. Andrews. *Journal of Social Science* (Saratoga papers of 1889). N. Y., Putnam, 1890.

Facts about Trusts. C. F. Beach, Jr. *Forum,* Sept., 1889.

Legality of Trusts. T. W. Dwight. *Political Science Quarterly,* Dec., 1888.

Michigan Salt Association. J. W. Jenks. *Political Science Quarterly,* March, 1888.

Trusts According to Official Investigations. E. B. Andrews. *Quarterly Journal of Economics,* Oct., 1888.

The Whiskey Trust. J. W. Jenks. *Political Science Quarterly,* June, 1889.

Conspiracy and Boycott Cases. E. P. Cheyney. *Political Science Quarterly,* June, 1889.

FIRE INSURANCE.

Griswold, J. Fire Underwriter's Text-book. Montreal, R. Wilson-Smith, 1889. 871 p. $10.

Hine, C. C. Fire Insurance, instructions for the use of agents in the United States. New ed. rev. and enl. N. Y., C. C. Hine, 1888. 157 p. O. $2.50.

Slow-Burning Construction is a chapter in E: Atkinson's Industrial Progress of the Nation [Capital and Labor] reprinted from *Century,* Feb., 1889.

The reports and circulars of information issued by the Boston Manufacturers' Mutual Fire Insurance Co., E: Atkinson, President, have high practical value.

LIFE INSURANCE.

Fackler, D. P. Agents' Monetary Life and Valuation Tables, and Explanations. 2d ed. rev. and enl. N. Y., C. C. Hine, 1888. 70 p. O. $1.50.

Willey, N. Principles and Practice of Life Insurance. N. Y., *Spectator* Co., 1886. 230 p. D. $2.

Walford's Cyclopædia of Insurance remains incomplete, the editor being deceased. 5 v. are published, A—Fir. Lond., C. & E. Layton, 1871. N. Y., *Spectator* Co.

Several States of the Union have Commissioners of Insurance, who issue annual reports; of these reports those of Mass. are deemed the best.

Workmen's Insurance in Germany. F. W. Taussig. *Quarterly Journal of Economics,* Oct., 1887. Also, *Forum,* Oct., 1889.

INTERNATIONAL TRADE.

The Reports of the various Departments at Washington, as referred to in detailed notes, furnish the best sources of fact on this subject. Evans' and Heyl's compilations of Duties are the best. Of advocates for Protection, Carey, List and [R. E.] Thompson are eminent. On the other side of the question Wells, Sumner and Taussig are leading writers. The writings of Cobden, and the volumes on his life and times by Morley and Rogers, throw much light on the Free-Trade movement in England. Its principal critics include Byles and Sullivan. The official documents relating to proposals of reciprocity with South American republics are of interest.

TARIFFS AND FOREIGN COMMERCE, HISTORICAL AND GENERAL WORKS.

Adams, G: HUNTINGTON, *comp.* **Tariff of 1890.** A Handbook of the U. S. Tariff under the acts of 1890 and the Bond and Warehouse Systems. New York, Baker, Voorhis & Co., 1890. 331 p. O. $3.

<small>Contains all the Treasury decisions and rulings now in force, arranged under the several schedules, with alphabetical index of articles.</small>

Comparison of the Customs Law of 1883 with New Law of 1890. With Administrative Customs Law of 1890. Washington, W. H. Morrison, 1890. pap. 25c.

Downing, R. F., *comp.* **United States Customs Tariff.** N. Y., R. F. Downing & Co. 348 p. S. $1.

<small>Gives duties alphabetically, also the McKinley Customs Administrative Act, and the Customs Tariff Act of 1890.</small>

Evans, C. H., *comp.* **Imports—Duties** from 1867 to 1883 inclusive. Washington, Gov. Pr. Office, 1884. 937 p. O.

<small>Really several works bound together: U. S. imports and duties, 1867-1883, showing by articles (alphabetical) for each year, quantity, value, rate and amount of duty, price and ad valorem rate, with other tables (671 p.); exports American colonies to Great Britain, 1689-1789, and exports U. S. to all countries, 1789-1883, etc. (266 p.).</small>

Furber, H. W., *ed.* **Which? Protection, Free Trade, or Revenue Reform?** Hartford, Park Publishing Co., 1884. 528 p. D. $2.

<small>Forty chapters give speeches, articles, extracts from books, etc., of as many leading authorities on all sides, American, English, and French.</small>

Heyl, LEWIS. **United States Duties on Imports.** 30th ed. V. 1, 1882, 410 p. V. 2, 1883, 339 p. O. Washington, W. H. Morrison, 1883. $6.00.

<small>Approved and in use by Treas. Dept. V. 1 is superseded by v. 2. (pts. 1, 3, 4). V. 2 includes Pt. 1, Digest of Statutes prior to Dec. 1, 1873 (158 p.) 2, Act of March 3, 1883 (51 p.) 3, Schedule of Duties, alphabetical, annotated (113 leaves). 4, Table of rates, statistics, regulations, etc. (129 p.). Most valuable. The same editor has prepared a "Pocket Tariff."</small>

Mason, D. H. **Short Tariff History of the United States.** Part 1, 1783-89. Chicago, David H. Mason, 1884. 157 p. D. $1.

<small>Holds that the only trial of nearly absolute free trade between the United States and foreign countries was disastrous, and that the protective power conferred in the Constitution was alien to the purpose of raising revenue.</small>

Sumner, W: G. **History of Protection in the United States.** N. Y., Putnam, 1877. 64 p. O. 75 c.

<small>Lectures delivered before the International Free Trade Alliance.</small>

Talbott, H:, *ed.* **Tariff from the White House,** extracts from the Messages. Handbooks of the Tariff, no 1. Washington, Gray & Clarkson, printers, 1888. 109 p. O. pap. 25 c.

Those parts of Presidents' Messages bearing on the tariff, Washington to Cleveland.

Tariff of 1883. The duty on every article and the free list, with a brief review of tariff legislation of the U. S. from the beginning of the Government. Also, imports, dutiable, with duties collected, and free for 1883 and 1887; with the total imports of each year since 1791. Also, a summary of the Mills Bill and the Senate Tariff Bill. N. Y., Tribune Assoc., 1888. 20 p. O. 12 c.

Taussig, F. W. Tariff History of the United States, 1789-1888. Questions of the Day, no. 47. N. Y., Putnam, 1888. 269 p. D. $1.25.

Comprises the material contained in "Protection to Young Industries" and "History of the Present Tariff," together with the revisions and additions needed to complete the narrative. A valuable record of facts. Author a tariff reformer.

Terrill, W. G., *ed.* **Appeal to the American People as a Jury.** Chicago, Belford, 1888. 12°, cl. $1 ; pap. 50 c.

Speeches in House of Rep. in "the great debate," April 17-May 19, 1888.

Thompson, R. W. History of Protective Tariff Laws. N. Y., Hill & Harvey, 1888. 526 p. O. $2.

The author is a protectionist.

Williams, C. F. Tariff Laws of the United States. Boston, Soule & Bugbee, 1883. 193 p. O. $1.50.

A commentary with explanatory notes, decisions of the courts and Treasury Department.

Wright, CARROLL D. **Scientific Basis of Tariff Legislation.** Boston, Cupples. Upham & Co., 1884. 20 p. O. pap., 20 c.

Reprinted from *Journal of Social Science*, 1884.

Young, E: Special Report on the Customs Tariff Legislation of the United States. Washington, Gov. Pr. Office, 1872. 205+137 p. O.

The first part a valuable résumé of tariff debates, with votes, from 1789; the second statistical. Afterward extended in successive editions (1874, etc.) to include later tariffs. The author was Chief of Bureau of Statistics (Treas. Dept.) and is of protectionist leanings.

Chisholm, J. C. Handbook of Commercial Geography. Lond. and N. Y., Longmans, 1889. 9+515 p. O. with 29 maps, $5.

An extremely interesting work of great value.

Hall, HUBERT. **Customs Revenue in England from the earliest times to the year** 1827. 2 v. O. V. 1, 327 p., Constitutional History; v. 2, 288 p., Fiscal History. Lond., Elliot Stock, 1885. 21s.

The best book on the subject.

Noble, J. Fiscal Legislation, 1842-1865. Lond., Longmans, 1867. 8°, 7s. 6d.

A clear and comprehensive account of the fiscal legislation of Great Britain during the period of twenty-three years which included the transition from a protective to a free-trade policy, the repeal of the navigation laws, etc., etc.

Roscher, W. Ueber Kornhandel und Theuerungspolitik. 3d ed. Stuttgart, 1852.

Also tr. into French, Paris, M. Block, 1854.

Cusumano, V. La teoria del commercio dei grani in Italia. Bologna, 1877.

The first tariff act, approved July 4, 1789, is the second chapter in the first volume of U. S. laws, " Acts Passed at the First Congress of the U. S. A." (Phila., F. Childs, 1795). Rates under this and succeeding tariffs are tabulated in Young's "Customs Tariff Legislation."

The Tariff Commission of 1882 reported in 2 v., 8vo, 2617 p., including testimony. The Commission Tariff, as finally shaped by Conference Committee, is given in Heyl, Williams, etc., in Treasury pamphlet, in pamphlet issued by N. Y. *Tribune*, etc.

Under the lettering "Old and New Tariffs Indexed," the Treas. Dept. bound together (1883) tariffs of 1880 and 1883, with Hawaiian reciprocity treaty, each indexed.

The Ways and Means Com. of 1884 (Morrison horizontal reduction bill) issued its bill, with estimated duties by C. H. Evans, also Arguments before Committee, in a volume of 417 p.

The Revision of the Tariff was reported upon by the Secretary of the Treasury, D: Manning, Washington, Feb. 16, 1886, in a volume of 675 p., including a series of letters of manufacturers, etc.

The Ways and Means Com. of 1886 (2d Morrison bill) issued a Report with testimony.

The Ways and Means Com. of 1888 (Mills bill) issued several editions of its bill, majority and minority reports, tabulated comparisons, etc. The Senate substitute of 1888 was printed by the Senate, as also pamphlet containing majority report by Senator Aldrich and minority report by Senator Beck; also Testimony taken before its sub-committee, in 4 v. 8°. A report giving law of 1883 and Mills bill, with tables showing estimated effects on revenues, was prepared by Clerk of W. and M. Com., H: Talbott. A folio series of tables showing present duties (1888) and estimates of House and Senate bills, by C: H. Evans, was also presented—a valuable and now scarce document.

The Ways and Means Com. of 1889-90 (McKinley bill) issued the bill, majority and minority reports, also hearings before Com., in 1 v., 8°. A folio series of tables showing present duties, notes explanatory of proposed changes, and estimates of results, was prepared also for this bill, as presented to the Senate, by C: H. Evans. A Conference Report with bill was also printed.

The Tariff of 1890 (McKinley bill) is published by the Treas. Dept., with comparison of Tariff of 1883, and (McKinley) Administrative Customs Act; also in pamphlets by the *Tribune*, New York (51 p. O. pap. 10 c.), by the Reform Club, and others; and a "McKinley Alphabet," showing duties and increase of same alphabetically, is issued by the *Evening Post*, New York (20 p. D. pap. 3 c.).

"Comparative Duties and the Relation of the Treas. Dept. to Tariff Legislation," was a special report by Jas. Nimmo, Jr., Chief of Bureau of Statistics, Feb. 20, 1883, issued by Treas. Dept.

A Synopsis of Decisions on construction of tariff and other laws is issued monthly and bound up annually by Treas. Dept. The decisions of the U. S. General Appraisers are also printed (weekly or occasionally) by the Treas. Dept.

Report of the Secretary of the Treasury on the Collection of Duties was issued by the Treas. Dept. as second volume of the Treasury Report in 1885-86.

See the *Congressional Record* for Congressional speeches on the tariff, many of which are also reprinted separately.

"Foreign Commerce and Navigation, Immigration, and Tonnage of the United States," for each fiscal year ending June 30, are covered in an annual report of the Bureau of Statistics of the Treasury Dept., which also issues quarterly and monthly statements of imports, etc.

"Causes of the Reduction of American Tonnage and the decline of navigation interests" were treated in a Special Report of House Select Committee, Feb. 17, 1870. (41st Congress, 2d Session, Ho. Rep., no. 28. 21+294 p.)

"Foreign Tariffs; discriminations against the importation of American products," were treated in full in a Report of the Senate Com. on Foreign Relations, 1884. (48th Congress, 1st Session, Senate Rep. no. 551. 576 p.)

"Tables showing the commerce between the U. S. and Canada," with special reference to the operations of tariff laws, for a series of years, were issued by the Bureau of Statistics, Treas. Dept., in 1887.

"Commerce of the U. S. with Mexico, Central America, the West Indies, and South America," is issued as a separate annual report of Bureau of Statistics, Treas. Dept.

Reports of the Commission upon more intimate relations between U. S. and Central and South America, were issued by State Dept. in 1 v., 8°, 1886.

The State Dept. issues annually a Report upon the Commercial Relations of the U. S. with Foreign Countries.

The Special Report on "Wool and Manufactures of Wool," issued by Bureau of Statistics, Treas. Dept., in 1887 (93+231 p. O.) is of great value in the tariff discussion, as are also the Census volumes on Manufactures, etc.

"Sugar and Molasses" were reported on in tables showing imports and exports of U. S. since 1789, production and consumption, tariff rates, etc., for a series of years, issued by Bureau of Statistics, Treas. Dept., in 1887.

"Cotton Textiles in Foreign Countries"—reports from Consuls of U. S. on imports into their districts—was published by State Dept., in 1 v., 1890.

Of the "Consular Relations of the U. S." U. S. Consular Reports to Dept. of State (Wash., Gov. Pr. Office), no. 12 (Oct., '81) is Mr. Blaine's report on "Cotton Goods Trade of the World;" no. 26½ is "Tariffs of Spain, Italy, Norway, Hawaii, and British Guiana;" no. 52 is "Declared Exports for U. S., 1884;" no. 53½ is "Tariff Laws of Mexico, 1885;" no. 73½ is "Customs Duties Imposed by Foreign Nations upon American Produce and Manufactures," transmitted by the President to the Ho. of Rep. (very valuable); no. 85 is "Statistical Abstract for Foreign Countries, 1873-83;" no. 108 includes "Subsidies to British Steamships;" no. 112 is "Steamship Subsidies by Foreign Countries." For important reports on tariff questions in ther numbers, see Indexes to Consular Reports nos. 1–59, 1880-5 (issued 1887), and to nos. 60–111, 1886-9 (issued 1890), under "Tariff," "Subsidies," names of countries, etc.

See "U. S. Statistical Abstract" yearly for imports, Spofford's "American Almanac" yearly for condensed tariff returns of preceding fiscal year.

See in "Economic Fact-Book," "References to Tariff Legislation in U. S." by W. E. Foster, an invaluable and impartial chronological summary.

The recent "Campaign Text-Books" of the Democratic and Republican parties, particularly those for 1888 (both published in that year by Brentano, New York) are devoted largely to the tariff.

The Financial Reform Almanac (Lond., Simpkin, Marshall & Co., Q. 1s.) contains each year valuable historical and present information concerning the English tariff. See also the British " Statistical Abstracts."

The Canadian Customs Tariff is issued as a Dominion publication, also in handy shape by W: Bryce, Toronto, and others.

The Department of Customs at Ottawa publishes an annual report of Canadian Trade and Navigation. Its statistics are of interest in showing how large a proportion of the Dominion's trade is with the United States.

"The Tariff: Protection and Free Trade," is the special subject in *The Bibliographer*, v 1, no. 3 (July, 1888), issued by Moulton, Wenborne & Co., Buffalo, N. Y. This has 732 references, largely to articles in periodicals, and many descriptive notes, of somewhat protectionist tendency.

FOR PROTECTION.

Baird, H: C. Brief Tracts on Some Economic Questions (1871-1888). 1st, 2d and 3d series. 3 pts. Phila., H. C. Baird, 1888. pap. 30 c.

Baird, H: C. Rights of American Producers, and Wrongs of British Free-Trade Revenue Reform. Phila., H: C. Baird, 1872. pap. 5 c.

Bigelow, E. B. The Tariff Question considered with regard to the policy of England and the interest of the U. S. New ed. Boston, Little, Brown & Co., 1877. 61 p. 8°, cl. 75 c.; pap. 50 c.

Carey, H: C. Harmony of Interests, Agricultural, Manufacturing, and Commercial. 1852. 3d ed. Phila., H: C. Baird, 1872. 229 p. 8°, $1.50.

This and the other works of Carey [see General Political Economy, 'American] afford the ablest American expositions of Protection.

Hall, H: American Navigation, with some account of its recent decay and of the means by which the prosperity may be restored. N. Y., Appleton, 1878. 91 p. O. pap. 50 c.

A plea for subsidies.

Hamilton, ALEX. Report on Manufactures. In Works in 7 v. (p. 123, v. 3.) N. Y., C. S. Francis & Co., 1851.

Hartshorn, E. A. Wages, Living, and the Tariff. 2d ed. Troy, W. H. Young, 1884. 101 p. T. pap. 25 c. Also, Amer. Prot. Tariff League, 1888. 2 c.

Hayes, J. L., and others. The Wool and Woolen Tariff of 1883. Cambridge, Mass., 1883. 65 p. 8°, pap. 50 c.

Hoyt, H. M. Protection *vs.* Free Trade: the scientific validity and economic operation of defensive duties in the United States. N. Y., Appleton, 1888. D. cl. $2; pap. 50 c.

Kelley, W. D. Industrial and Financial Questions. Phila., H. C. Baird, 1872. 514 p. O. $3.

Speeches, addresses, and letters, chiefly explaining and defending Protection.

McKee, T: H., *ed.* Protection Echoes from the Capitol. Washington, McKee & Co., 1888. 590 p. D. pap. $1.

Alphabetical arrangement of 1252 numbered extracts from Congressional speeches, etc., in favor of protection, with "'present law' and Mills bill compared," and general and Congressional (name) indexes.

Patten, S. N. Economic Basis of Protection Phila., Lippincott, 1890. 12°, $1.

Poor, H: V. **Twenty-two Years of Protection.** N. Y., H. V. and H. W. Poor, Sept., 1888. 222 p. O. pap.
<small>A protective view of "the period of Restoration," 1865-87, with statistics, prefaced by a review from the beginning.</small>

Porter, ROBERT P. **Protection and Free Trade to-day,** at home and abroad, in field and workshop. Boston, J. R. Osgood & Co., 1884. 48 p. S. pap. 10 c.

Porter, ROBERT P. **Free-Trade Folly.** N. Y., J. S. Ogilvie & Co., 1886. 96 p. Q. pap. 20 c.

Roberts, ELLIS H. **Government Revenue,** especially the American system, an argument for industrial freedom against the fallacies of free trade. N. Y., Houghton, Mifflin & Co., 1884. 389 p. D. $1.50.
<small>Based on lectures delivered at Cornell Univ. and Hamilton Coll. Full index. Author editor of Utica *Herald*.</small>

Seaman, EZRA C. **Refutation of Free-Trade Maxims.** Cambridge, Mass., 1883. 8°.

Stebbins, GILES B. **American Protectionists' Manual.** 17th thousand, revised. Chicago, C. H. Kerr & Co., 1888. 192 p. D. 75 c.; pap. 40 c.
<small>Contains many quotations from industrial witnesses and comparative figures.</small>

Thompson, R. E. **Protection to Home Industry.** N. Y., Appleton, 1886. O. $1.
<small>Lectures delivered at Harvard Univ., Jan., 1885.</small>

Wharton, JOSEPH. **International Industrial Competition.** Phila., H: C. Baird, 1872. 32 p. pap. 25 c.

Wharton, JOSEPH. **National Self-Protection.** Phila., H. C. Baird & Co., 1875. 37 p. 8°, pap. 25 c.

Byles, *Sir* J: BARNARD. **Sophisms of Free Trade and Popular Political Economy Examined.** 5th American from 9th English ed. Phila., H: C. Baird, 1872. 291 p. D. $1.25.

Sullivan, E: **Free-Trade Bubbles.** Lond., Stanford, 1883. 12°, 1s.

Borain, JULES. **Les enormités du libre echange anglais.** Bruxelles, 1878. 276 p.O.

Horace Greeley, Van Buren Denslow and R. E. Thompson, and F. List in his National System of Political Economy [Political Economy, General], argue for protection.

The *American Economist*, organ of the American Protective Tariff League, is published weekly at 23 W. 23d St., New York, $2.00 yearly. V. 1 (July, 1887–June, '88), and 2 (July–Dec., '88), were issued as *Tariff League Bulletin*. The American Protective Tariff League, same address, issues 32 numbers of its "Defenders" of the Tariff, pamphlets of from 2 to 32 pages, any one of which is mailed for 2 c. These include papers by Hartshorn, Draper, Harriman, Lawrence, Dudley, Boutwell, Porter, Ammidown, Weeks, Dodge and others, Porter's "Reply to the President's Free-Trade Message, 1887," Blaine's Reply to Gladstone, several prize essays, etc.

Among protectionist literature should be noted the (quarterly) *Bulletin* of the Nat. Assoc. of Wool Manufacturers (1864–1890), Boston, and the publications of the American Iron and Steel Association and Industrial League, Phila.

The literature of the Fair Trade movement in England is essentially protective.

The *Tribune*, New York, (weekly ed., $1 yearly,) is the leading advocate of Protection, and issues numerous extras and other pamphlets in its advocacy.

Benefits of Protection. J: Roach, and others. *North American Review*, Oct., 1884.

H: C. Carey. C: H. Levermore. *Political Science Quarterly*, Dec., 1890.

Free-Trade and Protection. W: E. Gladstone and James G. Blaine. *North American Review*, Jan., 1890. Continued in Feb. no. by Roger Q. Mills; in March by Senator J. S. Morrill; in April by W. C. P. Breckinridge.

Free-Trade Isolated. E: Sullivan, and Duke of Manchester. *Nineteenth Century*, v. 10, p. 161.

Protection and Free-Trade. J. Wharton. *Penn. Monthly*, v. 10, p. 219.

Protective Questions Abroad. R. E. Thompson. *Penn. Monthly*, v. 1, p. 436.

Protection and the Farmer. Senator S. M. Cullom. *Forum*, Oct., 1889.

FOR FREE TRADE OR TARIFF REFORM.

Bowker, R: R. Economic Fact-Book and Free Trader's Guide. N. Y., Free Trade Club, 1885. 146 p. D. pap. 25 c.

An introduction outlines the programme of revenue reform agitation, and gives directions for organizing clubs for revenue reform. A summary of protectionist points and free-trade facts, in the form of a dialogue, follows. Political platforms, extracts from advocates of free trade, and statistical tables make up the body of the work. Now out of print; the promised revised edition has not yet been issued.

Bowker, R: R. Free Trade the Best Protection. N. Y., Free Trade Club, 1880. 16 p. [of separate tracts] D. 5 c.

Brace, C: L. Free Trade as Promoting Peace and Good Will Among Men. Economic monograph, no. 16. N. Y., Putnam, 1879. 19 p. D. pap, 25 c.

Butts, I. Protection and Free Trade. Economic monograph, no. 2. N. Y., Putnam, 1875. 190 p. D. $1.25.

A brief, simple, cogent statement of the main points in the controversy, but out of print.

Chamberlain, *Rev.* N. H. **What's the Matter? or, Our Tariff and its Taxes.** Bost., De Wolfe, Fiske & Co., 1890. 268 p. D. pap. 50 c.; cl. $1.

A popular exposition in a series of conversations.

Codman, J: Free Ships; the Restoration of the American Carrying Trade. Economic monograph, no. 6. N. Y., Putnam, 1878. 54 p. D. pap. 25 c.

Codman, J: Shipping Bounties and Subsidies. Reform Club series, no. 7. N. Y., Putnam, 1890. 19 p. D. pap. 25 c.

Cox, S. S. Free Land and Free Trade: the lessons of the English Corn Law applied to the United States. Questions of the Day, no. 2. N. Y., Putnam, 1880. 126 p. D. 75 c.

Earle, A. L. Our Revenue System and the Civil Service. Economic monograph, no. 5. N. Y., Putnam, 1878. D. pap. 25 c.

Ely, R: T. Problems of To-day: a discussion of protective tariffs, taxation, and monopolies. N. Y., T. Y. Crowell & Co., 1888. 222 p. D. $1.50.

George, H: Protection or Free Trade: an examination of the tariff question with especial regard to the interests of labor. Land and Labor Library, no. 40. N. Y., H: George & Co., 1887. 359 p. S. cl. $1.50 ; pap. 35 c.

Mr. George leads up to the doctrine that ultimate free trade means free access to land through the operation of the " single tax."

Grosvenor, W. M. Does Protection Protect ? An examination of the effect of different forms of tariff upon American industry. N. Y., Appleton, 1871. 365 p. D. $3.

A very thorough statistical examination of the doctrine of protection as exemplified in American history. Long out of print.

Kelley, J. D. J. The Question of Ships ; the Navy and Merchant Marine. N. Y., Scribner, 1864. 6+229 p. D. $1.25.

A valuable work by a U. S. Navy lieutenant, from free-trade point of view.

Leib, HERMANN. The Protective Tariff: what it does for us ! Chicago, Belford, Clarke & Co., 1888. 232 p. D. cl. $1 ; pap. 50 c.

A criticism of protection by a leading German-American.

Miller, J. BLEECKER. Unconstitutionality of Protection. Reform Club series, no. 5. N. Y., Putnam, 1889. 35 p. D. pap. 25 c.

Moore, J. S. Friendly Sermons to Protectionist Manufacturers. Economic monograph, no. 3. N. Y., Putnam, 1878. 81 p. D. pap. 25 c.

Moore, J. S. Friendly Letters to American Farmers and Others. N. Y., Reform Club, 1888. Also Questions of the Day, no. 50. N. Y., Putnam, 1888. 101 p. D. pap. 25 c.

National Conference of Free Traders and Revenue Reformers [Proceedings of] under the auspices of the Amer. Free Trade League, Chicago, Nov. 11-12, 1885. N. Y., Free Trade Club, 1885. 160 p. pap. 15 c.

Contains addresses of Beecher, Wells. Hurd, Shearman, Smith, Hazard, Sargent, Vinton, and others, also separately published. Now out of print.

Philpott, H. J. Tariff Chats. Questions of the Day, no. 52. N. Y., Putnam, 1888. 39 p. D. pap. 25 c.

The President's Message, of Grover Cleveland, 1887; with annotations by R: R. Bowker. Reform Club series, no. 2. Also, Questions of the Day, no. 48. N. Y., Putnam, 1888. 38 p. pap. 25 c.

Raguet, CONDY. Principles of Free Trade. 2d ed. Phila., 1840. 439 p. O.

Report of a Committee of the Citizens of Boston opposed to a further increase of duties on importations. Boston, 1827. 196 p. 8°, pap.

Schoenhof, J. Destructive Influence of the Tariff upon Manufacture and Commerce, and the facts and figures relating thereto. N. Y., Free Trade Club pub. Also Questions of the Day, no. 9. N. Y., Putnam, 1884. 83 p. D. cl. 75 c.; pap. 40 c.

Schoenhof, J. Wages and Trade in Manufacturing Industries in America and in Europe. N. Y., Free Trade Club pub. Also, N. Y., Putnam, 1884. 25 p. D. pap. 15 c.

Facts and statistics adduced to prove that a protective tariff does not raise wages.

Shearman, T: G. The Distribution of Wealth. Land and Labor Library, no. 4. N, Y., H: George & Co., 1887. 16 p. 8°, pap. 5 c.

Out of print.

Sumner, W: GRAHAM. **Protectionism the ism which teaches that waste makes wealth.** N. Y., Holt, 1885. 172 p. S. $1.

The Tariff. N. Y., Reform Club, 1890. 412 p. D. $2.

A selection of numbers of *Tariff Reform* presenting Relations of the Tariff to Salt, Tinned Plate, Dairy-farming, Fruits, Shipping, Subsidies, Wages, Wool, Grapes, Copper, Brass, Farming, the Home Market, Coal, Iron, Steel, and Sugar. The tabulated facts are invaluable. Full analytical index. (Bound in half leather with above lettering, but without title-page.)

Trumbull, M. M. **The American Lesson of the Free-Trade Struggle in England.** Chicago, Schumm and Simpson, 1884. 290 p. D. cl. 75 c.; pap. 50 c.

Historical sketch of the English anti-corn-law movement, prefaced by commendatory letter from J: Bright.

Wells, D. A. **Creed of Free Trade.** Boston, H. O. Houghton & Co., 1877. 8°, pap. 25 c.

Reprinted from *Atlantic Monthly*, Aug., 1875.

Wells, D. A. **How Congress and the Public Deal With a Great Revenue and Industrial Problem.** N. Y., 1880. 269 p. O. pap.

Treats the taxation of sugar. Reprinted, with additions, from *Princeton Review*, Nov., 1880.

Wells, D. A. **Our Merchant Marine.** Questions of the Day, no. 3. N. Y., Putnam, 1882. 219 p. D. $1.

Wells, D. A. **Relation of the Tariff to Wages:** a simple catechism for those who desire to understand this matter. Questions of the Day, no. 54. N. Y., Putnam, 1888. 45 p. D. pap. 20 c.

Wells, D. A. **Sugar Industry of the United States and the Tariff.** N. Y., 1878. 119 p. O.

A report on the assessment and collection of duties on imported sugars from 1789-91 to 1878.

Wells, D. A. **The 'Decay of Our' Ocean Mercantile Marine,** its cause and cure. Reform Club series, no. 6. N. Y., Putnam, 1890. 48 p. D. pap. 25 c.

Wells, DAVID A. **Practical Economics.** A collection of essays respecting certain of the economic experiences of the United States. N. Y., Putnam, 1885. 259 p. O. $1.50.

The chapters presenting aspects of the tariff discussion are The True Story of the Leaden Images, Recent Phases of the Tariff Question, Tariff Revision, The Pauper-labor Argument.

Wells, D. A. **Primer of Tariff Reform.** N. Y., Free Trade Club pub. N. Y., Putnam, 1885. 39 p. T. pap. 10 c.

A primer in the form of a catechism, condensing in simple terms the arguments for tariff reform.

Wells, D. A. **Why We Trade and How We Trade.** Economic monograph, no. 1. N. Y., Putnam, 1878. 57 p. D. pap. 25 c.

White, HORACE. **The Tariff Question.** Economic monograph, no. 3. N. Y., Putnam, 1879. 30 p. D. pap. 25 c.

Ashworth, H: **Recollections of Richard Cobden and the Anti-Corn-Law League.** Lond. and N. Y., Cassell, 1876. 430 p. D, $3.50.

An appendix of returns by Board of Trade shows increase of foreign commerce since repeal of the corn and provision laws.

Baden-Powell, G: Protection and Bad Times, with special reference to the Political Economy of English Colonization. Lond., Trübner, 1879. 376 p. O.

Bastable, C. F. Theory of International Trade, with some of its applications to economic policy. Lond., Simpkin, Marshall & Co., 1887. 176 p. D.

Bright, J: Speeches on Questions of Public Policy, *ed.* by Prof. Thorold Rogers. Popular ed. Lond. and N. Y., Macmillan. 12°, $1.25.

Buxton, E. N. The A B C of Free Trade. Cobden Club tract. Lond. and N. Y., Cassell, 12 c.

Cobden, R. Political Writings. Cobden Club pub. Lond. and N. Y., Cassell, $3.10.

Fawcett, H: Free Trade and Protection. An inquiry into the causes which have retarded the general adoption of Free Trade since its introduction into England. 6th ed. Lond. and N. Y., Macmillan, 1888. xvi-173 p. D. $1.25.
The American arguments for protection are especially taken into account.

Farrer, T. H. Free Trade *vs.* Fair Trade. Cobden Club. Lond. and N. Y., Cassell, 1885. 2d rev. ed. 267 p. D. 2s. 6d.
An examination of the pleas for fair trade, as the protection incidental to retaliatory tariffs is called in England. Has very valuable statistical appendixes.

Leadam, J. S. What Protection Does for the Farmer: a chapter of agricultural history. Cobden Club tract. Lond and N. Y., Cassell, 1885. 25 c.

Medley, G: W. Fair Trade Unmasked. Cobden Club tract. Lond. and N. Y., Cassell, 1885. 42 p. D. pap. 25 c.

Mongredien, A: Free Trade and English Commerce. Cobden Club pub. Lond. and N. Y., Cassell, 1880. 102 p. 12mo, 25 c.

Mongredien, A: History of the Free-Trade Movement in England. Cobden Club pub. 10th thousand. Lond. and N. Y., Cassell, 1888. 188 p. T. 1s. Also, N. Y., Putnam, 1888. 50 c.

Mongredien, A: Pleas for Protection Examined. Cobden Club tract. New and rev. ed. Lond. and N. Y., Cassell, 1888. 48 p. D. pap. 25 c.

Morley, J: Life of R: Cobden. New ed. Lond., Chapman & Hall, 1883. 616 p. D. cl. 2s.; pap. 1s. Library ed. in 2 v., demy 8°, 32s.
Gives details of the Anti-Corn Law agitation, and negotiation of French treaty.

Pearce-Edgcumbe, E. R. Popular Fallacies Regarding Trade and Foreign Duties; the "Sophismes économiques" of F. Bastiat adapted to the present time. Lond. and N. Y., Cassell, 1885. 80 p. D. pap. 25 c.

Rathbone, W. Protection and Communism: a consideration of the effect of the American tariff on wages. Questions of the Day, no. 15. N. Y., Putnam, 1880. 42 p. D. pap. 25 c.
By a member of the British Parliament, who holds Protection to be communistic in tendency.

Rogers, J. E. Thorold. Cobden and Modern Political Opinion. Lond. and N. Y., Macmillan, 1873. 16+382 p. D. $3.

Thompson, Perronet. A Catechism of the Corn Laws. Lond., 1827.
One of the most remarkable publications ever made on the subject of free trade and protection. It was circulated at the time by thousands, but is now to be found only in the libraries. It contains the famous monkey illustration, and for wit has never been surpassed in economic literature.

Wise, R. B. Facts and Fallacies of Modern Protection. Lond., Trübner, 1879. 117 p. D. 2s. 6d.
Cobden Club prize essay, 1878.

Amé, M. Etude sur les tarifs de commerce. 2 v. Paris, Guillaumin, 1876.
The best French work.

Bastiat, F. Sophisms of Protection. With preface by Horace White. N. Y., Putnam, 1886. 398 p. 16°, cl. $1; pap. 50 c.

Chevalier, MICHEL. Examen du système commercial connu sous le nom de système protecteur. Paris, Guillaumin, 1852. 384 p. D.

Richelot, H: Histoire de la reforme commerciale en Angleterre. 2 v. Paris, Capelle, 1855. 494, 495 p. D.

In Chap. 7 "Recent Economic Changes," by David A. Wells, N. Y., 1889, will be found a comprehensive statement of the effect on the various States of Europe of governmental interference with international commerce, from 1870 to 1888. No similar review of the situation has heretofore been presented.

J. Schoenhof criticises protection in "The Industrial Situation," [see Labor and Capital, Wages].

See also "Free Trade," by Prof. Thorold Rogers, in Encycl. Britannica, 9th ed., v. 9; "Tariffs and Tariff Legislation," by D. A. Wells, in Lalor's Political Cyclopædia, v. 3.

The N. Y. Free Trade Club (Jas. Gaunt, Sec., 365 Canal St., New York), which is also publishing agent for the American Free Trade League, has published a variety of books and pamphlets, most of which are also included in the list of G. P. Putnam's Sons' publications. The smaller pamphlets include papers, speeches, etc., by Beecher, Bowker, Codman, Donnell, Hazard, Hurd, McAdam, Moore, Schoenhof, Shearman, Wells, White, and others.

The Reform Club, New York (2 E. 27th St.), issues the "Reform Club Series," also a series of tracts for *Tariff Reform*, with that title. A selection bound in 1 v. appears in list of books immediately foregoing.

The files of successive free-trade periodicals, *The American Free Trader*, *The New Century*, *The Million*, *The Peoples' Cause*, are of interest and value. The *Weekly Post*, New York, ($1 per year), and *Tariff Reform* ($1 per year), issued fortnightly by the Reform Club, New York, each issue treating a special subject, are now the leading periodicals on this side.

The Cobden Club, London, in its annual report, gives a list of and the number of books and tracts circulated by it from its start. It also publishes, through Cassell & Co., numerous pamphlets and leaflets.

Common Sense of the Tariff Question. E: Atkinson. *Popular Science Monthly*, Aug. and Sept., 1890.

How Customs Duties Work. E. J. Shriver. *Political Science Quarterly*, June, 1887.

Protectionism and Protectionists. F. A. Walker. *Quarterly Journal of Economics*, April, 1890.

COMMERCIAL UNION, RECIPROCITY.

Curtis, W: E. Trade and Transportation between the United States and Latin America. Washington, Gov. Pr. Office, 1890. 355 p. O.

Handbook of Commercial Union [United States and Canada]. Toronto, Williamson & Co., 1888. 360 p. D. 25c.

International American Conference. Minutes of the Conference. Washington, Gov. Pr. Office, 1890. 905 p. Q.

<small>In both Spanish and English. Corresponds to the Journal of the House of Representatives.</small>

International American Conference. Reports and Recommendations transmitted to Congress, with Message from the President, and letters from the Secretary of State. Washington, Gov. Pr. Office, 1890. 395 p. O.

<small>Contains Plan of Arbitration, 6 p.; Reciprocity Treaties with Latin America, 11 p.; Inter-continental Railway Line (with maps) 214 p.; Postal and Cable Communication, 68 p.; Sanitary Regulations, 13 p.; Customs Regulations, 18 p.; International Monetary Union, 2 p.; Patents and Trade Marks, 10 p.; Weights and Measures, 4 p.; Port Dues, 3 p.; International Law, 30 p.; Extradition of Criminals, 7 p.; International Bank, 7 p.; Memorial Tablet, 1 p.; Celebration of the Discovery of America, 1 p.</small>

International American Conference. Reports of Committees and Discussions thereon. Washington, Gov. Pr. Office, 1890. 1203 p. Q.

<small>Separately published in English and Spanish. To these reports is added, Report of the Tour of the Delegates through the United States; and an Historical Appendix—the Congress of 1856 at Panama and subsequent movements toward a Conference of American Nations.</small>

Our Continent; or, America for the Americans. Proceedings and reports of the Pan-American Congress; letters from South America relating to the trade of the East, West, and North coasts; and letters from Newfoundland on the Fisheries dispute. N. Y., Tribune Assoc., 1890. 96 p. D. pap., 25 c.

In November, 1890, the Bureau of American Republics was established by the Department of State at Washington. It will issue at frequent intervals, for free distribution to the public, pamphlets or bulletins, containing : 1, Existing customs tariffs of the several countries, with all changes of the same as they occur. 2, Regulations affecting entrance and clearance of vessels, importation and exportation of merchandise. 3, Ample quotations from commercial and parcel-post treaties between any of the American republics. 4, Important statistics of commerce and other information of special interest.

The Hawaiian Reciprocity Treaty is included in " Old and New Tariffs Indexed," issued by Treas. Dept., Washington, 1883.

The literature of Commercial Union can be had from Mr. Erastus Wiman, 314 Broadway, New York.

Can we Coerce Canada? Erastus Wiman. *North American Review*, Jan., 1891.

Capture of Canada. Erastus Wiman. *North American Review*, August, 1890.

Perplexities that Canada Would Bring. A. R. Carman. *Forum*, July, 1890.

PUBLIC FINANCE.

The first authority on American taxation is Wells, whose reports are invaluable. Ely's and Seligman's monographs deserve high commendation. The works of Dowell and Noble are the best English contributions to the literature of public finance. Pres. E. B. Andrews prescribes the following course for a student: Cossa's Taxation, then Marzano. From him, being now ready for a real comprehension of the subject, he could proceed to the third volume of Schönberg's Handbuch der politischen Oekonomie [see Political Economy, Works of Reference]. Thence to enrich his view by fresh and large exposition, joined with abundant historical application, he might pass to Cohn. He could then advance to Roscher, Wagner, Stein, and Leroy-Beaulieu.

REVENUE TAXATION, SINGLE-TAX.

Adams, C. F., Jr., **Williams,** W. H., and **Oberly,** J. H. **Taxation of Railroads and Railroad Securities.** N. Y., *Railroad Gazette*, 1880. 49 p. D. 50 c.

Reports on the systems of railroad taxation in the several States of the United States, also in Austria, British America, Belgium, England, France, Germany, Holland, Hungary, Russia. Switzerland.

Adams, H: CARTER. **Taxation in the United States** 1789-1816. Baltimore, Johns Hopkins Univ. Historical Series, 1884. 79 p. O. pap. 50 c.

Andrews, G: H., *Commissioner of Taxes.* **Twelve Letters on the Future of New York.** N. Y., 1877. O.

These papers and Mr. Minot's contain valuable information respecting the inequalities and inefficiencies of the systems of local taxation now existing in this country, with more particular reference to those of Massachusetts and New York. They cannot be easily purchased, but can usually be obtained for reference

Bolles, ALBERT S. **Financial History of the United States.** N. Y., Homans Pub. Co. 3 v. O. V. 1, 1774-89, 371 p. $2.50. V. 2, 1789-1860, 621 p. $3.50. V. 3, 1861-85, 585 p. $3.50.

Defective in method and arrangement. Contains some statistics not to be found in convenient shape elsewhere.

Bourne, E. G. **History of the Surplus Revenue of 1837.** Questions of the Day, no. 24. N. Y., Putnam, 1885. 161 p. D. $1.25.

Shows the disasters which resulted from distributing among the States a surplus of $40,000,000 from the Federal treasury.

Burroughs, W. H. **Law of Taxation.** N. Y., Baker, Voorhis & Co., 1877. O. shp. $6.50; supplement to 1883, $2.50.

Offers to the student or the lawyer full information on the laws of taxation in the United States, Federal, State, and municipal, with reviews and citations of court decisions.

Canfield, JAMES H. **Taxation.** Economic tract, no. 9. N. Y., Soc. for Political Education, 1883. 48 p. D. pap. 15 c.

Cooley, T: M. **Law of Taxation,** including the Law of Local Assessments. 2d ed. enl. Chicago, Callaghan & Co., 1886. 88+991 p. O. $7.50.

Crocker, G: G. **Exposition of the Double Taxation** of Personal Property in Massachusetts. Boston, 1885. 15 p. O. pap.

Davies, JULIEN T., *comp.* **System of Taxation in the State of New York.** Troy, 1888. 111+494 p. O.

Constitutional provisions, statutes, and cases relating thereto.

Ely, R: T., *and* **Finley,** J. H. **Taxation in American States and Cities.** N. Y., T. Y. Crowell & Co., 1888. 544 p. D. $1.75.

A popular work describing taxation as it is, with suggestions for reform. Presents much illustrative information. Holds that a referendum should decide proposed loans in cities. P. 94-101 give a bibliography of taxation.

Ensley, ENOCH. **The Tax Question:** what should be taxed, and how it should be taxed. Nashville, 1873. 27 p. O. pap.

Gouge, W: M. **Fiscal History of Texas.** Phila., Lippincott, 1852. 327 p. O.

An interesting chapter in American financial history. The errors of older communities were repeated with disastrous results.

Hilliard, FRANCIS. **The Law of Taxation.** Bost., Little, Brown & Co., 1875. O. $6.

Jones, W: H. **Federal Taxes and State Expenses.** Questions of the Day, no. 39. N. Y., Putnam, 1887. 135 p. D. $1.

Kearny, J: **Sketch of American Finance, 1789-1835,** N. Y., Putnam, 1887. 160 p. D. $1.

Minot, W. JR. **Taxation in Massachusetts.** Bost., A. Williams & Co., 1877. O. pap. 25 c.

Quincy, JOSIAH P. **Double Taxation in Massachusetts.** Boston, Houghton, Mifflin & Co., 1889. 24 p. O. pap.

Reports on Taxation from Consuls of the United States. Consular Reports, nos. 99 and 100. Washington, Gov. Pr. Office, 1888. 791 p. O.

Schwab, J: CHRISTOPHER. **History of the New York Property Tax:** an introd. to the History of State and Local Finance in New York. Baltimore, American Economic Assoc., 1890. 108 p. O. $1.

Seligman, E. R. A. **Finance Statistics of the American Commonwealths.** Boston, American Statistical Assoc., 1889. 120 p. O. pap. $1.

Seligman, E. R. A. **General Property Tax.** N. Y., Ginn & Co., 1890. 40 p. O. pap. 40 c.

Reprinted from *Political Science Quarterly*, March, 1890. Gives 2 p. American bibliography—reports, pamphlets, and monographs.

Seligman, E. R. A. **Taxation of Corporations.** N. Y., Ginn & Co., 1890. 110 p. O. pap. 75 c.

Reprinted from *Political Science Quarterly*, June, Sept., Dec., 1890. Fully discusses the general subject of double taxation. Contains a bibliography.

Shaw, ALBERT, *ed.* **The National Revenues.** Chicago, A. C. McClurg & Co., 1888. 245 p. S. $1.

Contains Protective Tariffs as a Question of National Economy, by Prof. W. W. Folwell; Surplus Financiering, by Prof. H. C. Adams; The Tariff and Trusts—Expenditures for Internal Improvements, by Prof. R. T. Ely; Shall the Internal Revenue be Retained? by Prof. R. M. Smith; A Defence of the Protective Policy, by Prof. R. E. Thompson; The Readjustment of the Revenues, by Prof. E. R. A. Seligman; The Theory and Practice of Protection, by Prof. Jesse Macy; The Certainties of the Tariff Question, by Prof. J. B. Clark; Taxation and Appropriation, by Prof. Woodrow Wilson; Equality in Taxation—Commercial Union with Canada, by Prof. A. D. Morse; Steamship Subsidies as a Means of Reducing the Surplus, by Prof. A. T. Hadley; Protection and American Agriculture, by Pres. F. A. Walker; The Tariff and the Western Farmer, by Prof. J. H. Canfield; International Taxation and a Revenue Tariff, by Prof. A. Yager; A Plan of Tariff Reduction, by Prof. E. W. Bemis; Wages and the Tariff, by Prof. J. L. Laughlin; The Scientific Basis of Tariff Legislation, by Carroll D. Wright. Statistical tables are appended.

Sherman, I. Exclusive Taxation of Real Estate and the Franchises of a few specified moneyed Corporations and Gas Companies. N. Y., 1875.

Sherman, J. Speeches and Reports on Finance and Taxation from 1859 to 1878. N. Y., Appleton, 1879. 8°, $2.50.

Sumner, W: G. Life of Alexander Hamilton. N. Y., Dodd, Mead & Co., 1890. 10+281 p. D. 75 c.

Has special reference to his financial measures.

Thompson, R. E. Relief of Local and State Taxation through Distribution of the National Surplus. Phila., E. Stern & Co., 1883. O. 28 p. pap. 25 c.

What Shall We Do with It? (meaning the surplus.) N. Y., Harper, 1888. D. 68 p. pap. 25 c.

Contains President Cleveland's message to Congress, Dec. 6, '87, under the title "Taxation and revenue discussed;" together with the letter of Hon. J. G. Blaine, and articles by Hon. G. F. Edmunds and H. Watterson.

Wells, DAVID A. First and Second Reports of the Commissioners appointed to revise the Laws for the Assessment and Collection of Taxes in New York, 1871 and 1872. Albany, Argus Co. 154, 102 p. O.

Contain some of the best discussions of taxation published in America. The former was published in 8vo, N. Y., 1871, 50 c. The latter is out of print in this country, but editions have been published in England and in France, in the latter country by the government.

Wells, DAVID A., *Special Commissioner of the Revenue.* 1st, 2d and 3d annual reports, with appendices. Washington, Treasury Department, 1867-69. 233 p. O.

Worthington, T. K. Historical Sketch of the Finances of Pennsylvania. Baltimore, American Economic Assoc., 1887. 108 p. O. 75 c.

Baxter, R. D. Taxation of the United Kingdom. Lond., Macmillan, 1869. O. 4s. 6d.

A work now out of print and obtainable only in the larger libraries. It gives an analysis of British taxation, and discusses with great ability some of the most important questions in connection with the subject.

Buchanan, DAVID. Inquiry into the Taxation and Commercial Policy of Great Britain. Edinburgh, W: Tait, 1844. 340 p. O.

Dowell, STEPHEN. History of Taxation and Taxes in England from the earliest times to the present day. 2d. ed. rev. Lond. and N. Y., Longmans, 1885. 4 v. O. $15.

The best work on the subject.

Fawcett, H. Indian Finance. Lond., Macmillan, 1880. 187 p. O. 7s. 6d.

Gladstone, W: E. Financial Statements of 1853, 1860-1863. Lond., Murray, 1863. 462 p. O.

Includes also a speech on Tax bills, 1861, and on Charities, 1863.

Goschen, G: J. Reports and Speeches on Local Taxation. Lond., Macmillan, 1872. 218 p. O. 5s.

In many respects the ablest English work on the topic.

Local Government and Taxation. Lond. and N. Y., Cassell, 1875. O. $2.

A series of essays published by the Cobden Club; presents a good exposition of the systems of taxation in countries other than England and the United States—namely, Scotland, Ireland, Australia, Holland, Belgium, France, Russia, and Spain.

McCulloch, J: R. **Taxation and the Funding System.** 3d ed. Lond., 1863. O.

This was the best work on the subject, but is now only of historical value. It is now out of print, but can be referred to in the larger libraries.

Noble, J: **Local Taxation,** a criticism of fallacies and a summary of facts. Lond., H. S. King & Co., 1876. O.

Noble, J: **The Queen's Taxes;** an inquiry into the amount, incidence, and economic results of the taxation of the United Kingdom. Lond., Longmans, 1873. O. 3s. 6d.

Now out of print; the larger public libraries have it.

Northcote, *Sir* STAFFORD H. **Twenty Years of Financial Policy** [1843-1861]. Lond., Saunders, Otley & Co., 1862. 16+399 p. O. 14s.

A summary of the chief financial measures of Great Britain passed between 1842 and 1861, with a table of budgets.

Palgrave, R. H. I. **Local Taxation in Great Britain and Ireland.** Lond., Murray, 1871. 124 p. O. 5s.

Peto, *Sir* S. MORTON. **Taxation, Its Levy and Expenditure.** Lond., Chapman & Hall, 1863. 418 p. O. 10s. 6d.

Tennant, C: **The People's Blue-Book. Taxation as it is and as it ought to be.** 4th ed. Lond., Longmans, 1872. D. 7s. 6d.

Very complete in respect to the tax laws of Great Britain and their administration; and also discusses in a very readable and generally correct manner the facts of taxation. Not a scientific book however.

Wilson, A. J. **The National Budget:** The National Debt, Taxes, and Rates. English Citizen series. Lond. and N. Y., Macmillan, 1882. 176 p. D. $1.

In small compass gives a view of the whole English system of taxation.

Wright, R. S., *and* **Hobhouse,** H: **Outline of Local Government and Local Taxation in England and Wales.** Lond., W. Maxwell & Son, 1884. 130 p. O. 5s.

London is excluded. Some considerations for amendment are presented.

Bonnet, VICTOR. **La question des impôts.** Paris, Guillaumin, 1879. 8+230 p. S.

De Flaix, E. FOURNIER. **Traité de critique et de statistique comparée des institutions financières,** systèmes d'impôts, et reformes fiscales des divers états au XIXme siècle. 1me tome. Paris, Guillaumin, 1889. 56+587 p. O.

Denis, H. **L'Impôt.** 1me serie. Bruxelles, Veuve Monnom, 1889. 309 p. 8°, 25 plates.

To be completed in a 2d v. An excellent work.

De Parieu, F. E. **Histoire des impôts généraux sur la propriété et le revenu.** Paris, Guillaumin, 1856. 339 p. D.

A general sketch of direct taxation in the principal nations.

De Parieu, F. E. **Traité des impôts.** 4 tomes. Paris, Guillaumin, 1866–67. 17+522, 516, 522, 500 p. D.
<small>Deserves high commendation.</small>

Guyot, YVES. **L'impôt sur le revenu.** Paris, Guillaumin, 1887. 347 p. D. 3.50 francs.
<small>Discusses in a most attractive style direct and indirect taxation. The author is a practical statesman as well as an eminent economist.</small>

Leroy-Beaulieu, PAUL. **Traité des science des finances.** 4me ed. corr. et aug. 1me tome. Des revenus publics. Paris, Guillaumin, 1888. 26+791 p. D
<small>The best French work. Replete with learning and research.</small>

Menier, A. **L'impôt sur le capital.** Paris, Guillaumin, 1874. 642 p. O.

Say, LEON, *ed.* **Dictionnaire des finances.** Paris, Berger-Levrault & Cie.
<small>Eminent collaborators are engaged on this work. Begun 1883, to be completed in 25 pts. in 1891. 3.50 fr. per pt.</small>

Say, LEON. **Les solutions democratique de la question des impôts.** Paris, Guillaumin, 1886. 2 tomes, 260, 299 p. S.
<small>An incisive criticism of proposals to use the taxing power to equalize the fortunes of men.</small>

Vignes, E: **Traité des impôts en France.** 2 tomes. Paris, Guillaumin, 1880. 5+556, 499 p. D.

Cohn, GUSTAV. **Finanzwissenschaft.** Stuttgart, F. Enke, 1889. 804 p. D.
<small>V. 2 of his System. This v. consists of an introd. and 4 pts. Of these the 2d and 3d are the most interesting; they describe the present system of taxation in the German Empire, and set forth the author's doctrine of taxation. "Professor Cohn writes judiciously, and with much less of confidence than certain of his compeers."</small>

Held, ADOLF. **Die Einkommensteuer.** Bonn, A. Marcus, 1872. 12+354 p. D.

Hock, C. F. von. **Die öffentlichen Abgaben und Schulden.** Stuttgart, Cotta, 1863. 11+381 p. D.

Kaizl, JOSEF. **Die Lehre von der Ueberwälzung der Steuern.** Leipzig, Duncker & Humblot, 1882. 8+131 p. D.
<small>Excellent history of the doctrines of incidence of taxation.</small>

Meyer, ROBERT. **Principien der gerechten Besteuerung.** Berlin, W: Hertz, 1884. 9+413 p. D.

Neumann, F. T. **Progressive Einkommensteuer.** Leipzig, Duncker & Humblot, 1874. 238 p. D.

Roscher, W: **System der Finanzwissenschaft: ein Hand- und Lesebuch für Geschäftsmänner und Studierende.** 3d ed. enl. Stuttgart, J. G. Cotta, 1886. 783 p. D. 12 marks.
<small>V. 4 of his Economic System. An excellent treatise on methods of national finance.</small>

Schaeffle, A. E. F. **Die Grundsätze der Steuerpolitik.** Tubingen, 1880. 659 p. D.

Schanz, G: **Die Steuern der Schweiz in ihrer Entwickelung seit Beginn des 19 Jahrhunderts.** Stuttgart, Cotta, 1890. 5 v.
<small>A history of taxation in Switzerland during this century, of special value to the student from Switzerland's diversity, geographically, ethnologically, and politically.</small>

Stein, LORENZ von. **Finanzwissenschaft.** Leipzig, Brockhaus, 1886. 2 v. D.

Vocke, W: Die Abgaben, Auflagen und die Steuer, vom Standpunkte der Geschichte und der Sittlichkeit. Stuttgart, J. G. Cotta, 1887. 24+625 p. O. 10 marks.
A philosophical treatise on taxation.

Vocke, W: Geschichte der Steuern des Britischen Reiches. Leipzig, A. Felix, 1866. 642 p. O.
In some respects better than Dowell's History.

Wagner, ADOLPH. **Finanzwissenschaft.** 3 v. Leipzig, C. F. Winter. V. 1, 3d ed., 1883. V. 2, 2d ed., 1890. V. 3, 1889.
The most comprehensive work on taxation in any language. As yet uncompleted.

Allessio, GIULIO. **Saggio sul sistema tributario in Italia e sui suoi effetti economici e sociali.** Torino, Fratelli Bocca, 1887. 2 v. 393, 1007 p. O.
The best treatise on Italian taxation.

Cossa, LUIGI. **Primi elementi di scienza delle finanze.** 3d ed., corr. ed. acc. Milano, Ulrico Hoepli, 1882. 200 p. S.

—— Same. **Taxation, Its Principles and Methods;** with an introd. and notes by Horace White. N. Y., Putnam, 1888. 213 p. D. $1.
Clear in definition, simple in statement, comprehensive in classification. The editor's notes discuss from the American point of view the taxation of personal property, of mortgages, corporations, land values, and taxes on consumption; and present the progressive tax system which has been in force in the city of Basle, Switzerland, for fifty years. The appendix describes the tax systems of New York and Pennsylvania. A bibliography is given.

Marzano, F. Compendio di scienza delle finanze. Turin, 1887. 2d ed., p. 360.
"As a sketch of finance connected, well-written and sufficiently full for a first view. It is the best single treatise within my knowledge."—*E. B. Andrews.*

Mazzola, UGO. **I dati scientifici della finanza pubblica.** Rome, Loescher, 1890. 217 p. S°, 5 francs.
"One of the brightest, deepest, and most original among the numerous writings on economics which Italy has produced in recent years."—*E. B. Andrews.*

Pantaleoni, MAFFEO. **Teoria della translazione dei tributi.** Rome, A. Paolina, 1882. 355 p. O.
A capital treatise on the incidence of taxation.

During 1891 the American Economic Association, Baltimore, will begin publishing translations of the best foreign works on Public Finance.

Besides the N. Y. Reports of D. A. Wells see also Report of the Maryland Tax Commission, Baltimore, 1888; Report of the [Massachusetts] Commissioners appointed to inquire into the expediency of revising and amending the laws relating to taxation and exemption therefrom, Boston, 1875; Report of the Revenue Commission [of Illinois], Springfield, 1886; Report of the Tax Commissioners of Connecticut, Hartford, 1887; and Report of the Special Tax Commissioners of Maine, Augusta, 1890.

For a statement of the curious system of taxation existing in Mexico, and its influence on the trade and industries of that country, see David A. Wells' Study of Mexico. N. Y., Appleton, 1887.

In David A. Wells' Practical Economics [see International Trade] is a chapter on The Taxation of Distilled Spirits, describing one of the most interesting experiences of the U. S. Internal Revenue Department.

In South Kingstown, Rhode Island, two town meetings are held; one of all citizens, the other of taxpayers only, who alone have a right to vote to impose taxes or upon expenditures of money. The list of the latter is given in the Town's Year Book, published at Wakefield, R. I.

Historical and Comparative Science of Finance, by Prof. E. R. A. Seligman, is in preparation for the series in Systematic Political Science by the University Faculty of Pol. Science, Columbia College, N. Y.

The Financial Reform Almanac, (Lond., Simpkin, Marshall & Co., 1s.) contains important statistics with arguments for reform in taxation.

The Treasury Department, Washington, publishes an annual report of the receipts and expenditures of the United States.

Valuation and Taxation of Real and Personal Property in the United States, by States, Counties, Cities, etc., for 1880, is given in v. 7, Census Reports, Tenth Census. Washington, Gov. Pr. Office, 1884. 909 p. Q.

Agriculture and the Single Tax. Horace White. *Popular Science Monthly*, Feb., 1890.

Bases of Taxation. F. A. Walker. *Political Science Quarterly*, March, 1888.

Income and Property Taxes in Switzerland. Gustav Cohn. *Political Science Quarterly*, March, 1889.

Single Tax Debate. S: B. Clarke, Prof. T: Davidson, W: L. Garrison, Prof. J: B. Clark, Pres. E. B. Andrews, Prof. E. R. A. Seligman, L: F. Post, E: Atkinson. H: George, Prof. W: T. Harris, and James R. Carret. *Journal of the American Social Science Assoc.*, no. 27. Saratoga papers of 1890. N. Y., Putnam, 1890. 53-127 p. O. $1.

Taxation of Labor. C: B. Spahr. *Political Science Quarterly*, Sept., 1886.

The Direct Tax of 1861. C. F. Dunbar. *Quarterly Journal of Economics*, July, 1889.

The Single Tax. H: George and E. Atkinson. *Century Magazine*, July, 1890.

The Tobacco Tax, 1864-90. F. L. Olmsted. *Quarterly Journal of Economics*, Jan., 1891.

PUBLIC DEBTS.

Adams, H. C. Public Debts: an essay in the science of finance. 2d. ed. N. Y., Appleton, 1890. 407 p. O. $2.50.

A survey of the facts of Public Debt as they were in 1880, with a masterly statement of the economic principles which should limit public indebtedness and decide its form. Traces the growth of corporate monopoly to the failure, about 1850, of State treasuries in schemes of public improvement. Holds that States should be re-empowered to borrow money, and abandon their claim to sovereignty, so as to be suable for debt—as Prussia is. Recommends that State Governments take forestry in hand. Gives the constitutional inhibitions on State and local indebtedness. Would forbid by law subsidies to railroads or other enterprises, and would have natural monopolies undertaken by municipalities, or States, instead of by corporations.

Elliot, JONATHAN. Funding System of the United States and of Great Britain, with some tabular facts of other nations touching the same subject. Washington, 1845. 1299 p. O.

Green, G· WALTON. **Repudiation.** Economic tract no. 11. N. Y., Soc. for Political Education, 1883. 42 p. D. pap. 20 c.

Richardson, W. A. **Practical Information Concerning the Public Debt of the United States,** with the National banking laws. 2d ed. Washington, W. H. & O. H. Morrison, 1873. 186 p. O.

Baxter, R. D. **National Debts.** 2d ed. Lond., Bush, 1871. O. 4s. 6d.

Neymarck, ALFRED. **Public Debts of Europe;** tr. by O. A. Bierstadt. N. Y., Homans Pub. Co., 1888. 80 p. O. pap. 50 c.

Ricca-Salerno, GUISEPPE. **Teoria generale dei prestiti pubblici.** Milano, Ulrico Hoepli, 1879. 141 p. D.

A History of the National Debts of the Principal Nations, and of the National Loans of the United States, from July 4, 1796, to June 30, 1880, prepared by Rafael A. Bayley, is given in v. 7, Census Reports, Tenth Census. Washington, Gov. Pr. Office, 1884. 909 p. Q. The Eleventh Census will contain a valuable investigation as to wealth, debt, and taxation, carried on under direction of T. Campbell-Copeland. Census Bulletin no. 6, Aug. 4, 1890, gives Financial Condition of Countries; no. 6, same date, Indebtedness of the United States and the several States in 1880 and 1890.

Some Precedents Followed by Alexander Hamilton. C: F. Dunbar. *Quarterly Journal of Economics,* Oct., 1888.

SOCIAL SCIENCE AND SOCIOLOGY.

Bascom, J. **Sociology.** N. Y., Putnam, 1887. 264 p. D. $1.50.
A survey of sociology in its more general features, and of its present problems.

Egleston, N. H. **The Home and Its Surroundings.** [New ed. of Villages and Village Life.] N. Y., Harper, 1883. D. $1.
Contains valuable suggestions for the improvement of village life.

Ely, R: T. **Social Aspects of Christianity.** New ed. enl. N. Y., T. Y. Crowell & Co., 1889. 132 p. D. 90 c.
Contents: Social Aspects of Christianity, The Church and the World, Philanthropy, Ethics and Economics.

George, H: **Social Problems.** N. Y., H: George & Co., 1884. 342 p. S. cl. $1 ; pap. 35 c.

Hamilton, R. S. **Present Status of Social Science;** a review historical and critical. N. Y., H. L. Hinton & Co., 1874. 7+332 p. D.

Harrison, J. B. **Certain Dangerous Tendencies in American Life,** and other papers. Boston, Houghton, Osgood & Co., 1880. 260 p. D. $1.25.

Johnson, J: **Rudimentary Society Among Boys.** Baltimore, Johns Hopkins Univ. Hist. Series, 1884. 46 p. O. pap. 50 c.

Newton, *Rev.* R. HEBER. **Social Studies.** N. Y., Putnam, 1887. 380 p· S. $1.60.
Reviews the labor question, coöperation, intemperance, moral education, socialism, and communism. A list of books on socialism, etc., is appended. Author is pastor of the Protestant Episcopal Church of All Souls New York City.

Riis, JACOB A. **How the Other Half Lives.** N. Y., Scribner, 1890. 11+304 p. O. $2.50.
Studies among the tenements of New York by the reporter for Associated Press at Police Headquarters. Illustrated from photographs by the author.

Strong, JOSIAH, *D.D.* **Our Country,** its possible future and its present crisis. New ed. N. Y., Baker & Taylor Co., 1889. 229 p. D. cl. 50 c.; pap. 25 c.
    Author an eminent Congregational clergyman. Regards as the perils besetting our country undesirable immigration, Romanism, Mormonism, intemperance, socialism and the money power. Pleads for evangelization as the remedy for the evils described.

Sumner, W: G. **What Social Classes Owe to Each Other.** N. Y., Harper. 160 p. S. 60 c.
    Maintains that social classes owe each other not interference but simply justice. A trenchant argument for individualism.

Ward, LESTER F. **Dynamic Sociology.** N. Y., Appleton, 1883. 2 v. 20+706, 8+690 p. D. $5.
    A systematic exposition of sociology and a plea for the extension of the functions of organized society, that principles long understood may be applied to the advancement of the race.

Wright, CARROLL D. **Popular Instruction in Social Science.** Boston, G: E. Crosby & Co., 1886.

Blackley, *Rev.* W: L. **Thrift and Independence,** a Word for Workingmen. Lond., Soc. for Prom. Christian Knowledge. N. Y., E. & J. B. Young & Co., 1885. 189 p. S. 45 c.
    Reviews the Friendly Society and other systems, and proposes National insurance.

Booth, C:, *ed.* **Life and Labor in East London.** Lond., Williams & Norgate, 1889. V. 1, 598 p. O.
    One of the ablest practical contributions ever made to social science. A business-like investigation by a business man.

Helps, *Sir* ARTHUR. **Social Pressure.** New ed. Lond., Chatto & Windus, 1883. 412 p. S. 2s. 6d.
    A continuation of the "Friends in Council" series, discussing in a conversational way problems of modern social life. Excellent.

Jevons, W. STANLEY. **Methods of Social Reform.** Lond. and N. Y., Macmillan, 1883. 313 p. O. $3.
    Discusses, among other themes, Experimental Legislation, Amusements of the People, The Rationale of Free Public Libraries, and The Use and Abuse of Museums.

Ruskin, J: **Crown of Wild Olive:** lectures on Work, Traffic, War and the Future of England; with article on Economy of Kings of Prussia. Orpington, Kent, G: Allen, 1866. bds. 13s.

Spencer, HERBERT. b. 1820. **Social Statics.** N. Y., Appleton, 1883. p. D. $2.
    First published in 1863. An able work. Does not represent later views of author.

Spencer, HERBERT. **The Man vs. the State.** N. Y., Appleton, 1884. 113 p. D. pap. 30 c.
    An arraignment of tendencies of government alleged to be encroaching on individual liberty and prosperity. Criticised by E. De Laveleye, in his Socialism of To-day [Socialism].

Spencer, HERBERT. **The Study of Sociology.** N. Y., Appleton, 1880. xiv-426 p. D. $1.50.
    Explains the scope of the science, its utility and method, and gives some of its more important general principles. Author is the foremost sociologist living.

Spencer, HERBERT. **Principles of Sociology.** 3d ed. rev. and enl. 2 v, N. Y., Appleton, 1890. V. 1, Data and Inductions of Sociology, Domestic Institutions. 883 p. O. V. 2, Ceremonial and Political Institutions. 667+26 p. O. $4.

Spencer, Herbert. Descriptive Sociology. A Cyclopædia of social facts, representing the constitution of every type and grade of human society, past and present, stationary and progressive. N. Y., Appleton, 1880.—In folio with tables. 8 pts. nos. 1 to 7, $4 each ; no. 8, $7.

Stanley, Maude. Clubs for Working-Girls. Lond., Macmillan, 1890. 266 p. 8°, 6s.

Wilkinson, Rev. J. F. **The Friendly Society Movement**: its origin, rise, and growth ; its social, moral, and educational influences. Lond. and N. Y., Longmans, 1886. 229 p. D. 90 c.

Courcel-Seneuil, J. G. **Etudes sur la science sociale.** Paris, Guillaumin, 1862. 8+492 p. O.

Delaire, A., ed. **La reforme sociale, et le centenaire de la Revolution.** Travaux du Congrès tenu en 1889 par la Société d'Economie Sociale. Paris, Bureaux de la Reforme Sociale, 1890. 769 p. O. 10 fr.

Fouillée, A. J. E. La science sociale contemporaine. 2me ed. Paris, Hachette & Cie., 1885. 13+424 p. D.

Le Play, P. G. F. La reforme sociale. 7me ed. Tours, Mame, 1890.

Leroy-Beaulieu, Paul. Essai sur la répartition des richesses. Paris, 1881.

Treitschke, H. G. Die Gesellschaftwissenschaft, ein kritischer Versuch. Leipzig, C. Hirzel, 1859. 107 p. D.

Ellero, Pietro. La questione sociale. Bologna, 1874. 435+3 p. O.

Minghetti, M. **Dell' economia pubblica e delle sur attinenze colla morale e col diritto.** 2d ed. Florence, 1868.

Recommended by Luigi Cossa as a thoughtful and valuable work.

—— Same. **Des rapports de l'économie publique avec la morale et le droit.** Tr. par St. Germain Leduc. Introd. par H. P. Passy. Paris, Guillaumin, 1863. 23+560 p. O.

Toniolo, G. Sulla distribuzione della richezza. Verona, 1878.

The American Social Science Assoc., the leading organization of the kind in the U. S., publishes an annual *Journal*, no. 1, 1868. Membership, $5 per annum, entitles to publications. F. B. Sanborn, Secretary, Concord, Mass.

The Transactions of the National Assoc. for the Promotion of Social Science, London, were published annually until 1885. They are of high value.

La Reforme Sociale, published at 184 Boulevard St. Germain, Paris, is the most important Social Science periodical in the world. *L'Economie Sociale*, a monthly review published by Berger, Levrault & Cie., Paris, v. 1, 1888–9, finds its field in the relations of laborers to their employers and to each other. Its chief topics are accidents, insurance, popular banks, dwellings, sanitation, factory laws, trades-unions, labor associations, coöperation, and profit-sharing.

Sociology is treated in the Collected Essays of Prof. W. G. Sumner. N. Y., Holt, 1885.

Ad. Wagner's " Rede über die sociale Frage " will be found under Political Economy, Essays and Criticisms.

Method of Study in Social Science. W: T. Harris. *Journal of American Assoc. of Social Science*, 1879.

Preventable Causes of Poverty. H: D. Chapin. *Forum*, June, 1889.

Province of Sociology. F. H. Giddings. *Annals American Academy Political and Social Science*, July, 1890.

Threefold Aspect of Social Science in America. F. B. Sanborn. *Journal American Social Science Assoc.*, 1881.

SOCIALISM, COMMUNISM, ANARCHISM.

Bellamy, E: **Looking Backward, 2000-1887.** 1887. Boston, Houghton, Mifflin & Co., 1890. 470 p. D. cl. $1; pap. 50 c.
  This socialistic romance has given rise to the Nationalist movement.

Ely, R: T. **French and German Socialism in Modern Times.** N. Y., Harper, 1883. 274 p. S. 75 c.
  A popular, impartial presentation. Brief and clear.

Ely, R: T. **Recent American Socialism.** Baltimore, Johns Hopkins University Hist. Series, 1885. 74 p. O. pap. 75 c.

Gronlund, LAURENCE. **The Coöperative Commonwealth;** an exposition of modern socialism. Boston, Lee & Shepard, 1884. 278 p. D. $1. N. Y., J. W. Lovell Co., 1887. 278 p. S. pap. 30 c.
  A statement of the case for state socialism, with plans for its operation.

Gronlund, LAURENCE. **Our Destiny:** the Influence of Nationalism on Morals and Religion. Boston, Lee & Shepard, 1891. 219 p. D. cl. $1; pap. 50 c.

Gronlund, LAURENCE. **Socialism vs. Tax Reform;** an answer to H: George. N. Y., N. Y. Labor News Co., 1886. 35 p. D. pap. 10c.

James, C. L. **Anarchy.** Eau Claire, Wis., C. L. James, 1886. 32 p. D. pap. 25c.

Lum, DYER D. **History of the Great Trial of the Chicago Anarchists,** condensed from the official record. Chicago, Socialistic Pub. Co., 1886. 192 p. D.

Nordhoff, C: **Communistic Societies of the United States.** N. Y., Harper, 1875. 438 p. D. $4.
  Written from personal observation. Describes the peculiar features of the religious creeds and practices, the social and domestic customs, and the industrial and financial arrangements of each society.

Noyes, J. H. **History of American Socialisms.** Phila., Lippincott, 1870. 678 p. D. $3.50.

Parsons, ALBERT R. **Anarchism.** Chicago, 1887. 200 p. D.

Seligman, E. R. A. **Owen and the Christian Socialists.** N. Y., Ginn & Co., 1886. 45 p. O.
  Reprinted from *Political Science Quarterly*, June, 1886. Contains a full bibliography of Owen and the Christian Socialists.

Shaw, ALBERT. **Icaria,** a chapter in the history of communism. N. Y., Putnam, 1884. 10+219 p. S. $1.
  An impartial history of communes which have attempted to realize the rational, democratic communism of the Utopian philosophers, apart from any religious basis.

Smith, GOLDWIN. **False Hopes,** or fallacies, socialistic and semi-socialistic, briefly answered. N. Y., J. W. Lovell Co. 69 p. D. pap. 15 c.

SOCIAL SCIENCE AND SOCIOLOGY.

Sprague, *Rev.* PHILO W. **Christian Socialism, What and Why?** N. Y., E. P. Dutton & Co., 1891. 204 p. S. cl. 75c.; pap. 50 c.
With appended address of the Bishop of Durham on Socialism.

Woolsey, THEODORE D. **Communism and Socialism;** their history and theory. N. Y., Scribner, 1880. 309 p. D. $1.50.
Describes phases of socialism, especially as developed in Germany.

Barnet, *Rev.* and *Mrs.* SAMUEL A. **Practicable Socialism.** Lond. and N. Y., Longmans, 1888. 212 p. S. 2s. 6d.
Essays written from 15 years' experience in East End of London.

Bax, E. B. **Ethics of Socialism.** Lond., Swan Sonnenschein, n. d. 6+210 p. D.

Bax, E. B. **Religion of Socialism.** Lond., Swan Sonnenschein, 1886. 11+177 p. D. 4s. 6d.

Booth, A. J. **Memoir of R: Owen.** Lond., Trübner, 1869. 5s.

Carpenter, E: **England's Ideal,** and other papers on social subjects. Lond., Swan Sonnenschein, 1889. 1s.
Presenting the ethical side of socialism.

Dawson, W. H. **Bismarck and State Socialism.** Lond., Swan Sonnenschein, 1890. 171 p. D.

Dawson, W: H. **German Socialism and Ferdinand Lassalle;** a biographical history of German socialistic movements during this century. Lond., Swan Sonnenschein, 1888. 12+300 p. D. 4s. 6d.

Donisthorpe, WORDSWORTH. **Individualism, a System of Politics.** Lond. and N. Y., Macmillan, 1890. 393 p. O.
An able critical review of socialistic proposals.

Graham, W: **Socialism, New and Old.** International Scientific Series, no. 68. N. Y., Appleton, 1891. 416 p. D. $1.75.
An able historical and critical review of socialism, with an examination of proposed remedies for low wages and unemployed labor, and of the eight hours working day. Author is Professor of Political Economy and Jurisprudence, Queen's College, Belfast.

Graham, W: **The Social Problem** in its economical, moral, and political aspects. Lond., Kegan Paul, 1886. 479 p. D. 14s.

Hyndman, H. M. **Historical Basis of Socialism in England.** Lond., Kegan Paul, 1883. 492 p. D. 8s. 6d.

Hyndman, H. M., *and* **Morris,** W: **Summary of the Principles of Socialism.** Lond., 1884. 62 p. D. pap. 6d.

Kaufmann, *Rev.* M. **Christian Socialism.** Lond., Kegan Paul, 1888. 232 p. D. 4s. 6d.

Kempner, M. **Common-Sense Socialism:** The Inadequacy of the Reward of Labor, The Depression of Trade, and the Organization of Material Progress. Lond., Swan Sonnenschein, 1887. 8+308+18 p. D. 7s. 6d.

Kirkup, T: **Inquiry into Socialism.** Lond. and N. Y., Longmans, 1887. 188 p. D. $1.50.
The clearest statement as yet made by any English author. Expects more from the development of coöperation than from direct interference from the State. Sees in the development of great corporations managed by paid superintendents a step toward socialistic production and a pledge of its future success.

Kropotkin, *Prince* PIERRE. **War, Law and Authority, Expropriation.** Three anarchistic essays. Lond., International Pub. Co., 1886. pap. D. 4d.

Mill, J: STUART. **Socialism.** 1st pt. of Socialism and Utilitarianism. Chicago, Belford, Clarke & Co., 1879. 3+136+152 p. D. $1.25.

Morris, W: **Signs of Change,** seven lectures delivered on various occasions. Lond., Reeves & Turner, 1888. 8+202 p. D. 4s. 6d.

Contains: How we live, and how we might live; Whigs, Democrats, and Socialists; Feudal England; Hopes of Civilization; Aims of Art; Useful work *vs.* useless toil; Dawn of a new epoch. Author famous as poet and artist.

Rae, J: **Contemporary Socialism.** Lond., Isbister, 1884. 7s. 6d. N. Y., Scribner, 1884. 455 p. D. $2.

States and criticises in a masterly way the principles of Lassalle, Marx, Karl Marlo, the Socialists of the Chair, the Christian Socialists, the Russian Nihilists, and H: George; with a general chapter on Socialism and the Social Question.

Shaw, G. BERNARD, *ed.* **Fabian Essays in Socialism.** Lond., Fabian Soc., 1889. 233 p. D. cl. 6s.; cheap pap. ed. 1s.

Contains: The Basis of Socialism, by G. B. Shaw, Sidney Webb, W: Clarke, and Sydney Olivier; The Organization of Society, by G. Wallas and Annie Besant; The Transition to Social Democracy, by G. B. Shaw; and The Outlook, by Hubert Bland.

Smith, H. L. **Economic Aspects of State Socialism.** Lond., Simpkin, Marshall & Co., 1887. 120 p. D.

Cobden prize essay, 1886.

Webb, SIDNEY. **Socialism in England.** Baltimore, American Economic Assoc., 1889. 73 p. O. pap. 75c.

—— Same. Rev. and enl. ed. Lond., Swan Sonnenschein, 1890. 133 p. 8°, 2s. 6d.

Blanc, L: **Organisation du travail.** Paris, 1848. 284 p. S.

Cabet, M. **Voyage en Icarie.** Paris, 1848. 8+600 p. S.

By the founder of the American Icaria [see Shaw, Albert].

Comte, AUGUSTE. **Positive Philosophy.** Tr. and condensed by Harriet Martineau. Lond., Trübner, 1876. 2 v. 8°, 25s.

Comte, AUGUSTE. **Positive Polity.** Lond., Longmans, 1875-77. 4 v. 8°, 80s.

Courtois, ALPHONSE, *fils.* **Anarchisme théorique et collectivisme pratique.** Paris, Guillaumin, 1885. 16+127 p.

Fouillé, ALFRED. **La science sociale.** Paris, Hachette & Cie., 1885.

Fourier, C: **Oeuvres complètes.** Paris, A. Dupont, 1870. 6 v. D.

Godin, M. **Social solutions;** tr. by Marie Howland. N. Y., J. W. Lovell Co., 1887. 326 p. D. $1.50.

The author founded the famous Familistère in Guise, France. Describes his coöperative principles in their detailed application.

Jannet, C. **Le socialisme d'état et la réforme sociale.** 2me ed. Mise au courant des statistiques et des lois les plus récentes. Paris, Plon & Nourrit. 626 p. D. 7.50 fr.

Author Professor of Political Economy in the Catholic Institute of Paris. Declares that no Catholic can be a Socialist. Presents interesting studies of the Peasant Unions of Germany, reform of the law of inheritance, compulsory insurance of workingmen, Catholic associations, etc.

Kropotkin, *Prince* PIERRE. **Paroles d'un Revolté.** Elisée Reclus, ed. Paris, C. Marpon and E. Flammarion. 3.50 fr.

Laveleye, E. de. Le socialisme contemporain. Paris, Alcan, 1890. 3.50 fr.

New ed. cont. chapters on Socialism in England, on the State and the Individual, with reply to Herbert Spencer.

—— Same. **Socialism of To-day.** Tr. by G. H. Orpen. With Socialism in England, by G. H. Orpen. Lond., Field & Tuer, 1885. 44+331 p. D. 6s.

Lepage, A: **Histoire de la Commune.** Paris, A. Lemerre, 1871. 4+284 p. S.

By an eyewitness.

Le Play, F. **La réforme sociale.** Tours, France, Alfred Mame, 1887. 3 v. 16 fr.

A comprehensive and able treatise. Other works by this author are noted under Labor.

Leroy-Beaulieu, PAUL. **Le collectivisme; examen critique du nouveau socialisme.** Paris, Guillaumin, 1885. 449 p. O.

Leroy-Beaulieu. La répartition des richesses. Paris, Guillaumin, 1888.

Proudhon, P. J. **Oeuvres.** Paris, A. Lacroix, Verboeckhaven & Cie., 1866. 22 v.

What is Property? included in foregoing, has been translated by B. R. Tucker [see Property, Capital].

Saint-Simon, H: **Oeuvres.** Paris, E. Dentu, 1866. 7 v. O.

Say, LEON. **Le socialisme d'état.** Angleterre, Allemagne, Italie. Paris, Levy, 1890. 216 p. D. 3.50 fr.

Sudre, ALFRED. **Histoire du communisme, ou refutation historique des Utopies socialistes.** Paris, Guillaumin, 1856. 8+487 p. S.

Gives within a moderate compass a good historical outline and summary of socialistic and communistic systems to 1856. An adverse criticism.

Testut, OSCAR. **Le livre bleu de l'Internationale,** rapports et documents officiels les aux congrès de Lausanne, Bruxelles et Bade par le conseil général de Londres et les délégues de touts les sections de l'Internationale. Paris, E. Lachaud, 1871. 324 p. D.

Thonissen, J. J. **Le socialisme depuis l'antiquité** jusqu'a la constitution française du 14 Janvier, 1852. Paris, Sagnier & Bray, 1852. 8+567, 595 p. D.

Villetard, E. **History of the International.** Tr. by Susan M. Day. New Haven, Conn., G. H. Richmond & Co., 1874. 9+259 p. D.

Adler, G: **Die Grundlagen der Karl Marx'schen Kritik der bestehenden Volkswirthschaft.** Tübingen, Laupp'schen Buchhandlung, 1887. 294 p. D. 6 marks.

An able criticism of Karl Marx's theories.

Bebel, AUGUST. **Woman in the Past, Present, and Future.** Tr. by H. B. Adams Walther. Lond., The Modern Press. 5s.

Contains exposition of the principles and practical ideas of German Social Democrats.

Held, ADOLF. **Zwei Bucher zur Socialen Geschichte Englands.** Leipzig, Duncker & Humblot, 1881. 776 p. O.

Best social history of England from the middle of the 18th century to 1830.

Held, ADOLF. **Sozialismus, Sozialdemokratie und Sozialpolitik.** Leipzig, Duncker & Humblot, 1878. 8+156 p. D.

Lassalle, FERDINAND. **Working Man's Programme.** Tr. with introd. by E. Peters. Lond., The Modern Press, 1884. 6d.

Lilienfeld, P. **Gendanken über die Socialwissenschaft der Zukunst.** B. 1, Gesellschaft ; B. 2, Gesetze ; B. 3, Psychophysik ; B. 4, Physiologie ; B. 5, Religion. Hamburg, G. Behre, 1873-81. 10+400, 10+404, 25+490, 30+496, 10+592 p. O.

Marlo, KARL. **Untersuchungen über die Organisation der Arbeit.** Kassel, W: Appel, 1850-53-57. 3 v. 502, 711, 862 p. D.

Marx, KARL, *and* **Engels,** FREDERICK. **Manifesto of the Communist Party.** Tr. and annotated by Engels. 2d ed. Lond., W. Reeves, 1888.
  An important document in the history of modern Socialism, whose policy it has virtually shaped.

Rodbertus-Jagetzow, C: **Werke.** Berlin, Puttkammer & Mühlbrecht, 1885. 3 v. O.

Schäffle, A. E. F. **Aussichtslosigkeit der Socialdemokratie.** Tübingen, 1885. 112 p. D.

Schäffle, A. E. F. **Capitalismus und Socialismus.** Tübingen, 1878. 15+575 p. D.

Schäffle, A. E. F. **Quintessenz des Socialismus.** Gotha, F. A. Perthes, 1879. 7+69 p. D.

—— Same. **Quintessence of Socialism.** N. Y., Humboldt Pub. Co., 1890. 55 p. D. 15 c.

Scheel, H. v. **Die Theorie der Sozialen Frage.** Jena, Friedrich Mauke, 1871. 159 p. D.

Schmoller, H. **Ueber einige Grundfragen des Rechts und der Volkswirthschaft.** Jena, 1875.
  An able reply to Treitschke.

Stein, L. **Der Socialismus und Communismus des heutigen Frankreichs.** Leipzig, O. Wigand, 1848. 16+592 p. O.

Treitschke, H. v. **Der Socialismus und seine Gönner.** Berlin, G. Reimer, 1875. 4+142 p. O.
  A criticism of socialistic arguments from the liberal standpoint.

Waltershausen, A. S. F. v. **Der moderne Sozialismus in den Vereinigten Staaten von Amerika.** Berlin, H. Bahr, 1890. 422 p. D.
  In some respects the ablest history of Socialism in the United States. A history of labor agitations as well as of Socialism. Describes the strikes of 1877, the Chicago anarchist uprising of 1887, the George and eight-hour movements.

Mazzini, JOSEPH. **Thoughts upon Democracy in Europe and The Duties of Man.** Lond., Alexander & Shepherd. 6d.
  A review (in part) of the aims and spirit of Socialists and Communists, in their various parties.

Karl Marx's Das Kapital [see Capital] expounds an elaborate plan of State Socialism. There is a new English translation. (N. Y., Humboldt Pub. Co., 1890. 18+506 p. D. pap. $1.20 ; cl. $1.75.)

Economic Socialism. H. Sidgwick. *Contemporary Review*, Nov., 1886.

Ethics of Socialism. F. H. Giddings. *International Journal of Ethics*, Jan., 1891.

Ferdinand Lassalle. L. J. Huff. *Political Science Quarterly*, Sept., 1887.

First Steps Toward Nationalism. E: Bellamy. *Forum*, Oct., 1890.

Influence of Socialism upon English Politics. W: Clarke. *Political Science Quarterly*, Jan., 1888.

Scientific Anarchism. H. L. Osgood. *Political Science Quarterly*, March, 1889.

Scientific Socialism, Rodbertus. H. L. Osgood. *Political Science Quarterly*, Dec., 1886.

Socialism in England. Percival Chubb. *Journal of Social Science* (Saratoga papers of 1889). N. Y., Putnam, 1890.

Some Experiments on Behalf of the Unemployed. Amos G. Warner. *Quarterly Journal of Economics*, Oct., 1890.

State Control of Industry in the 4th Century. W. A. Brown. *Political Science Quarterly*, Sept., 1887.

An account of Roman socialism.

State Socialism and Popular Right. J: Rae. *Contemporary Review*, Dec., 1890.

The Coming Anarchy. Prince Kropotkin. *Nineteenth Century*, Aug., 1887.

The Industrial Village of the Future. Prince Kropotkin. *Nineteenth Century*, Oct., 1888.

What Nationalism Means. E: Bellamy. *Contemporary Review*, July, 1890.

POPULATION, CENSUS.

Bonar, JAMES. **Malthus and His Work.** Lond. and N. Y., Macmillan, 1888. 430 p. O. $4; also, N. Y., Harper, 1885, 224 p. S. pap. 25c.

Presents Malthus' contributions to political economy, and traces his influence upon recent economic thought. Reviews his critics. The best survey of the discussion on population.

Doubleday, T: **True Law of Population** shewn to be connected with the food of the people. Lond., Smith, Elder & Co., 1853. 16+338+62 p. D.

Godwin, W: **Enquiry Concerning the Power of Increase in the Numbers of Mankind.** Lond., Longman, 1820. 626 p. O.

An adverse criticism of Malthus.

Malthus, T: R. 1766-1834. **Essay on the Principle of Population;** view of the past and present effects on human happiness. 2 v. Lond., 1807.

The foremost work on population. *Contents:* V. 1 Of the checks to population in less civilized parts of the world, and in past times and in modern Europe. V. 2, Of different expedients, as they affect the evils arising from the principle of population: systems of equality, emigration, poor laws, increasing wealth, moral restraints, etc. He opposed the poor laws.

—— Same. Lond. and N. Y., Ward, Lock & Co., 1890. 614 p. 8°, $2.

Reprinted from the last ed. rev. by the author; with a biography, full analysis, and critical introd. by G. T. Bettany.

Sadler, M. T: **Law of Population:** a treatise in disproof of the superfecundity of human beings, and developing the real principles of their increase. Lond., Murray, 1830. 2 v. 16+639, 690 p. D.

Thornton, W: T: **Over-Population and Its Remedy.** Lond., Longmans, 1846. 11+446 p. O.

Neumann, F. J. Beiträge zur Geschichte der Bevölkerung in Deutschland, seit dem Anfange dieses Jahrhunderts. Tübingen, 1883-87. 2 v. 8+368 284 p. O.

Garnier, JOSEPH. **Du principe du population.** 2me ed. Paris, Guillaumin, 1885. 63+552 p. D.

Messedaglia, AUG. **Della teoria della popolazione principalmente** sotto l'aspetto del metodo. V. 1. Verona, 1858.

Some consideration of the population question will be found in every systematic treatise on political economy. J: Stuart Mill and H: Fawcett adopt Malthusian views with qualification. H: George in Progress and Poverty dissents strenuously. Herbert Spencer in Biology, v. 2, discusses the population question. W: Roscher devotes a chapter to it of much interest in his Political Economy. H: C. Carey's review in Principles of Social Science is specially important [see Political Economy, General].

Tenth Census Reports, Washington (Gov. Pr. Office, 1883-88), include, besides the Compendium, quarto volumes as follows: V. 1, Population. V. 2, Manufactures. V. 3, Agriculture. V. 4, Transportion. V. 5 and 6, Cotton Production. V. 7, Valuation, Taxation, and Public Indebtedness. V. 8 Newspapers, Periodicals, Alaska, Fur-seal Islands, Shipbuilding. V. 9, Forest Trees of North America. V. 10, Petroleum, Coke, and Building Stones. V. 11 and 12, Mortality and Vital Statistics. V. 13, Precious Metals. V. 14, Mining Laws. V. 15, Mining Industries, excluding precious metals. V. :6 and 17, Water Power. V. 18 and 19, Social Statistics of Cities. V. 20, Wages, Necessaries of Life, Trades Societies, Strikes and Lockouts. V. 21, Defective, Dependent, and Delinquent Classes. V. 22, Power and Machinery Employed in Manufactures, and Ice Industry.

The [Eleventh] Census Bureau, Washington, issues bulletins giving preliminary reports. Those published in 1890 were on Financial Condition of Counties; Indebtedness of States in 1880 and 1890; Slate Mining; Pig-iron Production; Quicksilver Mining; Rapid Transit in Cities; Population of the United States, 1890; Steel Production; Census of Alaska; Education; Vital Statistics of the Jews.

COLONIES, COLONIZATION.

Cotton, J. S., *and* **Payne,** E: J. **Colonies and Dependencies.** India. J. S. Cotton; The Colonies, E: J. Payne. English Citizen Series. Lond. and N. Y., Macmillan, 1883. 6+164 p. D. $1.

Dilke, *Sir* C: W. **Problems of Greater Britain.** Lond. and N. Y., Macmillan, 1890. 738 p. D. $4.

Gives a comprehensive survey of the political and social questions of Great Britain's colonies and dependencies. A work of the very first rank.

England and Her Colonies: five Essays on Imperial Federation. Lond., Swan Sonnenschein, 1889. D. cl. 2s.; pap. 1s.

Essays selected as the best offered London Chamber of Commerce in prize competition— J. A. Froude, Prof. Seeley, and Sir Rawson W. Rawson being judges.

Merivale, HERMAN. **Colonization and Colonies.** Lond., Longmans, 1842. 2 v. O.

Contains much valuable history, and treats of the disposal of land in new colonies.

Payne, E: J. History of European Colonies. Lond. and N. Y., Macmillan, 1877. 11+408 p. S. $1.10.

Seeley, J: R. Expansion of England: two courses of lectures. Lond. and N. Y., Macmillan, 1888. 8+309 p. D. $1.50.

A survey of the British colonial empire. Excellent.

Leroy-Beaulieu, PAUL. De la colonisation chez les peuples modernes. 3me ed., aug. Paris, Guillaumin, 1886. 19+766 p. O.

Rambaud, ALF. La France coloniale, histoire, géographie, commerce. Paris, A. Colin & Cie., 1886. 38+714 p. O.

Vignon, L. Les colonies Françaises, leur commerce, leur situation economique, leur utilité pour la metropole, leur avenir. Paris, Guillaumin, 1886. 236 p. O.

Roscher, W: Kolonien, Kolonialpolitik und Auswanderung. 2d ed. Leipzig, 1856. 8+455 p. D.

The first of J. E. Cairnes' "Political Essays" is on Colonization and Colonial Government. (Lond., Macmillan, 1873.)

Recent Experiments in Colonization. A. White. *Contemporary Review*, Nov., 1890.

IMMIGRATION AND RACE QUESTIONS.

IMMIGRATION.

Bromwell, W: J. History of Immigration into the United States. N. Y., Redfield, 1856. 225 p. O.

Kapp, F: Immigration and the Commissioners of Emigration of the State of New York. N. Y., 1870. 240 p. O.

Report of the Standing Committee on Immigration, with the discussion thereon, read before the National Conference of Charities and Correction at Washington, June 9, 1885, by Dr. C: S. Hoyt. Washington, Gov. Pr. Office, 1885.

Smith, RICHMOND MAYO. Emigration and Immigration. N. Y., Scribner, 1890. 316 p. D. $1.50.

An historical and statistical survey. Discusses the political and social effects of immigration, as also the economic gain derived from it. Reviews the consequences to American labor of competition with recent immigrants having low standard of living. Recommends that "assisted" emigration be protested against as a breach of international comity, and that consular certificates be required from emigrants. Holds that if one nationality is to be built up in this country, one speech must be insisted upon. A bibliography is appended. An able and suggestive book, much the best on the subject.

Testimony and Reports of Committee of the House of Representatives to inquire into alleged violations of the Immigration Law, etc. Three Reports, Testimony, and Reports from Consuls. Washington, Gov. Pr. Office, 1889.

Bodio, LUIGI. Sulla condizione dell' emigrazione italiana. Roma, 1888.

Scalabrini, G. B. L'emigrazione italiana in America. Placenza, 1887.

The Bureau of Statistics, Treasury Department, Washington, includes in its monthly summary report of Imports and Exports, a statement of immigration by ports and nationalities. The Bureau includes Immigration in its Annual Report on Foreign Commerce and Navigation, and annual statistics are tabulated in U. S. Statistical Abstract [annual].

The Department of State, Washington, published the State and National laws relating to Immigration, 1887, and issues reports on Immigration.

Dr. J: B. Hamilton, Supervising Surgeon-General, has an important report on "The Immigration Service," included in the annual report U. S. Marine Hospital Service. [Washington, Gov. Pr. Office, 1890, 387 p. O.] He recommends restriction.

The Emigration Commissioners of New York issue an annual report. V. 1, 1847.

In Sir C: Dilke's Problems of Greater Britain [see Colonies] is much information regarding Immigration, Exclusion of Chinese, etc.

Anti-Chinese Legislation in Australasia. Joseph Lee. *Quarterly Journal of Economics*, Jan., 1889.

Anti-Chinese Legislation in British America. Joseph Lee. *Quarterly Journal of Economics*, April, 1889.

Chinese Exclusion Bill. H. L. Dawes. *Forum*, Jan., 1889.

Chinese Immigration. S. W. Williams. *Journal American Social Science Assoc.*, 1879.

Government by Aliens. Bishop A. Cleveland Coxe. *Forum*, Aug., 1889.

Immigration and Crime. W. M. F. Round. *Journal of Social Science* (Saratoga papers of 1889). N. Y., Putnam, 1890.

Invasion of Pauper Foreigners. Arnold White. *Nineteenth Century*, March, 1888.

Italian Immigration. Eugene Schuyler. *Political Science Quarterly*, Sept., 1889.

L'Emigration Europeen. E. Phillipovich. *Revue d'Economie Politique*, Aug., 1890.

Theory of Emigration. R. M. Smith. *Quarterly Journal of Economics*, Jan., 1891.

THE NEGRO.

Bill to Promote Mendicancy; facts and arguments showing that the South does not need Federal aid for her schools. N. Y., Evening Post Pub. Co., 1886. 20 p. O. pap. 5 c.

Blair, L. H. Prosperity of the South Dependent on the Elevation of the Negro. Richmond, Va., J. W. Randolph & English, 1890. 147 p. D. $1.
Lays stress on the need of education.

Brackett, JEFFREY R. **The Negro in Maryland:** a Study of the Institution of Slavery. Baltimore, Johns Hopkins Univ. series, 1889. 268 p. O. $2.
A valuable work, for the student of politics rather than the general reader.

Brackett, JEFFREY R. **Notes on the Progress of the Colored People of Maryland Since the War.** Baltimore, Johns Hopkins Univ. series, 1890. 96 p. O. $1.
A supplement to "The Negro in Maryland." The first, or at least the most satisfactory effort ever made to gather and arrange the statistics of an entire State on almost every feature of the negro's daily life. Without either argument or drawing of conclusions shows the best way to solve the problem of civilizing the negro.—*Frederic Bancroft.*

Bruce, PHILIP A. **The Plantation Negro as a Freeman:** Observations on his Character, Condition, and Prospects in Virginia. Questions of the Day, no. 57.   N. Y., Putnam, 1889.   9+262 p.   D. $1.25.
Takes an unfavorable view. Frederick Bancroft says: "Seems entirely blind to the prosperity, resources, and education of many of the negroes in such cities as Charleston, Washington, and Baltimore."

Cable, G: W. **The Negro Question.** N. Y., Scribner, 1890. 173 p. D. 75 c.

Cable, G: W. **The Silent South; the Freedman's Case in Equity,** and the Convict Lease System.   N. Y., Scribner, 1885.   180 p. D. $1.
Three articles reprinted from the *Century Magazine*. The first two plead for civil justice to the negro.

Fortune, T. T. **Black and White:** land, labor, and politics in the South. N. Y., Fords, Howard & Hulbert, 1884. 310 p. S. $1.
Claims that the Southern problem is not racial or political, so much as economic. A protest against land monopoly.

Mayo, A. D. **Third Estate of the South.** Bost., G: H. Ellis, 1890.
A sympathetic review of the negro's progress, by an Educational Commissioner. Delivered as an address to American Social Science Assoc., Saratoga, Sept. 2d, 1890.

Stetson, G. R. **Problem of Negro Education.** Boston, Cupples, Upham & Co., 1884.   21 p. O. pap. 10 c.

The Reports of the Hampton Normal and Agricultural Institute, Hampton, Va., Gen. S. C. Armstrong, Principal, are important. The Institute educates young negroes and Indians of both sexes, at nominal fees.

In Plain Black and White.   H: W. Grady.   *Century*, April, 1885.

The Republican Party and the Negro.   E. L. Godkin.   *Forum*, May, 1889.

THE INDIAN.

Harrison, J. B. **Latest Studies on Indian Reservations.** Phila., Indian Rights Assoc., 1887.   233 p. D. pap. 25 c.
A record of personal investigation from Omaha to Puget Sound and the lava-bed region of Southern Oregon.

Jackson, HELEN HUNT. **A Century of Dishonor.** Bost., Roberts Bros., 1888.   457 p. D. $1.50.
A sketch of the dealings of the United States Government with some of the Indian tribes.

Ludlow, HELEN W. **Ten Years' Work for Indians, 1878-88.** Hampton, Va., 1888.   80 p. D. pap. 15 c.
An account of the work of the Hampton Normal and Agricultural Institute, by a teacher.

Manypenny, G: W. **Our Indian Wards.** Cincinnati, R. Clarke & Co., 1880.   336 p. O. $3.
Author Commissioner of Indian Affairs, 1853-57, and Chairman of Sioux Com. of 1876. An historical and critical review, asking in the words of Chief Ouray: "Is not the Government strong enough to keep its agreement with us?"

An annual report is published by the Commissioner of Indian Affairs, Washington. A supplemental report on Indian Education was issued Dec. 1, 1889.

The Indian Rights Association issues reports and publications intended to diffuse information regarding the Indian problem, and enlist the sympathy and aid of all who wish the Indian's rights respected. The Assoc. issues an annual report (no. 1, 1883); also, an annual report of the Lake Mohonk Conference (no. 1, 1883). Herbert Welsh, Corresponding Secretary, 1305 Arch St., Philadelphia. Membership fee, $2 per annum, entitling subscribers to publications.

PAUPERISM AND POOR LAWS.

Brace, C: LORING. **Dangerous Classes of New York,** and Twenty Years' Work Among Them. N. Y., Wynkoop & Hallenbeck, 1872. 448 p. D. $1.25.

Hoyt, C: S., *M.D.* **Causes of Pauperism.** Albany, N. Y., State Pr. Office, 1877. 240 p. O.

Extract from report as Secretary State Board of Charities to Legislature of New York.

Booth, *General* W: **In Darkest England, and the Way Out.** N. Y., Funk & Wagnalls, 1890. 300 p. D. cl. $1 ; pap. 50 c.

By the founder and General of the Salvation Army. In the main a proposal that "the submerged tenth" be set to work in city refuges, farm colonies, and colonies over sea.

Eden, *Sir* F: MORTON. **State of the Poor** or, History of the Laboring Classes in England from the Conquest to the Present Period. Lond., 1797. 3 v.

A standard work. Gives details of diet, dress, fuel, and habitation; with the various plans proposed and adopted for the relief of the poor.

Fawcett, H: **Pauperism, its Causes and Remedies.** Lond., Macmillan, 1871. 5s. 6d.

Author in the later edition of his Political Economy [see Political Economy, English works] incorporated the substance of his special study of Pauperism.

Fowle, *Rev.* T. W. **The [English] Poor Law.** English Citizen series. Lond. and N. Y., Macmillan, 1881. 163 p. D. $1.

Nicholls, *Sir* G: **History of the English Poor Law.** Lond., Murray, 1854. 29+408, 467 p. D.

Nicholls, *Sir* G: **History of the Irish Poor Law.** Lond., Murray, 1856. 10+424 p. D.

Poor Laws in Foreign Countries. Reports to Local Government Board. Lond., Eyre & Spottiswoode, 1875. 482 p. O.

Laurent, EMILE. **Le paupérisme et les associations de prévoyance,** nouvelles études sur les sociétés de secours mutuels. 2 v. Paris, Guillaumin, 1865.

Monnier, ALEXANDRE. **Histoire de l'assistance publique.** 3me ed. Paris, Guillaumin, 1866. 8+568 p. O.

Aschrott, P. F. **Das englische Armenwesen** in seiner Historischen Entwickelung. Leipzig, Duncker & Humblot, 1886. 22+450 p. D.

—— *Same.* **English Poor Law System,** Past and Present. Tr. by H. Preston-Thomas, with preface by H: Sidgwick. Lond., Knight & Co., 1888. 18+332 p. D.

Fano, ENRICO. **Della carita preventiva.** Milano, 1868.

Poor Law Experiment at Elberfeld. Rev. W. W. Edwards. *Contemporary Review,* July, 1878.

Relief of the Poor in Germany. Amos G. Warner. *Pub. American Statistical Assoc.,* Dec., 1889.

CHARITIES AND CHARITY ORGANIZATION.

Adams, Herbert B. Notes on the Literature of Charities. Baltimore, Johns Hopkins Univ. Hist. Series, 1887. 48 p. O. pap. 25 c.
Contains as appendix " English Charity Organizations," by D. R. Randall.

Gurteen, *Rev.* S. H. Handbook of Charity Organization. Buffalo, N. Y., S. H. Gurteen, 1882. 254 p. O.

Handbook for Friendly Visitors Among the Poor. N. Y., Charity Organization Soc., 1883. 88 p. S. cl. 50 c.; pap. 35 c.

Handbook for Hospitals. N. Y., Putnam, 1883. 263 p. D. 75 c.
Prepared for the State Charities Aid Assoc.

Handbook for Visitors to the Poorhouse. 4th ed. rev. N. Y., Putnam, 1888. 90 p. D. pap. 25 c.
Ed. by a special committee State Charities Aid Assoc.

Lowell, Josephine Shaw. Public Relief and Private Charity. Questions of the Day, no. 13. N. Y., Putnam, 1884. 111 p. D. cl. 75 c.; pap. 40 c.

Methods of Assisting the Working Classes in the Enforcement of Their Legal Rights. N. Y., State Charities Aid Assoc., 1885. 27 p. O. *gratis.*

New York Charities Directory. N. Y., Charities Organization Soc., 1890. 400 p. S. $1.

Schuyler, *Miss* Louisa Lee. Importance of Uniting Individual and Associated Volunteer Effort in Behalf of the Poor. N. Y., State Charities Aid Assoc., 1878. 13 p. O. 15 c.

Wayland, Fcs. Out-Door Relief and Tramps. New Haven, Conn., 1877.
Read at Saratoga meeting Am. Social Science Assoc., 1877.

Charities' Register and Digest. 3d issue, rev. and enl. Lond. [for the Charity Organization Soc.], Longmans, 1890. 1200 p. O. 10s. 6d.

Loch, C. S. Charity Organization. Lond., Swan Sonnenschein & Co., 1890. 8°, 2s. 6d.

The Annual Proceedings of the National Conference of Charities and Correction, published at 141 Franklin St., Boston. *Mrs.* I. C. Barrows, ed., contain papers of interest to the student of social problems.

The State Charities Aid Assoc., 21 University Place, New York, issues a variety of pamphlets, price list on application. Its annual reports are *gratis.* The Association's library comprises works in every department of practical reform; catalogue, revised to April, 1886, and supplements, *gratis,* form a good bibliography.

The Charity Organization Society, 21 University Place, New York, issues a large variety of pamphlets for general information, *gratis.*

The Charity Organization Societies of New York, and the Society for Organized Charity, Philadelphia, publish periodicals and reports of value.

The Charity Organization Society, London, publishes a valuable *Review,* and reports.

PUBLIC HEALTH AND SANITATION.

Abel, MARY HINMAN. **Practical Sanitary and Economic Cooking** adapted to persons of moderate and small means. Rochester, N. Y., Essay Dept. Am. Public Health Assoc., 1890. 182 p. D. cl. 40 c.; pap. 35 c. English-German text, cl. 60 c.; pap. 55 c.

Buck, ALBERT H., *M.D., ed.* **Treatise on Hygiene and Public Health.** N. Y., W. Wood & Co., 1890. 2 v. 792, 657 p. O. $10.

Dr. J: S. Billings and other eminent physicians are contributors. V. 1 contains in part: Individual Hygiene, Habitations. V. 2, Occupations, Public Health. The best American work of its kind.

Gerhard, W: PAUL. **Guide to Sanitary House Inspection.** N. Y., J: Wiley & Sons, 1885. 145 p. S. $1.

Hints and helps regarding the choice of a healthful home in city or country, by an eminent sanitary engineer.

Plunkett, *Mrs.* H. M. **Women, Plumbers, and Doctors.** N. Y., Appleton, 1885. 248 p. D. $1.25.

Waring, G: E., *Jr.* **Sanitary Drainage of Houses and Towns.** Bost., Houghton, Mifflin & Co., 1881. 366 p. D. $2.

Battershall, J. P. **Food Adulteration and Its Detection.** Lond. and N. Y., Spon, 1887. 4+328 p. O. $3.50.

Contains a bibliographical appendix.

Bernays, ALBERT J. **Food.** Lond., Soc. for Prom. Christian Knowledge. N. Y., E. & J. B. Young & Co., 1890. 123 p. S. 40 c.

Chaumont, F. S. B. FRANCOIS de. **The Habitation in Relation to Health.** Lond., Soc. for Prom. Christian Knowledge ; N. Y., E. & J. B. Young & Co., 1890. 120 p. S. 40 c.

Hartley, W. NOEL. **Water, Air, and Disinfectants.** Lond., Soc. for Prom. Christian Knowledge ; N. Y., E. & J. B. Young & Co., 1890. 120 p. S. 40 c.

Jenkin, FLEEMING. **Healthy Houses.** N. Y., Harper, 1877. 122 p. S. pap. 25 c.

Adapted to American conditions by G: E. Waring, Jr.

Parkes, E: A., *M.D.* **Manual of Practical Hygiene.** N. Y., W. Wood & Co., 1884. 2 v. in 1. 368, 556 p. O. $5.

Ed. by F. S. B. F. de Chaumont. From last Lond. ed., with an appendix giving the American practice in matters relating to hygiene, by F. N. Owen.

Parkes, E. A., *M.D.* **Personal Care of Health.** Lond., Soc. for Prom. Christian Knowledge ; N. Y., E. & J. B. Young & Co., 1890. 120 p. S. 40 c.

Richardson, B: W., *M.D.* **Health and Occupation.** Lond., Soc. for Prom. Christian Knowledge ; N. Y., E. & J. B. Young & Co., 1890. 120 p. S. 40 c.

Richardson, B: W., *M.D.* **Household Health.** Lond., Soc. for Prom. Christian Knowledge ; N. Y., E. & J. B. Young & Co., 1886. 192 p. S. 45 c.

Richardson, B: W., *M.D.* **Hygeia, a City of Health.** Lond. and N. Y., Macmillan, 1876. 47 p. D. pap. 25

Teale, T. Pridgin. **Dangers to Health,** Pictorial Guide to Domestic Sanitary Defects. N. Y., Appleton, 1885. 172 p. O. $3.

Questions of sanitation are covered to a considerable extent in the Investigation by a Select Committee Ho. Rep., relative to the causes of the general depression in labor and business (A. S. Hewitt, Chairman. [45th Cong., 3d Sess. Ho. misc. doc., no. 29. [Washington, Gov. Pr. Office, 1879 675 p. O.] Also, in Report of Senate Com. upon relations between Capital and Labor, and testimony taken before com. (H. W. Blair, Chairman). [Washington, Gov. Pr. Office, 1885. 4 v. 1196+1412+729+857 p. O. V. 5 not yet published (Jan., 1891).]

Many of the States of the Union have Boards of Health. The Reports of the Boards of Massachusetts, Michigan, and New Jersey are especially valuable. Much important information concerning the sanitary condition of tenements and workshops is given in the Reports of the Bureaus of Statistics of Labor, Massachusetts, New Jersey, Connecticut, and New York.

The American Public Health Assoc. issues annual reports. These and other important publications are to be had from the Secretary, Dr. I. A. Watson, Concord, N. H. For 25 cents he forwards four important pamphlets: Healthy Homes and Foods for the Working Classes ; Sanitary Needs and Necessities of School Life ; Disinfection and Individual Prophylaxis against Infectious Diseases; Preventable Causes of Disease, Injury and Death in American manufactories and workshops, and best means of avoidance.

Water Supply of Cities. C: F. Wingate. *North American Review*, April, 1883.

WORKINGMEN'S DWELLINGS.

White, Alfred T. **Improved Dwellings for the Laboring Classes.** N. Y., Putnam. 1879. 45 p. O. 25 c.
Suggestions for their building on strictly commercial principles.

Galton, Douglas. **The Construction of Healthy Dwellings,** Houses, Hospitals, Barracks, Asylums, etc. Lond. and N. Y., Macmillan, 1884. $2.75.

Hill, Octavia. **Homes of the London Poor.** N. Y., State Charities Aid Assoc., 1875. 78 p. O. 25 c.

Report, First, of Royal Commission for Inquiring into the Housing of the Working Classes. [England and Wales.] Lond., Eyre & Spottiswoode, 1885.

Solly, *Rev.* H: **Rehousing of the Industrial Classes ;** or, Village Communities *vs.* Town Rookeries. Lond., Swan Sonnenschein, 1889. S. pap. 6d.

For works treating Building Associations see Coöperation [Capital and Labor.]

The American Economic Assoc., Baltimore, offers prizes of $300 and $200 for essays to be received by Nov. 15th, 1891, on the "Housing of the Poor in American Cities." The Assoc. will probably publish the prize essays.

The Report of the Tenement-House Building Co., New York, of which Prof. E. R. A. Seligman, Columbia College, is Secretary, will be published early in 1891. It will show the application of insurance to rent, and other interesting phases of the Company's work.

The Riverside Buildings of the Improved Dwellings Co., of Brooklyn, are described in an illustrated pamphlet, published 1890, *gratis*, by Alfred T. White, 130 Water St., New York.

Workingmen's Homes. R: R. Bowker. *Harper's Magazine*, April, 1884.

CRIME AND PRISONS.

Dugdale, R: L. **The Jukes:** a study in crime, pauperism, and heredity 4th ed., with introd. by W: M. F. Round. N. Y., Putnam, 1888. 121 p. D. $1

Falkner, ROLAND P. **Prison Statistics of the United States for 1888.** Phila., Univ. of Pa. series, 1889. 34 p. D. pap. 25 c.
A social study of the personal characteristics of prisoners.

Green, SANFORD M. **Crime:** its nature, causes, treatment, and prevention. Phila., Lippincott, 1889. 346 p. O. $2.

Round, W. M. F. **Our Criminals and Christianity.** N. Y. and Lond., Funk & Wagnalls, 1888. 16 p. O. pap. 15 c.

Smith, EUGENE. **Prison Science** with special reference to recent New York legislation. Economic tract, no. 30. N. Y., Society for Political Education, 1890. 24 p. D. pap. 10 c.

Wines, E. C., *D.D.* **State of Prisons and Child-Saving Institutions.** Cambridge, Mass., J. Wilson & Son, 1880. 23+719 p. O. $5.
An almost exhaustive history of prisons and child-saving institutions throughout the civilized world, based on facts carefully gathered during 18 years' close study and observation. Appendix submits a plan for giving breadth, stability, and permanence to the work of preventing and repressing crime.

Wright, CARROLL D. **Hand Labor in Prisons.** Boston, Wright & Potter Co., 1887.

Baker, T. B. L. **War with Crime.** Lond. and N. Y., Longmans, 1890. 300 p. O. $4.
Reprinted papers on crime, prison discipline, etc., ed. by H. Philips and E. Verney.

Du Cane, *Sir* EDMUND F. **The Punishment and Prevention of Crime.** English Citizen series. Lond. and N. Y., Macmillan, 1885. 235 p. D. $1.

Ellis, HAVELOCK. **The Criminal.** Contemporary science series, no. 1. N. Y., Scribner & W., 1890. 8+337 p. D. $1.
A review of results thus far reached by students of criminal anthropology in Italy, France, Germany, England, and the United States, with criticism.

Hoyle, W. **Crime in England and Wales in the 19th Century.** An historical and critical retrospect. Lond., E. Wilson, 1876. 2s. 6d.

Morrison, W. D. **Crime and the Prison System.** Lond., Swan Sonnenschein, 1890. 8°, 2s. 6d.

Pike, LUKE OWEN. **History of Crime in England.** Illustrating the changes in the laws in the progress of civilization. 2 v. Lond., Smith, Elder & Co., 1873-1876. 8°, 36s.

Rylands, L. G. **Crime, its Causes and Remedy.** Lond., 1889. 264 p.
Directs attention to the necessity for a more vigorous treatment of juvenile delinquents through industrial and reformatory schools.

Tallack, W. **Penological and Preventive Principles.** Lond., Howard Assoc., 1889. 414 p. D.
Embodies the result of long experience.

Wilson, ANDREW. **Science and Crime,** and other essays. N. Y., Humboldt Pub. Co., 1887. 45 p. O. pap. 15 c.

Aschrott, P. F. **Strafensystem und Gefängnisswesen in England.** Berlin, S. Guttentag, 1887. 311 p. D. 7 50 marks.
An admirable account of English penology.

Falkner, ROLAND P. **Die Arbeit in den Gefängnissen.** Jena, G. Fisher, 1888. 89 p. D. 2 marks, 40 pf.

Discusses the question of convict labor with an extensive use of American facts, in comparison with those of European countries.

Holtzendorff, *Baron* J. W. F. v., *and* **Jagemann,** EUG. v. **Handbuch des Gefängnisswesens,** in Einzelbeiträgen von A. Bar und andere. Hamburg, 1888. 2 v. O.

Lombroso, CESARE. **L'Uomo Delinquente.** Torino, 1889. 2 v. O.

Much the most important work on the criminal. Havelock Ellis says that it over-estimates atavism, and presses too strongly the epileptic affinities of crime.

The National Prison Association's reports, containing much information on penology, may be had from the Secretary of the N. Y. Prison Association, W. M. F. Round, 135 E. 15th St., New York. The latest report, for 1889, is $1.25.

The *Summary*, the best prison newspaper, is published weekly at the State Reformatory, Elmira, N. Y.

The Convict Lease System, by G: W Cable, in an essay in "The Silent South," [see The Negro.]

Prison Ethics is one of the "Essays, Moral, Political, and Æsthetic," of Herbert Spencer. N. Y., Appleton.

THE LIQUOR QUESTION.

Cyclopedia of Temperance and Prohibition. N. Y., Funk & Wagnalls, 1891. 750 p. D. $3.50.

An exhaustive work from the Prohibition standpoint, though written with the aim of making an authoritative rather than a partisan presentation. Abounds in statistical tables giving facts abroad and at home. Several important articles are contributed by specialists. Among subjects treated are Bible Wines, Compensation, Constitutional Prohibition, Cost of Drink Traffic, High License, Local Option, and Prohibition, general principles.

Fernald, JAMES C. **Economics of Prohibition.** N. Y., Funk & Wagnalls, 1890. 10+515 p. O. $1.50.

Presents statistics regarding the cost of the liquor habit.

Finch, J: B. **The People versus the Liquor Traffic.** N. Y., National Temperance Soc., 1888. 259 p. D. cl. 50 c.; pap. 30 c.

Speeches by the leading Prohibition orator of his day.

Gough, J: B. **Temperance Lectures.** N. Y., Am. Temp. Pub. House, 1879. 84 p. D. pap. 25 c.

Gustafson, AXEL. **The Foundation of Death: A Study of the Drink Question.** N. Y., Funk & Wagnalls, 1887. 598 p. D. $1.50.

From the total abstinence standpoint. A copious bibliography, 64 p., of works in various languages bearing on the drink subject, is appended.

Iles, G: **The Liquor Question in Politics.** Economic tract, no. 26. N. Y., Soc. for Political Education, 1889. 27 p. D. pap. 15 c.

Kerr, NORMAN, *M.D.* **Inebriety: Its Etiology, Pathology, Treatment, and Jurisprudence.** Lond., H. K. Lewis, 1888. 415 p. D.

Comes to teetotal conclusions.

Lees, F. R. Text-Book of Temperance. N. Y., National Temperance Soc., 1886. 312 p. D. cl. $1.25 ; pap. 50 c.

A comprehensive examination of most of the aspects of the question from a teetotal standpoint.

Oswald, FELIX L., M.D. The Poison Problem; or, The Cause and Cure of Intemperance. N. Y., Appleton, 1886. 138 p. D. cl. $1; pap. 25 c.

Pitman, ROBERT C. Alcohol and the State: A Discussion of the Problem of Laws as Applied to the Liquor Traffic. N. Y., National Temperance Soc., 1886. 411 p. D. cl. $1.50 ; pap. 50 c.

A standard work in advocacy of the policy of Prohibition. Author Associate Judge Superior Court of Massachusetts.

Prohibitionists' Text-Book. N. Y., National Temperance Soc., 1889. 414 p. D. cl. $1 ; pap. 50 c.

Wheeler, E. J. Prohibition: the Principle, the Policy, and the Party. N. Y., Funk & Wagnalls, 1889. 229 p. D. cl. 75 c.; pap. 25 c.

The best summary of the case for Prohibition. Appendix contains the U. S. Supreme Court decision in the Kansas cases (Ziebold and Hagelin, 1887) ; a table of " Police Statistics for 58 American Cities ; " a table of " Commitments to Jail for Crime in Connecticut ; " Governor (of Kansas) Martin's Letter to Associated Press, July 12, 1887, and the famous Bowman decision (1888) of the Supreme Court.

Caine, W. S., *and* Hoyle, W: Local Option. Imp. Parl. series, no. 4. Lond., Swan Sonnenschein, 1885. D. 1s.

Richardson, B: W., *M.D.* Temperance Lesson-Book: A Series of Short Lessons on Alcohol and Its Action on the Body ; Designed for Reading in Schools and Families. N. Y., National Temperance Soc., 1888. 220 p. D. cl. 50 c.; pap. 25 c.

Richardson, B: W., *M.D.* Ten Lectures on Alcohol. N. Y., National Temperance Soc., 1883. 190 p. cl. $1 ; pap. 50 c.

Several of Dr. Richardson's tracts are appended.

The National Temperance Society and Publication House, J: N. Stearns, Secretary, 58 Reade St., New York, issues a variety of publications in the interests of total abstinence, and publishes *The National Temperance Advocate*, monthly, $1 per annum, ranking next to the *Voice* in importance as a Prohibition periodical. It issues *The National Temperance Almanac*, giving latest statistics, by J. N. Stearns, pap. 10 c.

The Voice, New York, a weekly journal, $1 per annum, is the ablest and most widely circulated journal in the U. S. advocating Prohibition. Its publishers, Funk & Wagnalls, issue a variety of works having the same purpose as *The Voice*. Of these one of the most important is the *Political Prohibitionist*, published yearly, a compact digest of facts and figures for use in prohibition campaigns, 50 c.

The Church Temperance Society, Robert Graham, Secretary, 16 Fourth Avenue, New York, issues a variety of publications, in which temperance is understood to mean moderation. Especially important are " New York City and Its Masters," " Liquordom in New York City," and " Chattel Mortgages and Saloon Fixtures in New York City," all by Mr. Robert Graham.

The Joint Committee on High License, composed of representatives of the Citizens' Committee on High License, the Church Temperance Society, and the Society for the Prevention of Crime, J: B. Pine, Secretary, 50 Pine St., New York, has issued a number of leaflets and circulars on behalf of High License and the reform of the Excise Laws. The Committee was superseded Jan. 14, 1891, by the formation of the Excise Reform Association, having a similar object. J: Jay Chapman, 49 Exchange Place, Secretary.

The U. S. Brewers' Assoc., New York, issue the following works by the Manager of their Literary Bureau, G. Thomann, *gratis:* Liquor Laws of the U. S., their Spirit and Effect; Colonial Liquor Laws; Reports of Temperance Congress held at Antwerp and Zurich; Alleged Adulterations of Malt Liquors; Inebriety and Crime; Real and Imaginary Effects of Intemperance; The Effects of Beer upon Those Who Make and Drink It; The Nation's Drink Bill, economically considered; The System of High Licenses, how it can be made successful; Solution of the Temperance Problem. Also, Papers on Prohibition, by G. C. Low; Intemperance in the Light of Cosmic Laws, by Dr. Bowditch; The Art of Drinking, by G. G. Gervinus; The Connection of Disease with Habits of Intemperance, by Brit. Medical Assoc.; Mistakes of Prohibitionists, by J: Mudie.

The leading English periodicals advocating total abstinence and prohibition are the *Alliance News*, Manchester, and *National Temperance League's Annual*, London: the latter reports the progress of the anti-liquor movement in Great Britain and dependencies.

The Original Package Case. C. Stuart Patterson. *Annals Am. Acad. Pol. and Soc. Science*, Phila., Oct., 1890.

POLITICAL SCIENCE: GENERAL WORKS.

Atkinson, W. P. **The Study of Politics.** Boston, Roberts Bros., 1888. 63 p. S. 50 c.
An introductory lecture delivered to the senior class at the Mass. Inst. of Technology.

Burgess, J. W. **Political Science and Comparative Constitutional Law.** N. Y., Ginn & Co., 1891. 2 v. V. 1, Sovereignty and Liberty. 20+337 p. O. V. 2, Government. 20+404 p. O. $5.
An epoch-making work in the literature of political science. The State as sovereign organization of the Nation, is sharply distinguished from the Government. Government, to the author, is but one of the means through which the State attains its ends. The other means is liberty. V. 1 treats of the Nation and the State, as concepts of political science. Under the head of Constitutional law, the author describes the organization of sovereignty, of liberty and of government. The latter topic occupies v. 2. The typical constitutions selected for comparison are those of France, Germany, England and the United States. The author's method is historical and comparative. Author is Professor of Constitutional and International Law and History, and Dean of the University Faculty of Political Science, Columbia College.

Crane, W., *and* **Moses,** BERNARD. **Politics;** an introduction to the study of comparative constitutional law. N. Y., Putnam. 184 p. D. $1.50.

Lieber, FRANCIS. **Civil Liberty and Self-Government.** Ed. by Theodore D. Woolsey. Phila., Lippincott, 1874. 8°, $3.50.

Lieber, FRANCIS. **Manual of Political Ethics.** 2d ed., rev. by Theodore D. Woolsey. Phila., Lippincott, 1875. 2 v. 8°. $6.
These two works are sound and very able, but originally written nearly forty years ago, they are now out of date. The editor's revisions do not give illustrations of how abundantly history has borne out the author's main positions.

White, ANDREW D. **European Schools of History and Politics.** Baltimore, Johns Hopkins Univ. Series, 1887. 89 p. O. pap. 25 c.

A survey of the recent growth of this department of study in Germany, France, and Great Britain.

Wilson, WOODROW. **The State; Elements of historical and practical politics.** Bost., D. C. Heath & Co., 1889. 36+686 p. D. $2.

A sketch of Institutional History and Administration from ancient times to the present day. Suffers from taking a field too wide for the limits of a single volume. Theories not always carefully considered.

Woolsey, THEO. D. **Political Science; or, The State, Theoretically and Practically Considered.** N. Y., Scribner, 1889. Rev. ed. 2 v. 586+626 p. O. $5.

The best systematic treatise which can be mentioned. The historical portion of it embraces a great deal of instructive information about the history of political institutions.

Bagehot, W. Physics and Politics. Thoughts on the application of the principles of "Natural Selection" and "Inheritance" to political society. N. Y., Appleton, 1876. 228 p. 12°, $1.50.

Applies the methods of natural science to some of the elementary problems of political science; it is to be highly recommended as opening up a new method of conceiving and treating the topics of political science.

Cairnes, J. E. Political Essays. Lond. and N. Y., Macmillan, 1873. 350 p. O. $2.50.

Comprising essays on colonization and colonial government, the revolution in America, international law, protection, free trade, etc.

Freeman, E. A. Comparative Politics. To which is added The Unity of History. Lond. and N. Y., Macmillan, 1874. 7+522 p. O. $3.50.

Contains: Range of the Comparative Sciences; Greek, Roman, and Teutonic; The state; The king; The assembly.

Greg, W. R. Political Problems. Lond., Trübner, 1870. 342 p. D. 10s. 6d.

Discusses social and political questions from a conservative standpoint.

Harrison, F. Order and Progress. Part 1, on Government; Part 2, on Studies of Political Crises. Lond., Longman, 1875. 8°, 14s.

Helps, ARTHUR. **Thoughts upon Government.** Bost., Roberts, 1872. 8°, $2.25.

Maine, *Sir* H: J. SUMNER. **Popular Government.** N. Y., Holt, 1886. 261 p. O. $2.75.

Four essays by the author of "Ancient Law," critical of democracy. He commends the safeguards of the Constitution of the United States.

Mill, J: S. **Considerations on Representative Government.** N. Y., Holt, 1875. 364 p. D. $2.

Well worth reading, although some of the topics discussed have lost their hold on public interest and attention.

Mill, J: S. **On Liberty.** N. Y., Holt, 1879. $1.25.

The classical work on the subject.

Morley, J: **On Compromise.** 2d ed. Lond. and N. Y., Macmillan, 1877. 10+227 p. O. $1.50.

An essay on the lines of Mill's Liberty, treating the question of compromise between principle and expediency.

Smith, BRUCE. **Liberty and Liberalism.** Lond. and N. Y., Longmans, 1888. 684 p. D. $2.25.

<small>A protest against the alleged growing tendency toward undue interference by the State with individual liberty, private enterprise, and the rights of property.</small>

Spencer, H. **Social Statics; or, the Conditions Essential to Human Happiness.** N. Y., Appleton. 1880. xviii+518 p. S°, $2.

<small>A very interesting and suggestive treatise; it is almost alone in the field it covers (elementary analysis and discussion of "rights"), but the author needs to rewrite it to adjust it to his own opinions at the present time. First published in 1850.</small>

Stephen, FITZ JAMES. **Liberty, Equality, and Fraternity.** N. Y., Holt, 1882. $2.

<small>A criticism of Mill's notions and an attempt to re-analyze them, and to give them greater precision.</small>

Twiss, *Sir* TRAVERS. **The Law of Nations Considered as Independent Political Communities.** Part 1, On the rights and duties of nations in time of peace. 2d ed. Lond. and N. Y., Macmillan. 1875. 60+620 p. O. $3.75.

Janet, PAUL. **Histoire de la science politique dans ses rapports avec la morale.** Paris, F. Alcan, 1887. 2 v. 20 fr.

<small>In many respects the best work on the subject.</small>

Leroy-Beaulieu, PAUL. **L'état moderne et ses fonctions.** Paris, Guillaumin, 1890. 463 p. 8°.

<small>Chiefly treats of the economic relations of the State. Author takes the *Laissez-faire* view.</small>

Montesquieu, M. DE S. **The Spirit of Laws.** Tr. by T. Nugent. Cincinnati, R. Clarke & Co., 1873. 2 v. 48+381, 12+445 p. D. $4.

<small>Contains memoir of the life and writings of the author, and an analysis of the work by D'Alembert.</small>

Bluntschli, J. K. **Politik als Wissenschaft.** Stuttgart, 1876. 8°.

Bluntschli, J. K. **Theory of the State.** Tr. from the 6th German ed. by R. Lodge. Lond. and N. Y., Macmillan, 1885. 518 p. O. $3.25.

Humboldt, Baron W. VON. **The Sphere and Duties of Government.** Tr. by Joseph Coulthard, Jr. Lond., J. Chapman, 1854. 15+203 p. D. 5s.

<small>One of the most influential essays ever written on the limits of the activity of the state.</small>

Sources and Literature of Political Science, by Mr. G. H. Baker, is in preparation for the series in Systematic Political Science by the Univ. Faculty of Pol. Science, Columbia College, N. Y.

POLITICAL SCIENCE: HISTORY AND EARLY INSTITUTIONS.

Lubbock, *Sir* J. **Origin of Civilization, and the Primitive Condition of Man.** N. Y., Appleton. 12°, $5.

Lubbock, *Sir* J. **Prehistoric Times,** as illustrated by ancient remains, and the manners and customs of modern savages. N. Y., Appleton. 8°, $5.

<small>Both the foregoing works are standard authorities.</small>

McLennan, J. FERGUSON. **Studies in Ancient History.** Lond. and N. Y., Macmillan, 1885. $4.

<small>Comprises a reprint of "Primitive Marriage."</small>

McLennan, J: Ferguson. **The Patriarchal Theory.** Lond. and N. Y., Macmillan, 1885. 335 p. O. $4.
<small>These two works tend to correct the one-sidedness of Maine's theory.</small>

May, *Sir* T: Erskine. **Democracy in Europe,** a History. N. Y., A. C. Armstrong & Son, 1886. 2 v. cl. $2.50; hf. cf. $6.

Pollock, *Sir* F: **Introduction to the History of the Science of Politics.** Lond. and N. Y., Macmillan, 1890. 130 p. D. 2s. 6d. Also, N. Y., Humboldt Pub. Co., 1883. 50 p. O. pap. 15 c.
<small>An outline covering the field of political science from Plato and Aristotle to J: S. Mill and Herbert Spencer.</small>

Tylor, E. B. **Primitive Culture.** N. Y., Holt, 1877. 2 v. 502–468 p. O. $7.
<small>Researches into the development of mythology, philosophy, religion, language, art and custom. One of the best authorities.</small>

Wilson, Daniel. **Prehistoric Man;** or, Researches into the Origin of Civilization. 3d ed. rev. and enl. Lond. and N. Y., Macmillan, 1880. 2 v. $8.

Guizot, F. P: G. **History of the Origin of Representative Government in Europe.** Tr. by A. R. Scoble. (Bohn's Standard Library.) Lond., G. Bell & Sons, 1861. 20+538 p. D. 3s. 6d.

Bluntschli, J. K. **Geschichte des Allgemeinen Staatsrechts und der Politik.** Munich, J. G. Cotta, 1867. 667 p. O.
<small>From Machiavelli to modern times. A most important treatise, especially with respect to the German literature of the subject.</small>

Mohl, Robert v. **Geschichte und Literatur der Staatswissenschaften.** Erlangen, F. Enke, 1858.
<small>A most important work, although now a little antiquated.</small>

Waitz, T. **Grundzüge der Politik.** Göttingen [*Kiel*], 1862. 4.50 marks.
<small>Brief, but very satisfactory.</small>

A History of Political Theories, by Mr. W: A. Dunning, is in preparation for the series in Systematic Political Science, by the Univ. Faculty of Pol. Science, Columbia College, N. Y.

In C: K. Adams' "Manual of Historical Literature" (N. Y., Harper, 1889, 39+720 p. O. $2.50) are capital brief descriptions of the most important histories in English, French, and German.

See [under Land] Sir H. J. Sumner Maine's "Early History of Institutions" and "Village Communities;" also, F: Seebohm's "English Village Community." The last is a most scholarly work, based on original investigation. It argues that the manor, not the mark system, was original and universal in England.

AMERICAN GOVERNMENT.
ELEMENTARY WORKS.

Among several excellent books for elementary study those of Fiske and Macy may be chosen as the best. The beginner can then take up with profit Wilson's "Congressional Government" [Essays and Criticism]. Next Bryce, who is especially full in his analysis of State Governments. For a discussion of American institutions from the comparative standpoint, Burgess [Political Science, General Works] is for advanced students the best author. The most important commentaries on the Federal Constitution are Story's, as edited by Cooley [Advanced Works]; "The

Constitutional History of the United States, as seen in the development of American law," is valuable in this connection [American Political and Constitutional History.] The reader who wishes to understand the English Constitution, so as to compare it with that of the United States, will find the best works to be those of Hannis Taylor, Bagehot, and Stubbs.

Alden, J. **Science of Government** in connection with American institutions. N. Y., Sheldon & Co., 1876. 304 p. D. $1.
> An elementary text-book on political science and the constitutional law of the United States. Out of date.

Alton, EDMUND. **Among the Lawmakers.** N. Y., Scribner, 1886. 12+308 p. D. $2.50.
> Author when a boy was page in U. S. Senate. Describes the three Departments of the general Government in an interesting way. A book for youths.

Bowker, R: R. **Primer for Political Education.** Economic tract, no. 21. N. Y., Society for Political Education, 1886. 42 p. D. pap. 15 c.

Clement, R. E. **Civil Government in the United States.** N. Y., A. Lovell & Co., 1888. 232 p. D. $1.
> Studies of the Federal Constitution, arranged for use in public schools.

Cocker, W. J. **The Government of the United States.** N. Y., Harper, 1889. 274 p. S. 72 c.
> A clear and concise introductory text-book.

Constitution of the United States, Declaration of Independence, and Articles of Confederation. Phila., T. & J. W. Johnson & Co., 1887. 46 p. D. pap. 10 c.

Dawes, ANNA LAURENS. **How We Are Governed :** an explanation of the constitution and government of the United States. Boston, D. Lothrop Co., 1885. 423 p. D. $1.50.

Fiske, J: **Civil Government in the United States,** considered with some reference to its origins. N. Y., Houghton, Mifflin & Co., 1890. 360 p. D. $1.
> A concise manual, historical in method, bringing out the relationships of the subject distinctly, and referring to more elaborate treatises, monographs, and documents for those who wish to pursue the study at greater length. Questions are appended to each chapter. Eminently adapted to use in schools as a text-book.

Flanders, H. **Exposition of the Constitution of the United States.** 4th ed. rev. Phila., T. & J. W. Johnson & Co., 1885. 318 p. D. $1.25.
> Compact and accurate. Suitable as a text-book for advanced pupils.

Ford, WORTHINGTON C., *ed.* **American Citizen's Manual.** N. Y., Putnam, 1886. 334 p. D. $1.25.
> Part 1, Governments (National, State, and Local), the Electorate, and the Civil Service. Part 2, The Functions of Government, considered with special reference to taxation and expenditure, the regulation of commerce and industry, provision for the poor and insane, the management of the public lands, etc. Clear, simple, and comprehensive. Author argues for free trade and gold standard.

Furey, FRANCIS T. **An Explanation of the Constitution of the United States.** N. Y., Catholic Pub. Soc. Co., 1889. 156 p. D. bds. 50 c.
> Prepared for use in Catholic schools, academies, and colleges.

Giffin, W. M. **Civics for Young Americans.** N. Y., A. Lovell & Co., 1888. 117 p. D. 60 c.
> A brief description of our government. with an explanation of the important clauses of the Constitution.

AMERICAN GOVERNMENT.

Macy, JESSE. **Our Government:** how it grew, what it does, and how it does it. New ed. rev. and enl. N. Y., Ginn & Co., 1890. 289 p. D. $1.

Gives a concise account of the origin of our governmental institutions. Describes local and federal government, and the administration of justice. Discusses the national and state constitutions. An appendix gives the Articles of Confederation, and the Constitution of the United States. This edition brings down to date the facts regarding the Australian ballot and other recent legislation of importance. Specially adapted for schools.

Mills, WALTER T. **The Science of Politics.** N. Y., Funk & Wagnalls, 1887. 204 p. D. $1.

An untechnical statement of the fundamental principles of American civil life, and of the methods and conditions of their successful application to the conduct of affairs, under the forms and usages of our government. A commentary on our institutions rather than a description of them.

Mowry, W. A. **Studies in Civil Government.** Bost., Silver, Rogers & Co., 1887. 250 p. D. $1.25.

A simple text-book, treating first of the local government, then of the state and the nation. Taxation, the public schools, and banking are explained in an interesting way. Author is editor of *Education*.

Nordhoff, C: **Politics for Young Americans.** N. Y., Harper, 1877. 195 p. D. $1.

A good book for the first elements of the subject. Written as letters to his son. From the standpoint of free trade and gold standard.

Story, JOSEPH. **Familiar Exposition of the Constitution.** N. Y., Harper, 1884. 372 p. D. 90 c.

Written in 1840.

Thorpe, F. N. **Government of the People of the United States.** Phila., Eldredge & Bro., 1889. 308 p. D. 90 c.

A school text-book. Includes the Declaration of Independence, the Articles of Confederation, the Constitution of the U. S., and other documents. Author is a professor in Manual Training School, Phila.

Stürenburg, E., *and* **Steiger,** E. **Auskunft und Rath für Deutsch-Amerikaner** in den wichtigsten fragen des Offentlichen, Rechts-, Geschäfts-, und Privat- Lebens. N. Y., E. Steiger & Co., 1888. 310 p. D. cl. 80 c.; pap. 60 c.

Old South Leaflets, reprints of important historical and other documents, twenty-two in number, are published by D. C. Heath & Co., Boston, single nos., 5 c. per copy; double nos., 6 c.

ADVANCED WORKS.

Calhoun, J: C. **Works.** Ed. by R. K. Crallé. N. Y., Appleton, 1853-56. $15.

V. 1 contains a disquisition on Government, and an examination of the Constitution and Government of the United States wherein the States Rights view is maintained.

Cooley, T: M. **Treatise on Constitutional Limitations** which rest upon the legislative powers of the States of the American Union. 6th ed. enl. with results of recent cases by Alexis C. Angell. Bost., Little, Brown & Co., 1890. 98+885 p. O. $6.

The standard work on the subject.

Patterson, C. S. **Federal Restraints on State Action.** Phila., T. & J. W. Johnson & Co., 1888. 32+290 p. O. $3.50.

Contains: The United States and the States under the Constitution, treating of the relations of the Government of the United States and the Governments of the several States with regard to Taxation ; The Regulation of Commerce ; The Impairment of the Obligation of Contracts ; The Protection of the Rights of Person and of Property, and The Exercise of Judicial Powers. Author is Professor in Law Department, Univ. of Pa.

Story, JOSEPH. **Commentaries on the Constitution of the United States.** With notes and additions by T: M. Cooley. Bost., Little, Brown & Co., 1873. 2 v. shp. $12.

Tiedeman, CHRISTOPHER G. **The Unwritten Constitution of the United States,** a philosophical inquiry into the fundamentals of American Constitutional law. N. Y., Putnam, 1890. 3+165 p. D. $1.

Shows how public opinion has given all the importance of written law to certain rulings in our government, which are presented and discussed.

Wilson, WOODROW. **State and Federal Governments of the United States.** Bost., D. C. Heath & Co., 1890. 131 p. D. 50 c.

The longest chapter in " The State," by same author.

Bryce, JAMES. **The American Commonwealth.** N. Y., Macmillan, 1889. Rev. ed. 2 v. 1493 p. D. $6.

The ablest exposition of the Government of the United States. Explains very fully the State Governments, and their relations to the Federal Government. Bestows much attention on municipal problems. Takes a comprehensive view of the industrial and social, as well as the political life of the people. Accurate, candid, and sympathetic. Its forecasts are well argued and of profound interest. Author an eminent Member of the British House of Commons. Seth Low contributes a chapter on Municipal Government.

Comparative Constitutional Law of the American Commonwealths, by F. W. Whitridge, is in preparation for the series in Systematic Political Science by the Univ. Faculty of Pol. Science, Columbia College, N. Y.

ESSAYS AND CRITICISM.

Adams, H: C. **Relation of the State to Industrial Action.** Baltimore, American Economic Assoc., 1887. 85 p. O. pap. 75 c.

Sets forth work the state as such can do better than individuals. Very suggestive.

Draper, J: W: **American Civil Policy.** N. Y., Harper, 1865. 4+317 p. D. $2.

Eaton, DORMAN B. **Secret Sessions of the Senate;** their origin, motive, object, and effect. N. Y., Soc. for Political Education. 80 p. pap. *gratis.*

A criticism of what is held to be a grave defect and danger in the national legislature.

Hall, C. H. **Patriotism and National Defence.** N. Y., Soc. for Political Education, 1885. 43 p. D. pap. 15 c.

Lockwood, H. C. **Abolition of the Presidency.** N. Y., R. Worthington, 1884. 331 p. O. $1.50.

An argument based on the fear than an autocrat may fill the Presidential chair.

Lowell, JAMES RUSSELL. **The Independent in Politics.** Reform Club series, no. 1. N. Y., Reform Club, 1888. 27 p. pap. 10 c.

An address delivered before the Reform Club of New York, April 13, 1888.

Mason, E: CAMPBELL. **The Veto Power.** Harvard Historical monograph, no. 1. N. Y., Ginn & Co., 1890. 232 p. D. $1.

Traces the origin, development, and function of the veto power in the Government of the United States, 1789-1889. The vetoes are classified and discussed, and the State constitutional provisions as to the veto are given.

Mulford, E. The Nation. The foundation of civil order and political life in the United States. N. Y., Houghton, Mifflin & Co., 1886. xiv-418 p. 12°, $2.50.

An attempt to find a basis for political science in broad ethical considerations outside the letter of the law. Originally published in 1870 and now somewhat out of date.

Roosevelt, THEODORE. Essays on Practical Politics. N. Y., Putnam, 1888. 74 p. D. 25 c.

Describes the Albany Legislature and machine politics in New York City. Author was a member of N. Y. Assembly.

Stickney, ALBERT. Democratic Government: a study of politics. N. Y., Harper, 1885. 166 p. D. $1.

Mantains that politicians by machine methods control elections, and so control government. To freely choose the best men for office author proposes to revive the town-meeting, a group of four or five hundred voters to select a delegate, and the delegate to elect the office-holders. Would increase the responsibility of heads of departments, and substitute viva voce voting for secret ballot. Incidentally a sharp criticism of current methods in politics.

Stickney, ALBERT. The Political Problem. N. Y., Harper, 1890. 189 p. D. $1.

Stickney, ALBERT. A True Republic. N. Y., Harper, 1879. 271 p. D. $1.

Holds that the United States cannot be a true republic until its Constitution is reformed. Proposes the abolition of the term system. Would give to Congress all the legislative and removing power, and no appointing power. Would have full appointing power in the hands of the Chief Executive and his heads of departments.

Sterne, SIMON. Defective and Corrupt Legislation; the Cause and Remedy. Questions of the Day, no. 22. N. Y., Putnam, 1885. 26 p. D. pap. 25 c.

A trenchant criticism of the legislation of the State of New York. Proposes that by Constitutional Amendment local and special laws be divided from general laws. Would institute cabinet or ministerial responsibility.

Storey, MOORFIELD. Politics as a Duty and as a Career. Questions of the Day, no. 58. N. Y., Putnam, 1889. 33 p. D. pap. 25 c.

Brings out the immense influence exerted by associations aiming at specific political reforms, in giving direction to routine-ridden politicians. A particularly good pamphlet.

Wilson, WOODROW. Congressional Government. Bost., Houghton, Mifflin & Co., 1885. 333 p. S. $1.25.

Analyzes congressional government, and points out defects. Advocates the abolition of standing committees, recommends that the Cabinet should have seats in Congress, and be advisers of both President and Congress.

De Tocqueville, ALEXIS. Democracy in America. Tr. by H: Reeve. Ed. with notes by Fcs. Bowen. 6th ed. 2 v. Bost., J: Allyn, 1876. $5.

—— *Same.* Ed. with notes by J. C. Spencer. N. Y., A. S. Barnes & Co., 1886. 875 p. D. $2.50.

De Tocqueville, ALEXIS. American Institutions. Tr. by H: Reeve. Ed. with notes by Fcs. Bowen. 7th ed. Bost., J: Allyn, 1874. $1.75.

—— *Same.* Ed. with notes by J. C. Spencer. N. Y., A. S. Barnes & Co., 1886. 460 p. D. $1.

V. 1 of " Democracy in America."

Political Ideas of the Puritans. Herbert L. Osgood. *Political Science Quarterly*, March and June, 1891.

The American Commonwealth : Changes in its Relation to the Nation. J: W. Burgess. *Political Science Quarterly*, March, 1886.

AMERICAN POLITICAL AND CONSTITUTIONAL HISTORY.

Bancroft, G: History of the Formation of the Constitution of the United States. N. Y., Appleton, 1885. In 1 v., $2.50; in 2 v., $5.

Benton, T: H. Thirty Years' View of the Workings of the American Government, 1820-50. N. Y., Appleton, 1854. 2 v. $6.

Constitutional History of the United States, as seen in the development of American law. N. Y., Putnam, 1889. 296 p. D. $2.50.

A course of lectures before the Political Science Assoc., Univ. of Mich. Contains: The Federal Supreme Court, by T: M. Cooley; Influence of Chief Justice Marshall, by H: Hitchcock; Influence of Chief Justice Taney, by G: W. Biddle; Decisions of Supreme Court since 1865, by C: A. Kent; The State Judiciary, by Daniel H. Chamberlain.

Cooper, T. V., *and* **Fenton, H. T.** American Politics: a non-partisan history of American political parties, with their platforms, notable speeches, etc. Phila., Fireside Pub. Co., 1887. 1097 p. O. $5.

Curtis, G: T. History of the Constitution of the United States. New ed. V. 1, From the Declaration of Independence to the close of the Civil War. N. Y., Harper, 1889. 12+774 p. O. $3.

To be completed in a 2d v., which will probably be published in May, 1891.

Curtis, G: Ticknor. Implied Powers of the Constitution. Washington, R. H. Derby, 1885. 24 p. O. pap. 50 c.

Davis, Horace. American Constitutions: the relations of the three departments as adjusted by a century. Baltimore, Johns Hopkins Univ. series, 1885. 70 p. O. pap. 50 c.

Points out the existence and danger of the preponderance of the legislative branch of the Government as against the executive.

The Federalist: a commentary on the Constitution of the United States; being a collection of essays written in support of the constitution agreed upon Sept. 17, 1787, by the Federal Convention; reprinted from the original text of Alex. Hamilton, John Jay, and James Madison; ed. by H. Cabot Lodge. N. Y., Putnam, 1888. 628 p. O. $2.

These celebrated essays are introduced by an article on the authorship, the bibliography, and the texts of the *Federalist*, and supplemented by the Articles of Confederation and the Constitution of the United States.

Fiske, J: American Political Ideas viewed from the standpoint of universal history. N. Y., Harper, 1885. 158 p. D. $1.

Treats of the town-meeting, the federal union, and "manifest destiny."

Foster, W: E. References to the Constitution of the United States. N. Y., Society for Political Education, 1890. 50 p. D. pap. 25 c.

Refers to the sources of the Constitution, in Teutonic, British, and Colonial institutions;

gives ample references to every important step in the formal drafting and adoption of the Constitution; and indicates every important book, public document, and magazine article or review elucidating constitutional provisions, commenting upon them, or comparing them with the fundamental law of foreign countries. An appendix briefly sets forth the decisions of the United States Supreme Court on questions of National or State supremacy since 1865.

Foster, W: E. References to the History of Presidential Administrations, 1780-1885. N. Y., Soc. for Political Education, 1885. 58 p. D. pap. 25 c.

Hare, J. I. CLARK. American Constitutional Law. Bost., Little, Brown & Co., 1889. 2 v. 1400 p. O. shp. $12.

An exposition of the body of legal doctrine to which the Constitution of the United States has given rise. Careful and keen in discrimination. A work of the first importance.

Hitchcock, H. American State Constitutions; a study of their growth. N. Y., Putnam, 1887. 61 p. D. 50 c.

Houghton, WALTER R. Conspectus of the History of Political Parties and the Federal Government. Indianapolis, Granger, 1880. $5.

Contains colored historical charts, the platforms of all parties, and a concise narrative of political events, etc.

Howard, G: E. Introduction to the Local Constitutional History of the United States. V. I. Development of the township, hundred, and shire. Baltimore, Johns Hopkins Univ. series, 1889. 526 p. O. $3.

A work of immense research, the only comprehensive treatise on the subject, but evidence not always complete or fully digested. Overlooks, for example, the influence of the Puritan clergy in early legislation in America.

Jameson, J. A. Treatise on Constitutional Conventions. 4th ed. Chicago, Callaghan & Co., 1887. 684 p. O. shp. $5.25.

Gives the facts relating to these conventions; the chief cases and opinions bearing upon them are discussed. A standard work.

Johnston, A. History of American Politics. New and enl. ed. N. Y., Holt, 1890. 7+355 p. S. 80 c.

A brief handbook of political history to 1889, giving facts, dates, and figures in outline.

McPherson, E: Political History of the United States During the Great Rebellion, a record of legislation and important political action, National and State, 1860-4. 4th ed. Washington, J. J. Chapman, 1882. 653 p. O. $5.

McPherson, E: Political History of the United States During the Period of Reconstruction, from April 15, 1865, to July 15, 1870, a record of legislation and important political action, National and State. 3d ed. Washington, J. J. Chapman, 1880. 648 p. O. $5.

McPherson, E: Handbook of Politics, a record of important political action, National and State. Washington, J. J. Chapman. V. 1, July 15, 1870–July 15, 1872; v. 2, July 15, 1872–July 15, 1874; v. 3, July 15, 1874–July 15, 1876; v. 4, July 15, 1876–Aug. 1, 1878; v. 5, July 1, 1878–July 1, 1880; v. 6, July 1, 1880–July 31, 1882; v. 7, July 31, 1882–July 31, 1884; v. 8, July 31, 1884–July 31, 1886; v. 9, July 31, 1886–Aug. 31, 1888; v. 10, Aug. 31, 1888–July 31, 1890. V. 1-3, $2.50 each; v. 4-10, $2 each.

Stanwood, E. History of Presidential Elections. New ed., rev. to 1888. Bost., Houghton, Mifflin & Co., 1889. 407 p. D. $1.50.

Stephens, ALEX. H. **Constitutional View of the Late War Between the States.** Phila., Nat. Pub. Co., 1868–70. 2 v. 8°, $5.50.

<small>Author was Vice-President of the Southern Confederacy.</small>

Sterne, SIMON. **Constitutional History and Political Development of the United States.** New and rev. ed. N. Y., Putnam, 1888. 361 p. D. $1.25.

<small>A capital introductory work.</small>

Von Holst, H. E. **Verfassung und Demokratie der Vereinigten Staaten von Amerika.** Dusseldorf, 1873–84. 6 v.

—— *Same.* **Constitutional and Political History of the United States.** Tr. by J. J. Lálor. Chicago, Callaghan & Co., 1885. 6 v. $20.

<small>Is unrivalled as a political history, and contains, in its critical passages, a great deal of sound political philosophy. V. 6 brings the narrative to 1859. Translation not always perfect, and typographical errors are many.</small>

<small>In Lalor's Cyclopædia of Political Science, Prof. Alex. Johnston contributed articles which are among the best political literature of America.</small>

<small>A record of political events, American and foreign, commencing with Oct. 1, 1888, is contained in the *Political Science Quarterly*, beginning with the no. for June, 1889.</small>

<small>Theory and Practice of Elections, Presidential Elections, and Civil Service Reform are treated in the Collected Essays of Prof. W: G. Sumner. N. Y., Holt, 1885.</small>

<small>The Constitution of the United States in Civil War. W: A. Dunning. *Political Science Quarterly*, June, 1886.</small>

<small>The Constitution of the United States in Reconstruction. W: A. Dunning. *Political Science Quarterly*, Dec., 1887.</small>

<small>Constitutions of the State of New York. J. Hampden Dougherty. *Political Science Quarterly*, Dec., 1888, and June, 1889.</small>

ENGLISH CONSTITUTION AND GOVERNMENT.

Taylor, HANNIS. **Origin and Growth of the English Constitution.** 2d ed. Bost., Houghton, Mifflin & Co., 1890. Part 1, 616 p. D. $4.50.

<small>This work, to be completed in a second part, is intended to show, in the light of the most recent researches, the gradual development of the English Constitutional system, and the growth therefrom of the Federal Republic of the United States.</small>

Amos, SHELDON. **A Primer of the English Constitution and Government.** 3d ed. Lond. and N. Y., Longmans, 1877. 243 p. D. $1.75.

Amos, SHELDON. **Fifty Years of the English Constitution, 1830-80.** Bost., Little, Brown & Co., 1880. 32+495 p. O. $3.

Anson, *Sir* WILLIAM R. **Law and Custom of the Constitution.** Part 1, Parliament. Lond. and N. Y., Macmillan, 1886. 19+336 p. O. $2.75.

<small>An authoritative exposition. Part 2 will deal with the executive. Should accompany the study of Professor Dicey's work on the Law of the Constitution.</small>

Bagehot, W. **The English Constitution,** and other Essays. N. Y., Appleton, 1876. 8+468 p. D. $2.

<small>A capital popular exposition.</small>

Chalmers, M. D. **Local Government.** English Citizen series. Lond. and N. Y., Macmillan, 1883. 160 p. D. $1.

Craik, H: **The State and Education.** English Citizen series. Lond. and N. Y., Macmillan, 1884. 166 p. D. $1.

Creasy, E. S. **The Rise and Progress of the English Constitution.** 4th ed. rev. N. Y., Appleton, 1886. 11+359 p. D. $1.50.

Cunningham, W. **Politics and Economics,** with survey of recent [British] legislation. Lond., Kegan Paul, 1885. 16+275 p. D. 5s.

Favorable to State interference.

Dicey, A. V. **Lectures Introductory to the Study of the Law of the Constitution.** Lond. and N. Y., Macmillan, 1885. 7+407 p. O. $3.50.

The best introductory book on the English Constitution. Contains a thoughtful analysis of the Constitution of the United States.

Farrer, *Sir* T: H. **The State in Its Relation to Trade.** English Citizen series. Lond. and N. Y., Macmillan, 1883. 11+181 p. D. $1.

An admirable little book.

Freeman, E. A. **The Growth of the English Constitution from the Earliest Times.** 4th ed. Lond. and N. Y., Macmillan, 1884. 234 p. D. $1.75.

Hallam, H: **Constitutional History of England** from the Accession of Henry VII. to the death of George II. New ed. N. Y., A. C. Armstrong & Son, 1885. 3 v. O. cl. $5.25 ; hf. cf. $10.50.

Jevons, W: STANLEY. **The State in Relation to Labor.** English Citizen series. Lond. and N. Y., Macmillan, 1882. 166 p. D. $1.

Low, SIDNEY J., *and* **Pulling,** F. S., *eds.* **Dictionary of English History.** Lond. and N. Y., Cassell, 1885. 1119 p. O. $6.

Contains many articles on Constitutional subjects which state in brief form the results of latest scientific research. It has an able list of writers.

May, *Sir* T: ERSKINE. **Constitutional History of England, 1760-1860,** with a new chapter, 1861-71. N. Y., A. C. Armstrong & Son, 1885. 2 v. O. cl. $2.50 ; hf. cf. $6.

Continuation of Hallam.

Skottowe, B. C. **A Short History of Parliament.** N. Y., Harper, 1887. 345 p. D. $1.25.

An introductory work.

Stubbs, W: **Constitutional History of England.** Lond. and N. Y., Macmillan, 1878. 3 v. 713-708-680 p. O. Library ed., $12 ; Students' ed., $7.80.

The best work on the subject. Thoroughly judicial.

Taswell-Langmead, T: P. **English Constitutional History.** 3d ed. rev. and enl. Bost., Houghton, Mifflin & Co., 1886. 826 p. O. $7.50.

An excellent manual, well fitted for use as a text-book.

Todd, ALPHEUS. **On Parliamentary Government in England:** its origin, development, and practical operation. 2d ed., edited by his son. Lond. and N. Y., Longmans, 1889. 2 v. 844, 964 p. O. $17.50.

The best work on the subject.

Todd, ALPHEUS. **Parliamentary Government in the British Colonies.** Bost., Little, Brown & Co., 1880. 12+607 p. O. $5.

The standard authority.

Boutmy, E. Le développement de la constitution et de la société politique en Angleterre. Paris, E. Plon, Nourrit & Cie., 1887. 352 p. D. 3.50 francs.

Combines the legal with the historical aspect of English constitutional history.

De Franqueville, *Comte.* **Le gouvernement et le parlement britanniques.** Paris, Rothschild, 1887. 3 v. 595, 567, 575 p. D. 24 francs.

Gneist, RUDOLPH. **Das englische Parlament.** Berlin, Allgemeiner Verein für Deutsche Literatur, 1886. 407 p. O. 7 marks.

An analysis tracing out the sources of the English Parliament's stability, with comment on the dangers now held to be threatening that stability. Of interest to those who believe influences to be at work in opposition to American institutions for local self-government.

—— *Same.* **The English Parliament.** Tr. by R. J. Shee. Bost., Little Brown & Co., 1886. 420 p. O. $3.50.

A faulty translation.

—— *Same.* Tr. by E. H. Keane. N. Y., Putnam, 1887. 462 p. O. $3.

The preferable version.

Gneist, RUDOLPH. **Das englische Verwaltungsrecht der Gegenwart in Vergleichung mit den deutschen Verwaltungssystemen.** 3te nach deutscher systematik umgestaltete Aufl. Berlin, 1884. O.

The only comprehensive work on English administrative law.

Gneist, RUDOLPH. **History of the English Constitution.** N. Y., Putnam, 1886. 2 v. O. $8.

Two principles are brought out with special prominence—that the national Government of England has been for generations supreme over every personal body throughout the State, and that Englishmen are determined to be ruled by law.

Gneist, RUDOLPH. **Self-Government. Communalverfassung und Verwaltungsgerichte in England.** Berlin, J. Springer, 1871. 1028 p. O.

Jellinek, GEORG. **Gesetz und Verordnung.** Freiburg, J. C. B. Mohr, 1887. 412 p. O. 10 marks.

A disquisition on the encroachments of the administrative upon the legislative authority in England, France, Germany, Austria, and Belgium; with analogies from the history of Greece, Rome, and the United States.

English Local Government Bill. Frank J. Goodnow. *Political Science Quarterly,* June, 1888.

Local Government in England. Frank J. Goodnow. *Political Science Quarterly,* Dec., 1887.

CANADIAN CONSTITUTION AND GOVERNMENT.

Bourinot, J: G: **Federal Government in Canada.** Baltimore, Johns Hopkins Univ. series, 1889. pap. $1.

Bourinot, J: G: **Manual of the Constitutional History of Canada.** Montreal, Dawson Bros., 1888. 238 p. D. $1.25.

A revision of the author's "Parliamentary Practice and Procedure in Canada." By the chief authority on Canadian Constitutional questions.

Colby, C: C. **Parliamentary Government in Canada.** Montreal, Dawson Bros. 57 p. S. 50 c.

An outline of the Canadian political system by a Member of Parliament. Omits to describe the Constitution and procedure of the two Houses of the Legislature.

Munro, J. E. C. **Constitution of Canada.** Lond. and N. Y., Macmillan, 1889. 356 p. O. $3.
<small>A comprehensive treatise.</small>

Smith, GOLDWIN. **Political Destiny of Canada.** With a reply by Sir Francis Hincks, and a rejoinder. Toronto, Williamson & Co., 1878. $1.
<small>Holds annexation to the United States to be Canada's political destiny. Sir Francis Hincks was for some years a Minister of the Crown.</small>

Canada and the United States, a study in comparative politics. J. G. Bourinot. *Annals Am. Acad. Pol. and Soc. Science,* Phila., July, 1890.

OTHER FOREIGN GOVERNMENTS AND CONSTITUTIONS.

Hart, A. B. **Introduction to the Study of Federal Governments.** Harvard Historical monograph, no. 2. N. Y., Ginn & Co., 1890. 218 p. D. $1.
<small>Brief sketches of the principal federal governments, from the Amphictyonic Council to Brazil, with brief critical accounts of the literature upon each. Includes a parallel conspectus of the texts of the constitutions of Canada, Germany, Switzerland, and the United States.</small>

James, E. J., *tr.* **Federal Constitution of Germany.** Phila., Wharton School of Finance and Economy, 1890. 43 p. D. pap. 50 c.

James, E. J., *tr.* **Federal Constitution of Switzerland.** Phila., Wharton School of Finance and Economy, 1890. 46 p. D. pap. 50 c.

Lockwood, H. C. **Constitutional History of France.** N. Y., Rand, McNally & Co., 1890. 442 p. O. $2.50.

Moses, BERNARD. **Federal Government of Switzerland.** Oakland, Cal., Pacific Press Pub. Co., 1889. 256 p. D. $1.50.
<small>Concisely presents the fundamental ideas of central government, not only of Switzerland, but of important confederations in both hemispheres. Not entirely satisfactory.</small>

Adams, Sir F. O., *and* **Cunningham,** C. **The Swiss Confederation.** Lond. and N. Y., Macmillan, 1889. 8°, $4.

—— *Same.* **La Confederation Suisse.** Ed. française avec notes et additions par H. G. Loumeyer. Basle, H. Georg, 1890. 319 p. 8°.
<small>The notes and additions confer new value on this important work.</small>

Demombynes, G. **Constitutions Européennes.** 2 v. L. Larose & Forcel, 1881.
<small>Résumé of the legislation concerning the Parliaments, the Councils Provincial and Communal, and judicial organization in the different countries of Europe, with a note on the Congress of the United States.</small>

Hélie, M. FAUSTIN-ADOLPHE. **Les Constitutions de la France.** Paris, A. M. Ainé, 1880. 1468 p. O.
<small>The best history of French constitutions, with excellent commentary.</small>

Schültze, HERMANN. **Lehrbuch des deutschen Staatsrechts.** Leipzig, Breitkopf & Härtel, 1881-6. 2 v. in 1. 21 marks.
<small>An account of the historical development of the German state, and the comparative constitutional and administrative law of the twenty-five states within the empire.</small>

Local Government in Prussia. Frank J. Goodnow. *Political Science Quarterly,* Dec., 1889, March, 1890.

GOVERNMENT ADMINISTRATION.

The best work in this department is Kirchenheim's ; Carlier's is very valuable. Many works already mentioned as treating Constitutional Government also deal with Administration, as for example. Woodrow Wilson's " The State " [Political Science, General Works], and De Franqueville's " Le gouvernement et le parlement britanniques," [English Constitution and Government.] Lamphere's Description of the Government of the United States is the best.

GENERAL WORKS.

Elmes, WEBSTER. Executive Departments of the United States at Washington. Washington, W. H. & O. H. Morrison, 1879. 557 p. D. $4.

Lamphere, G: N. The United States Government, its Organization and Practical Workings. Phila., Lippincott, 1880. 297 p. O. $2.50.

Aucoc, J: L. Conferences sur l'administration et le droit administratif. Paris, Dunod, 1886. 3 v. O.

V. 1 will be found the most valuable to the general reader. The others are technical.

Batbie, A. P. Traité theorique et pratique de droit public et administratif. Paris, Cotillon, 1862–68. 7 v. O.

Block, MAURICE, ed. Dictionnaire de l'administration française. 2d ed. Paris, Berger, Levrault & Cie., 1878. 1856 p. O. Supplement, 1878–84. 446 p. O.

Each article gives a bibliography, and compares French with other systems.

Carlier, AUGUSTE. Droit public des états unis. Paris, Guillaumin, 1890.

A masterly review.

Couturier, R. Organisation politique, administrative et judiciaire de la France. 2me ed. Lyon, L'auteur, 1886. 68 p. O. 2 fr.

Monnet, EMILE. Histoire de l'administration provinciale, departmentale et communale en France. Paris, A. Rousseau, 1885. 7+565 p. O.

Vivien, A. F. A. Etudes administratives. 3me ed. Paris, Guillaumin, 1859. 2 v. D.

Bornhak, CONRAD. Preussisches Staatsrecht. Freiburg, 1888–90. 3 v. O.

V. 1 and 2 are especially devoted to administration.

Gneist, RUDOLF. Das Englische Verwaltungsrecht der Gegenwart. Berlin, J. Springer, 1884. 2 v. in 1.

Gneist, RUDOLF. Das Englische Verwaltungsrecht mit Einschluss des Heeres, der Gerichte und der Kirche. 2te Aufl. Berlin, J. Springer, 1867. 2 v. O.

The best general work on English administration.

Kirchenheim, A. v. Einführung in das Verwaltungsrecht. Stuttgart, F. Enke, 1885. 7+174 p. O.

The best work on the subject. It compares the administrations of Germany, France, and England. Contains a complete bibliography of 20 p.

Laband, PAUL. Das Staatsrecht des deutschen Reichs. Freiburg, 1887–90.

Of this one v. and 2 pts. of a second v. have appeared. A clear, complete and logical work.

Rüttimann, H. Das Nordamerikanische Bundestaatsrecht. Zurich, Drell, 1867–76. 2 v. O.

Sarwey, O. v. **Allgemeines Verwaltungsrecht.** Tübingen, H. Laupp, 1887.

Stein, Lorenz v. **Handbuch der Verwaltungslehre.** Stuttgart, J. G. Cotta, 1876. 27+898 p. O.

Zorn, Ph. **Das Staatsrecht des deutschen Reichs.** Berlin, F. Guttentag, 1880-83. 2 v. S.

Comparative Administrative Law and Science, by Prof. F. J. Goodnow, is in preparation for the series in Systematic Political Science, by the Univ. Faculty of Pol. Science, Columbia College, N. Y.

In J. F. Jameson's " Constitutional History of the U. S., 1775-89," [Bost., Houghton, Mifflin & Co., 1889.] Mr. Guggenheimer has a chapter on "The Development of the Executive Departments."

THE SUFFRAGE.

ELECTION SYSTEM, ELECTORAL REFORM.

Bowker, R: R. **Electoral Reform,** with the Massachusetts Ballot Reform Act, and New York (Saxton) Bill. Economic tract, no. 25. N. Y., Soc. for Political Education, 1889. 49 p. D. pap. 15 c.

McKnight, D. A. **Electoral System of the United States;** a critical and historical exposition of its fundamental principles, and of the acts and proceedings of Congress enforcing it. Phila., Lippincott, 1878. 433 p. O. $3.

McMillan, D. C. **Elective Franchise in the United States,** with a pref. by Horatio Seymour. N. Y., Putnam, 1880. 198 p. D. $1.

A review of the effects of the caucus system on the civil service, and the principles and policies of parties. Proposes the control of primary elections by law.

O'Neil, C: A. **American Electoral System.** An Analysis of its Character and History. N. Y., Putnam, 1887. 9+284 p. D. $1.50.

A discussion of the defects in the methods of choosing the President and Vice-President of the United States, with suggestions for reform.

Stanwood, E· **History of Presidential Elections.** Rev. ed. Bost., Houghton, Mifflin & Co., 1888. 5+407 p. $1.50.

Stanton, *Mrs.* Elizabeth Cady, Anthony, Susan B., and Gage, Matilda J., *eds.* **History of Woman Suffrage.** N. Y., Fowler & Wells, 1882. 3 v. O. $5.

Sterne, Simon. **Suffrage in Cities.** Economic monograph, no. 7. N. Y., Putnam, 1878. 41 p. D. pap. 25 c.

A sharp criticism. Proposes that only citizens who pay taxes shall vote.

Wigmore, J: H. **The Australian Ballot System** as embodied in the legislation of various countries ; with an historical introd. Bost., C. C. Soule, 1889. 155 p. O. $1.

Dilke, *Mrs.* Ashton, *and* Woodall, W., *M.P.* **Woman Suffrage.** Imp. Parl. series, no. 5. Lond., Swan Sonnenschein, 1885. D. 1s.

Lubbock, *Sir* J: **Representation.** Imp. Parl. series, no. 2. Lond., Swan Sonnenschein, 1885. 3+90 p. D. 1s.

Walpole, Spencer. **The Electorate and the Legislature.** English Citizen series. Lond., Macmillan, 1881. 160 p. D. $1.

Borgeaud, CHARLES. Histoire du plébiscité. V. 1. Le plébiscite dans l'antiquité. Paris, E. Thorin, 1887. 200 p. 3.50 fr.

The first volume in a series. The author thinks that the people will soon directly make laws as they now pass upon constitutional amendments—through the ballot-box.

Guer, E. G. de. Manuel électoral. 2me ed. Paris, Berger-Levrault, 1881. 372p. D.

A practical guide to elections municipal, departmental, legislative, and consular ; also to the elections of councils of *prud'hommes*. Endorsed by the French Minister of the Interior.

Prins, ADOLPHE. La démocratie et le régime parlementaire. Bruxelles, C. Muquardt, 1887. 220 p. D. 4 fr.

A criticism of democratic government, with a suggestion that the suffrage be limited and representation distributed according to economic interests—those of farmers, laborers, artisans, etc.

See *Mrs.* M. G. Fawcett on "Why women require the franchise," in Essays and Lectures by H: and M. G. Fawcett. Lond., Macmillan, 1872. 262–91 p.

The leading journal in the United States for the advocacy of Woman Suffrage is the *Woman's Journal*, weekly, $2.50 per year, published at 3 Park Street, Boston.

The City Reform Club of New York issues an Annual Record from its office, 41 Park Row, giving a review of a session of the Legislature at Albany, a biographical sketch of each representative and senator of New York City, with an account of his conduct as a legislator, his votes, and the bills (if any) introduced by him.

The Ballot in England. E. Goadby and H. H. Asquith. *Political Science Quarterly*, Dec., 1888.

The Ballot in New York. A. C. Bernheim. *Political Science Quarterly*, March, 1889.

Compulsory Voting as a Means of Correcting Political Abuses. F: S. Holls. *Annals Am. Acad. Pol. and Soc Science*, Phila., April, 1891. Also, separately, 50 c.

Electoral Reform Legislation. C: Claflin Allen. *Arena*, Dec., 1890.

With special reference to Corrupt Practices Acts.

The Federal Election Bill. H. C. Lodge and T. V. Powderly. *N. A. Review*, Sept., 1890.

National Control of Elections. Sen. W. E. Chandler. *Forum*, Aug., 1890.

MINORITY REPRESENTATION.

Buckalew, C. R. Proportional Representation. Ed. by John G. Freese. Phila., 1872. 8°, $3.

Treats of the representation of successive majorities in the federal, state, municipal, corporate, and primary elections. With an appendix.

Dutcher, SALEM. Minority or Proportional Representation, its nature, aims, history, processes, and practical operation. N. Y., U. S. Pub. Co., 1872. 165 p. O. $1.50.

Quincy, J. P. Protection of Majorities; or, Considerations Relating to an Electoral Reform, with other papers. Bost., Roberts, 1876. 163 p. D. $1.

Sterne, SIMON. Representative Government and Personal Representation. Phila., Lippincott, 1871. D. $1.75.

Hare, T: Election of Representatives, parliamentary and municipal. 4th ed. Lond., Longmans. 1873. 47+380 p. D. 7s.

Representation of Minorities. D: D. Field. *Journal Am. Social Sci. Assoc.*, 1871.

CIVIL SERVICE AND ITS REFORM.

Bernard, G: S. Civil Service versus The Spoils System. N. Y., J: B. Alden, 1885. 128 p. S. pap. 10 c.

Articles reprinted from the *Index-Appeal* of Petersburg, Va.

Bonaparte, C: J. Civil Service Reform as a Moral Question. N. Y., National Civil Service Reform League, 1889. 8 p. D. pap. 2 c.

Bowker, R: R. Civil Service Examinations. Economic tract, no. 22. N. Y., Soc. for Political Education, 1886. 45 p. D. pap. 15 c.

Introduction stating the principles of Civil Service Reform examinations, followed by question papers representing national, state, and municipal examinations, with actual answers of successful and unsuccessful candidates.

Brown, WILLARD. Civil Service Reform in the New York Custom-House. N. Y., N. Y. Civil Service Reform Assoc., 1882. 19 p. D. pap. 5 c.

Bugbee, JAMES M. The Selection of Laborers. N. Y., National Civil Service Reform League, 1885. 8 p. D. pap. 2 c.

By a member of the Massachusetts Civil Service Commission. Also published in German at same price.

Civil Service Question-Book. Syracuse, N. Y., C. W. Bardeen, 1888. 282 p. S. $1.50.

Intended to be a sufficient review in all subjects upon which questions are asked in civil service examinations; with full answers and directions as to applications for examinations and positions.

Clarke, W. H. The Civil Service Law. N. Y., L. K. Strouse & Co., 1888. 200 p. D. $1.

A defence of the law passed by Congress Jan. 16, 1883, with corroborative evidence from the works of eminent American statesmen.

Comstock, J. M. Civil Service in the United States. N. Y., Holt, 1885. 602 p. D. $2.

A catalogue of non-elective positions and information in regard to competitive examinations, under the Act of 1883. Also, a description of the Civil Service of New York and Massachusetts and of their municipalities.

Curtis, G: W: Address to the Voters of the United States. N. Y., National Civil Service Reform League, 1882. 10 p. S. pap. 2 c.

Eaton, DORMAN B. Civil Service in Great Britain: A History of Abuses and Reforms, and Their Bearing upon American Politics. With an introd. by G: W: Curtis. N. Y., Harper, 1879. 14+469 p. O. $2.50. Also, 1881 (Franklin Square Library.) 82 p. Q. pap. 25 c.

The most comprehensive and complete exposition of administrative abuses and reforms yet published, traced historically from Norman times. It sets forth the theoretical and practical effects of the reform in Great Britain and India, and explains the bearing of that experience upon the administration of this country.

Eaton, Dorman B. The Spoils System and Civil Service Reform in the Custom-House and Post-Office at New York. N. Y., N. Y. Civil Service Reform Assoc., 1881. 136 p. D. pap. 15 c.

Eaton, Dorman B. Term and Tenure of Office. 2d ed. abridged. N. Y., N. Y. Civil Service Reform Assoc., 1882. 76 p. D. pap. 15 c.

Foulkes, W: D. Civil Service Reform, its later aspects. Economic tract, no. 31. N. Y., Society for Political Education, 1890. 13 p. D. pap. 10 c.
The author was Chairman Special Committee National Civil Service Reform League.

Godkin, E. L. The Danger of an Office-Holding Aristocracy. N. Y., N. Y. Civil Service Reform Assoc. pap. 5 c.

Parton, James. Beginning of the Spoils System in the National Government, 1829-30. N. Y., N. Y. Civil Service Reform Assoc., 1882. 23 p. D. pap. 5 c.
Reprinted from Parton's "Life of Andrew Jackson."

Primer of Civil Service Reform. N. Y., N. Y. Civil Service Reform Assoc., 1885. 20 p. S. pap. 2 c.
Also published in German at same price.

Richmond, H: A. The Workingmen's Interest in Civil Service Reform. N. Y., N. Y. Civil Service Reform Assoc., 1888. 19 p. D. pap. 3 c.

Shepard, E: M. The Competitive Test and the Civil Service of States and Cities. Economic tract, no. 14. N. Y., Soc. for Political Education, 1884. 43 p. D. pap. 25 c.

The United States Civil Service Commission issues reports, (no. 1, 1884), also a compilation of laws. (Washington, Gov. Pr. Office.)

The Civil Service Commission of Massachusetts issues an annual report of especial value. The Civil Service Commission of New York (Albany) issues an annual report (no. 1, 1884).

The Supervisory Board of Commissioners of the New York Municipal Civil Service, City Hall, New York, issues an annual report, no. 1, 1885. Nos. 1 and 2 are out of print. These reports give the regulations of the New York City Civil Service, with details of their working. The schedules filled out by applicants are included.

The National Civil Service Reform League, W: Potts, Secretary, 56 Wall St., New York, is an organization of the local Civil Service Reform Associations throughout the Union, and is maintained by them. It publishes the proceedings of its annual meetings, 1882, 10 c. per copy; 1884-87, 5 c. per copy; 1889-90, 8 c. per copy, to be had from the Secretary, or from G: P. Putnam's Sons, New York. These give the annual addresses of G: W: Curtis, President of the League.

The New York Civil Service Reform Association, W: Potts, Secretary, 56 Wall St., New York, annual subscription, $5, publishes an annual report, (no. 1, 1883.) These and other publications of the Association may be had from the Secretary, or from G: P. Putnam's Sons, New York.

There are many other similar Associations throughout the United States. The most important of them are those of Baltimore, Boston, Brookline, Brooklyn. Buffalo, Cambridge, Indianapolis, Philadelphia, Rochester, and Syracuse.

Journals advocating the reform are *The Civil Service Chronicle*, Indianapolis, monthly, 50 c. per year; *The Civil Service Record*, Boston, monthly, 50 c. per year, and *The Civil Service Reformer*, Baltimore, monthly, $1 per year.

Do the People Wish Civil Service Reform? A. B. Hart. *Forum*, March, 1890.

Merit System vs. Patronage System. Theodore Roosevelt. *Century*, Feb., 1890.

An Object Lesson in Civil Service Reform. Theodore Roosevelt. *Atlantic Monthly*, Feb., 1891.

Obstacles to Civil Service Reform. W. M. Ferriss. *Forum*, July, 1890.

Some Popular Objections to Civil Service Reform. O. T. Morton. *Atlantic Monthly*, April and May, 1890.

Why Patronage in Offices is un-American. H. C. Lodge. *Century*, Oct., 1890.

POST OFFICE, TELEGRAPH SERVICE.

Francisco, M. J. **Review of Argument for Limited Post and Telegraph by the Postmaster-General.** Rutland, Vt., M. J. Francisco, 1891. 48 p. O. pap. *gratis*.

An adverse review.

Wells, DAVID A. **Relation of the Government to the Telegraph:** a review of propositions for changing the telegraphic service of the country. N. Y., 1873. 170 p. pap. O.

Hill, G. B. **Life of Sir Rowland Hill, and History of Penny Postage.** Lond., De La Rue, 1880. 2 v. 30s.

Lewins, W: **Her Majesty's Mails,** an historical and descriptive account of the British Post Office. Lond., 1864. 9+348 p. D.

Rothschild, ARTHUR. **Histoire de la poste aux lettres.** 2me ed. aug Paris, Hachette & Cie., 1873. 394 p. D.

König, B. E. **Geschichte der Deutschen Post,** von ihren Anfängen bis zur Gegenwart. Eisenach, 1889. 8+479 p. D.

Schöttle, G. **Der Telegraph in administrativer und finanzieller Hinsicht.** Stuttgart, 1883. 327 p. O.

An excellent work.

The Post-Office Department of the United States (Washington, Gov. Pr Office), issues an annual report.

The Postal Telegraph Service in Foreign Countries, a report compiled by R. B. Lines, is contained in v. 4, 19th Census Reports, Washington, Gov. Pr. Office, 1883.

Public Control of the Telegraph. Bronson C. Keeler. *Forum*, June, 1890.

WAR AND NAVY.

Cooper, J. F. **History of the Navy of the United States to 1853.** Continued to 1860. Bost., Mason, 1860.

Ingersoll, L. D. **History of the War Department of the United States.** Washington, F. B. Mohun, 1879. 613 p. O. $3.50.

Laws of the United States Governing the Granting of Army and Navy Pensions, together with the regulations relating thereto. Washington, Gov. Pr. Office, 1887. 140 p. D.

Regulations for the Army of the United States. Washington, Gov. Pr. Office, 1889. 8°.

Regulations for the Government of the United States Navy. Washington, Gov. Pr. Office, 1870-76. 2 v. D. and O.

Scott, R. N. Analytical Digest of the Military Laws of the United States. Phila., Lippincott, 1873. 510 p. O.

United States Navy Department, Compilation of Laws Relating to the Navy, Marine Corps. etc., prepared by J. W. Hogg. Washington, Gov. Pr. Office, 1883. 401 p. O.

United States War Department, Regulations of the Army of the United States and General Orders in force on 17th Feb., 1881. Washington, Gov. Pr. Office, 1881. 1385 p. O.

The Secretary of War and the Secretary of the Navy publish annual reports.

FORESTRY.

Brisbin, JAMES S. **Trees and Tree-Planting.** N. Y., Harper, 1882. $1.50.

Fernow, B. E. **Need of a Forest Administration for the United States.** Salem, Mass., Salem Press, 1888. 8 p. O.

Fernow, B. E. **Our Forestry Problem.** N. Y., 1887. 11 p. O.
Reprinted from *Popular Science Monthly*, Dec., 1887.

Forestry in Europe. U. S. Consular Report. Department of State, Washington, Gov. Pr. Office, 1887. 320 p. O.

Fuller, ANDREW S. **Practical Forestry.** N. Y., Orange Judd Co., 1884. 2+299 p. D. $1.50.
Valuable for concise descriptive notes on our timber trees.

Hough, FRANKLIN B. **Elements of Forestry.** Cincinnati, R. Clarke & Co., 1882. 10+351 p. D. $2.
Incomplete and out of date.

New York Forest Commission. Special Report. Transmitted to the Legislature, Jan., 1891. Albany, 1891. 42 p. O.
Discusses the establishment of a park in the Adirondack wilderness, and presents the Act proposed therefor. Illustrated with a map showing the forest of the wilderness as it was in 1884, and boundaries of the proposed Adirondack Park. Tables are appended showing the improved and unimproved areas of the wilderness in detail.

Reports of the Forestry Division. Washington, Department of Agriculture, 1877-90. 9 nos. pap.
Bulletin 1, The Relation of Railroads to Forest Supplies and Forestry, 1887. 150 p. Bulletin 2, The Forest Condition of the Rocky Mountains, etc., 1888. 252 p. Bulletin 3, Preliminary Report on the use of Metal Track on Railways as a Substitute for Wooden Ties, etc., 1889. 79 p. Bulletin 4, Report on the Substitution of Metal for Wood in Railroad Ties, etc., 1890. 363 p. Circulars of Information: No. 3, Increasing the Durability of Timber. No. 4, Information to Railroad Managers Concerning Railroad Ties. No. 5, Arbor Day Planting in Eastern States. No. 6, Instructions for Growing Tree-Seedlings. No. 7, Treatment of Tree-Seedlings in Nurseries.

Sargent, C: S. Silva of North America; a description of the trees which grow naturally in North America, exclusive of Mexico. Bost., Houghton, Mifflin & Co., 1890. 9+119 p. Q. $25.

V. 1 of a work to be completed in 12 v., two to be issued annually. Author is Director Arnold Arboretum, Harvard Univ. The work, splendidly illustrated, will on completion give the silva of North America ampler description than that of any other country in the world.

Schlich, W. Manual of Forestry. Lond., Bradbury, Agnew & Co., 1889. V. 1. 232 p. D. 7s. 6d.

This volume in Pt. 1 treats of the utility of forests, in Pt. 2 of the fundamental principles of sylviculture. The best summary on these subjects published. Work to be completed in 5 additional pts.

Schurz, Carl. Need of a Rational Forest Policy in the United States. Philadelphia, American Forestry Assoc., 1889. 12 p. O. pap.

An address delivered before the American Forestry Association, Oct. 15, 1889.

Boppe, Lucien. Traité de sylviculture. Paris et Nancy, Berger, Levrault & Cie, 1889. 444 p. O.

The best French treatise. Clear and concise.

Demontzey, Prosper. Traité pratique de reboissement et du gazonnement des montagnes. 2me ed. Paris, J. Rothschild, 1882. 528 p. D.

The classical authority on the correction of torrents.

Gayer, Karl. Der Waldbau. 3d ed. Berlin, Paul Parey, 1889. 619 p. D. 13 marks.

The standard German work on sylviculture.

Gayer, Karl. Die Forstbenutzung. 7th ed. Berlin, Paul Parey, 1888. 614 p. D. 13 marks.

The standard German work on forest utilization.

Hess, Richard. Der Forstschutz. 2d ed. Leipzig, B. G. Teubner, 1887. 2 v. 424, 445 p. O. pap. 18 marks.

One of the best books on forest protection.

Judeich, Friedrich. Die Forsteinrichtung. 4th ed. Dresden, G. Schönfeld, 1885. 514 p. D. 10 marks.

The standard German work on working plans in forestry.

Mayr, Heinrich. Die Waldungen von Nordamerika. Munich, M. Rieger, 1890. 448 p. O. pap. 18 marks.

The most extended treatment of North American forests from the forester's point of view.

Semler, Heinrich. Tropische und nordamerikanische Waldwirthschaft und Holzkunde. Berlin, Paul Parey, 1888.

Very valuable and comprehensive.

V. 9 of the Tenth Census Reports is on the Forest Trees of North America (exclusive of Mexico), by C: S. Sargent. Washington, Gov. Pr. Office, 1884. 612 p. Q.

Reports are published by the Forest Commissions of New York, New Hampshire, and Colorado; by the State Forest Association of Minnesota, State Bureau of Forestry of Ohio, and the State Board of Forestry of California. Of these reports one worthy of special mention is that of January 23, 1885, made to the Legislature of New York by Messrs. C: S. Sargent, D. Willis James, E: M. Shepard, and W. A. Poucher, a Commission appointed to investigate and report a system of forest preservation.

The American Forestry Association, which aims at the preservation of American forests, and the promotion of forestry as a science, meets annually and publishes its proceedings. Ed. Bowers. Safe Deposit Bldg., Washington, D. C., Corresponding Secretary. Annual subscription, $2. Life membership, $50.

Governmental Control of Forests in the U. S., by B. E. Fernow; Forest Policy Abroad, by Gifford Pinchot; and, Present Condition of Forests on the Public Lands, by Ed. Bowers, will be published during 1891 by the American Economic Assoc., Baltimore, as a no. in its series.

Forest Leaves is a monthly periodical published by the Pennsylvania Forestry Association, 25 Juniper St., Philadelphia, Pa., $1 per year.

Garden and Forest, 154 Nassau St., New York, is a weekly illustrated journal with a capital Forestry department, $4 per year.

IRRIGATION.

Campbell, D. W. Digest of Decisions of the Supreme Courts, States and Territories, arid region, and of the U. S. Circuit and Supreme Courts, in irrigation cases. Rev. and ed. by W. C. Pollock. Washington, 1889. 59 p.

Hall, W: H. Irrigation Development. Sacramento, Cal., State Printing Office, 1886. 622 p. O.
Sets forth the history, law, and administrative systems relating to irrigation, watercourses, and waters in France, Italy, and Spain. Forms introductory part of a report by State Engineer of California.

Hall, W: H. Irrigation in [Southern] California. Sacramento, Cal., State Printing Office, 1888. 672 p. O.
Illustrates and explains the field, water-supply, and works of irrigation in San Diego, San Bernardino, and Los Angeles Counties; with their organization and working. Forms part of a report by the State Engineer of California.

Hinton, R. J. Irrigation in the United States. A report prepared under direction of the Commissioner of Agriculture. (49th Cong., 2d sess., Senate misc. doc., v. 1, no. 15.) Washington, Gov. Pr. Office, 1887. 8°.

Ronna, A. Les irrigations. Paris, A. Muntz, 1888–89. 2 v. 8°.
V. 1, Water supply and machines for irrigation. V. 2, Canals and irrigation systems.

The Present Stage of the Irrigation Question. J. Bonner. *Overland Monthly*, June, 1889.

Water Storage in the West. W. G. Bates. *Scribner's Magazine*, Jan., 1890.

PARTIES AND PARTY HISTORY.

Brown, Everit, *and* Strauss, Albert. Dictionary of American Politics; comprising political parties, measures, and men. N. Y., A. L. Burt, 1888, 565 p. D. cl. $1; pap. 50 c.

Patton, J. Harris. The Democratic Party, a History. N. Y., Fords, Howard & Hulbert, 1884. 345 p. D. $1.

A Year of Republicanism. N. Y., Tribune Assoc., 1890. 72 p. O. 25 c.
Contents in part: *Tribune's* review of Pres. Harrison's first year of administration, articles by A W. Tourgee and G: W. Cable on Southern elections; by U. S. Senator W: M. Stewart and W. M. Grosvenor on Unlimited Silver Coinage.

Under American Political and Constitutional History will be found works incidentally giving the history of political parties.

CAUCUS, MACHINE.

Ivins, W. M. Machine Politics and Money in Elections in New York City. N. Y., Harper, 1887. 150 p. S. pap. 25 c.

An exposition by the City Chamberlain of New York; a plea for the Australian secret ballot.

Lawton, G: W. American Caucus System; its Origin, Purpose, and Utility. Questions of the Day series, no. 25. N. Y., Putnam, 1885. 107 p. D. $1.

Vickers, G. The Fall of Bossism, a History of the Committee of One Hundred in Philadelphia. Phila., N. C. Boyson, 1883. D. $1.25.

Whitridge, F: W. The Caucus System. Economic tract, no. 8. N. Y., Soc. for Political Education, 1882. 27 p. D. pap. 10 c.

Contains a bibliography, 1 p.

PARLIAMENTARY PRACTICE.

Cushing, L. S. Law and Practice of Legislative Assemblies in the United States. 9th ed. Bost., Little, Brown & Co., 1890. 8°, shp. $6.

Cushing, L. S. Manual of Parliamentary Practice. Bost., Thompson, Brown & Co., 1885. 75 c.

Jefferson, T: Manual of Parliamentary Practice. New ed. N. Y., Clark & Maynard, 1876. 12°, $1.

Brought down to practice of present day; with rules and orders of both houses Congress.

"A Deliberative Body." T: B. Reed. *N. A. Review*, Feb., 1891.

Limitations of the Speakership. T: B. Reed (Speaker), and J: G. Carlisle (ex-Speaker). *N. A. Review*, March, 1890.

Reforms Needed in the House. T: B. Reed. *N. A. Review*, May, 1890.

Reply to X. M. C. T: B. Reed and a Democratic Leader. *N. A. Review*, Aug., 1890.

Speaker Reed's Error. X. M. C. *N. A. Review*, July, 1890.

A Word as to the Speakership. James Bryce. *N. A. Review*, Oct., 1890.

CHURCH AND STATE.

Denominational Schools, a discussion of, at the National Educational Association, July, 1889, with papers by Cardinal Gibbons, Bishop Keane, E. D. Mead and John Jay. Syracuse, N. Y., C. W. Bardeen, 1889. 71 p. D. pap. 25 c.

Hecker, *Very Rev.* I. T. **The Church and the Age.** N. Y., Catholic Pub. Soc. Co., 1888. $1.25.

Intended to prove the compatibility of obedient faith and intelligent liberty. By the founder of the Order of Paulists.

Schaff, PHILIP, *D.D.* **Church and State in the United States;** or, The American idea of religious liberty and its practical effects. N. Y., Scribner, 1888. 183 p. O. $1.50.

Reprinted from Am. Hist. Assoc papers, V. 2, no. 4 · with official documents. Author Prof. of Church History in Union Theol. Seminary, New York. Sets forth the Am. theory of the relation of Church and State, compares the Am. system with other systems, reviews the basis of the Am. system in Federal and State Constitutions. Among topics of special interest are presented: The Oath, The official acts of Presidents, Exemption of Church Property from taxation, and connecting links between Church and State, Marriage, Sunday observance, Education. The progress of religious freedom in the several countries of Europe is sketched. Official documents are appended, together with opinions of B: Franklin, Judges Story and Cooley, Dr. Lieber, and G: Bancroft. Christianity is shown to be a part of the common law of Pennsylvania and New York.

Schaff, PHILIP, *D.D.* **Progress of Religious Freedom** as shown in the History of Toleration Acts. N. Y., Scribner, 1889. 124 p. O. $1.50.

Traces the history of the progress of the idea of religious liberty, from Galerius to the Constitution of the United States. Discriminates between religious liberty and religious toleration, showing that the United States is the only country enjoying the former. Gives the principal Edicts and Acts which have extended or withdrawn toleration.

Thompson, R. W. **Papacy and the Civil Power.** N. Y., Harper, 1877. 750 p. D. $3.

Elliot, ARTHUR. *M.P.* **The State and the Church.** English Citizen series. Lond. and N. Y., Macmillan, 1882. 181 p. D. $1.

Gladstone, W: E. **Vatican Decrees** and their bearing on civil allegiance. With replies of Archbishop Manning and Lord Acton. N. Y., Appleton, 1874. 96 p. O.

Richard, H., *M.P., and* **Williams,** J. CARVELL. **Disestablishment.** Imp. Parl. series, no. 6. Lond., Swan Sonnenschein, 1885. D. 1s.

Maistre, J. M., *Comte de.* Du Pape. 24me ed. Lyon, 1876. 508 p. D.

An argument for the spiritual and temporal sovereignty of the Pope.

Geffcken, F. H: Staat und Kirche. Berlin, W: Hertz, 1875. 673 p. O.

—— *Same.* **Church and State,** their relations historically considered. Tr. and ed. by E: F. Taylor. Lond., Longmans, 1887. 2 v. S°, 42s.

Janssen, JOHS. Kirche und Staat. Mainz, Kirchheim. 1861. 10+402 p. D.

By an eminent Roman Catholic authority.

Zeller, E: Staat und Kirche. Leipzig, Fues, 1873. 250 p. D.

Hammerstein, L. v. **De Ecclesia et Statu Juridice Consideratis.** Trier, Prussia, Paulinus-Druckerei, 1885. 3 marks, 20 pf.

An authoritative exposition from the Roman Catholic point of view.

"Church and State in Mexico," in U. S. Consular Report, no. 27. Washington, Department of State, 1887.

The National League for the Protection of American Institutions, J. M. King, General Secretary, 150 Nassau St., New York, issues tracts *gratis* in advocacy of the principle that no State shall found or maintain any institution which is wholly, or in part, under ecclesiastical control. Its special object is to keep the public schools free from such control.

American Christian State Schools. Rev. T: Jefferson Jenkins. *Catholic World,* Feb., 1891.

Keynotes from Rome. H. C. Lea. *Forum,* Feb., 1890.

The Old Know-Nothingism and the New. E: McGlynn, D.D. *N. A. Review,* Aug., 1887.

Religious Teaching in the Schools. Bishop McQuaid. *Forum,* Dec., 1889.

The Catholic University (Washington) and its Constitutions. *Catholic World,* July, 1880.

MUNICIPAL GOVERNMENT.

Allinson, E. P., *and* Penrose, Boies. Philadelphia, 1681-1887; a history of municipal development. Baltimore, Johns Hopkins Univ. series, 1887. 392 p. O. $3; shp. $3.50.
An account of a great municipality's growth, with special reference to the legislation of 1887, which largely transformed the city's government. A sketch of early systems of local administration is prefixed.

Billings, J: S., *M.D.* Municipal Government and Public Health. Phila., Am. Academy of Pol. and Social Science, 1891. 23 p. pap. 25 c.

Bugbee, James M. City Government of Boston. Baltimore, Johns Hopkins Univ. series, 1887. 60 p. O. pap. 25 c.

The Bullitt Bill—reorganizing the municipal government of Philadelphia, adopted December 16, 1886. Phila., T. & J. W. Johnson & Co., 1887. 36 p. O. pap. 25 c.

Hodder, F. H. References on Municipal Government in the United States. Ithaca, N. Y., Library Cornell Univ., 1888. 8 p. pap. 5 c.
A reference to books and articles on municipal government in the U. S., and in London, Berlin, Vienna and Paris.

Howe, W: W. City Government of New Orleans. Baltimore, Johns Hopkins Univ. series, 1889. 33 p. O. pap. 25 c.

James, Edmund J. Relation of the Modern Municipality to the Gas Supply. Baltimore, Amer. Economic Assoc., 1886. 76 p. O. pap. 75 c.
Argues that municipalities should retain functions, such as gas supply, which are necessarily monopolies.

Low, Seth. The Problem of City Government. Baltimore, Johns Hopkins Univ. series (Notes supplementary to Studies), 1889. pap. 5 c.

Mathews, Robert. Municipal Administration. Rochester, N. Y., R. Mathews, 1885. 16 p. O. pap.

Moses, Bernard. Establishment of Municipal Government in San Francisco. Baltimore, Johns Hopkins Univ. series, 1889. 83 p. O. pap. 50 c.

Municipal Reform. Cambridge, Civil Service Reform Assoc., 1884. 74 p. O.
The selection of Municipal officers, by T. H. Pease; Their appointment, by J: Prentiss; Their selection and tenure of office, by H: T. Terry. Three prize essays.

Relation of Modern Municipalities to Quasi-Public Works; a Report of the Committee on Public Finance to the Council of the American Economic Assoc. Baltimore, Amer. Econ. Assoc., 1888. 87 p. O. pap. 75 c.

Shaw, Albert. Municipal Government in England. Baltimore, Johns Hopkins Univ. series (Notes supplementary to Studies), 1889. pap. 5 c.

Snow, Marshall S. City Government of St. Louis. Baltimore, Johns Hopkins Univ. series, 1887. 40 p. O. pap. 25 c.

Birch, W. de G. Historical Charters and Constitutional Documents of the City of London. Lond., 1887. 48+338 p. O.

Firth, J: F. B. Municipal London. Lond., Longmans, 1876. 775 p. O. 25s.

Vine, J. R. S. English Municipal Institutions. Lond., Waterlow, 1879. 8+272 p. O. 10s. 6d.
Their growth and development from 1835 to 1879 statistically illustrated.

Block, MAURICE, *and* **Pontich**, H. de. **Administration de la ville de Paris et du departement de la Seine.** Paris, Guillaumin, 1884. 31 + 1032 p. O.

The Municipal Administration of Berlin, a communication by Hon. Andrew Dickson White, U. S. Minister to Germany, to the Secretary of State, forms part of a report of Mr. Coleman (2d Secretary of Legation at Berlin). "Foreign Relations." Washington, Gov. Pr. Office, 1881. p. 478–89.

A study of the organization and administration of municipal government of Vienna, by Hon. J: A. Kasson, U. S. Minister to Austria, is given in a communication to the Secretary of State. "Foreign Relations." Washington, Gov. Pr. Office, 1879. p. 64–79.

The Massachusetts Society for Promoting Good Citizenship, C. F. Crehore, M.D., Secretary, 87 Milk St., Boston, has published "Annotations on Works on Civil Government," 23 p. During the winter of 1888–9 it conducted a course of lectures on municipal government. Of the first seven, a syllabus is published; Hon. Mellen Chamberlain's lecture on Josiah Quincy, the Great Mayor, is published in full. During 1891 the Society plans to reprint from *Education* a series of articles on "Preparation for Citizenship in New England Colleges." Subscription, to the Society, $1 per year.

Municipal Ownership of Gas Works in the United States, by E: W. Bemis, will be published during 1891 by the American Economic Assoc., Baltimore.

Glasgow: a municipal study. Albert Shaw. *Century*, March, 1890.

The Government of American Cities. Andrew D. White. *Forum*, Dec., 1890.

How London is Governed. Albert Shaw. *Century*, Nov., 1890.

Municipal Finance. W: M. Ivins. *Harper's Magazine*, Oct., 1884.

Municipal Government. W: M. Ivins. *Political Science Quarterly*, June, 1887.

Municipal Government in Great Britain. Albert Shaw. *Political Science Quarterly*, June, 1889.

POLICE.

Horr, NELSON T., *and* **Bemis**, ALTON A. **Treatise on the power to enact, the passage, validity, and enforcement of municipal police ordinances.** Cincinnati, R. Clarke & Co., 1887. 312 p. O. shp. $4.

Full and authoritative.

Brayer, FELIX. **Manuel de police, administrative et judiciaire.** Paris, Bureau du *Journal des Commissaires de Police*, 1877. 3 + 423 p. D.

Held, OTTO. **Die bestehende Organisation und die erforderliche Reorganisation der preussichen Polizeiverwaltung.** Berlin, F. Ludhardt, 1886. 6 + 228 p. O.

INTERNATIONAL LAW, TREATIES, ARBITRATIONS, AND DIPLOMACY.

The best introductory works on international law are those of Woolsey and Maine. Field presents a capital summary of existing principles, and cites every eminent authority. Wheaton, Phillimore, Twiss, and Heffter are authoritative treatises for the advanced student, Wheaton especially. Kent's Commentary may follow in order. Bluntschli's is the best codification ever prepared,

Wheaton and Woolsey are the principal historians of international law. Martens is the chief compiler of treaties. Those of the United States are presented in an official volume, which should be accompanied in study by Wharton's excellent Digest. In diplomacy Schuyler's and K. Marten's works are the best.

Davis, G. B. **Outlines of International Law;** with an Account of its Origin and Sources, and of its Historical Development. N. Y., Harper, 1887. 469 p. D. $2.

An introductory text-book.

Field, D: DUDLEY. **Outlines of an International Code.** Book 1, On Peace. Book 2, On War. 2d ed. enl. N. Y., Baker, Voorhis & Co.; Lond., Trübner & Co., 1876. 3+45+712 p. O. shp. $6.50.

While this work is a project of law, it gives a concise statement of the principles of international law as now recognized by nations in their intercourse with each other. A full citation of treaties is presented, with ample notes on the leading authorities.

Gallaudet, E. M. **International Law.** New ed. N. Y., Holt, 1886. 20+321 p. D. $1.50.

Halleck, H. W. **International Law;** or, Rules Regulating the Intercourse of States in Peace or War. Phila., Lippincott, 1866. $2.50.

International American Conference. Plan of Arbitration for the Settlement of Disputes Between the American Republics. Report and Recommendations. Washington, Gov. Pr. Office, 1890. 6 p. O.

International American Conference. Report and Recommendations Concerning a Uniform Code of International Law. Washington, Gov. Pr. Office, 1890. 30 p. O.

Kent, JAMES. **Commentary on International Law.** Rev., with notes and cases, by J. T. Abdy. 2d ed. rev. Lond., G: Bell & Sons, 1877. 10s. 6d.

Includes: Naval Prize Act, 1864; Treaty of Washington and Geneva Award, 1871; Geneva Convention, 1864; Proclamation of Neutrality and Declaration as to Belligerents and Neutrals, 1877; Foreign Enlistment Act, 1870; and a tabulated list of the Russian and Turkish Treaties, 1699-1871.

Lyman, THEO. **Diplomacy of the United States.** Boston, Wells & Lilly, 1828. 2 v. 8°.

An important work. May be had in the chief public libraries.

Personal Instructions to diplomatic agents of the United States in foreign countries. (State Department), Washington, Gov. Pr. Office, 1885.

Pomeroy, J. N. **International Law in Time of Peace.** Ed. by Theo. D. Woolsey. Bost., Houghton, Mifflin & Co., 1886. 14+481 p. O. $5.

Lectures delivered in 1866-7; serves as a good introduction to the subject.

Schuyler, EUGENE. **American Diplomacy** and the Furtherance of Commerce. N. Y., Scribner, 1886. 469 p. O. $2.50.

Explains the workings of the Consular and Diplomatic Service.

Treaties and Conventions Between the United States and the Powers, 1776 to 1887. Washington, Gov. Pr. Office, 1889. 13+1334 p. O.

Contains notes, with reference to negotiations preceding the several treaties, to the executive, legislative, or judicial construction of them, and to the causes of some of them. A chronological list is given, and an analytical index.

Trescot, W. H. **Diplomacy of the Revolution,** an Historical Study. N. Y., Appleton, 1852.

Out of print. May be had in the larger public libraries.

INTERNATIONAL LAW, TREATIES, ETC.

Wharton, FRANCIS. **Digest of the International Law of the United States,** taken from documents issued by Presidents and Secretaries of State, from decisions of Federal Courts and Opinions of Attorneys-General. Senate misc. doc. no. 162, pts. 1-3. Washington, Gov. Pr. Office, 1886. 3 v.

Wheaton, H. Elements of International Law. 2d annotated edition by W: B. Lawrence. Bost., Little, Brown & Co.; Lond., Sampson Low, 1863. 2 v. 1095+47 p. O.

Wheaton, H. Elements of International Law. 8th ed. Ed. by R: H. Dana. Bost., 1866. 47+749 p. O.

Wheaton, H. Elements du droit international. 2 v. in 1. Leipzig, 1848.

Wheaton, H. History of the Law of Nations in Europe and America from the earliest times to the treaty of Washington, 1842. N. Y., 1845. 14+797 p. O.

Woolsey, THEODORE D. **Introduction to the Study of International Law.** 6th ed. N. Y., Scribner, 1891. $2.50.
Revised to date and enlarged by Theodore Salisbury Woolsey, Professor of International Law, Yale Univ. This work, specially designed as an aid in teaching and in historical studies, is the best introduction to the subject.

Amos, SHELDON. **Political and Legal Remedies for War.** N. Y., Harper, 1880. 2+364 p. O. $1.50.

Hosack, J: On the Rise and Growth of the Law of Nations from the Earliest Times to the Treaty of Utrecht. Lond., Murray, 1882. 12+394 p. O. 12s.

Levi, LEONE. **International Law, with Materials for a Code of International Law** International Scientific series, no. 60. N. Y., Appleton, 1888. 12+346 p. D. $1.50.
The chapters on treaties are very full.

Maine, *Sir* H: J. SUMNER. **International Law.** N. Y., Holt, 1888. 234 p. O. $2.75.
A series of twelve lectures introductory to the subject, characterized by the author's encyclopedic knowledge.

Phillimore, *Sir* ROBERT. **Commentaries upon International Law.** 2d ed. Lond., Butterworth, 1871-74. 4 v. O. 53s.
V. 4 treats of private international law.

Twiss, *Sir* TRAVERS. **Law of Nations Considered as Independent Political Communities.** Pt. 1, On the Rights and Duties of Nations in Time of Peace. 2d ed. Lond. and N. Y., Macmillan, 1875. 60+620 p. O. $3.75.

Westlake, J: Treatise on International Law, with principal reference to its practice in England. Lond., W: Maxwell & Son, 1880. 27+340 p. O. 15s.

Garden, GUILLAUME, *Comte* de. **Histoire générale des traités de paix,** et autres transactions principales entre tous les puissances de l'Europe, depuis la paix de Westphalie. Paris, 1848-59. 14 v.

Lefèvre, EMILE. **Réorganisation du consulat Français a l'étranger.** Bibliothèque du Cercle Parisien. Paris. E. Dentu, 1883. 160 p. Q.

Martens, G: F. v. **Cours diplomatique; ou, Tableau des relations extérieures des puissances de l'Europe tant entre elles qu'avec d'autres états dans les diverses parties du globe.** Berlin, 1801. 3 v. O.

Martens, G: F. v. **Précis du droit des gens modernes de l'Europe.** Augmenté des notes de Pinheiro-Ferreira, avec bibliographie pas Ch. Verge. 2me ed. aug. Paris, 1864.

Martens, G: F. v. **Recueil de traités des puissances et états de l'Europe, 1761-1808.** 2me ed. aug. Gottingue, 1817-35. 8 v. O.

Martens, G: F. v. **Nouveau recueil de traités des puissances et états de l'Europe, 1808-37.** Gottingue, 1817-41. 16 v. O.

Martens, G: F. v. **Nouveaux supplemens au recueil de traité des puissances et états 1761-1339.** Suivié d'un appendix par F: Murhard. Gottingue, 1837-42. 3 v. O.

Martens, G: F. v. **Nouveau recueil général de traités, 1840-73,** redigé par F: Murhard. Gottingue, 1843-75. 22 v. O.

Martens, G: F. v. **Nouveau recueil général de traités et autre actes relatif aux rapports de droits international.** Par C. Samwer et Jules Kopf. Gottingue, 1876. 14 v. O.

Martens, G: F. v. **Table générale du recueil des traités.** Gottingue, 1875-6. V. 1, Chronological. V. 2, Alphabetical.

Martens, K., *Freiherr* v. **Le guide diplomatique.** 5me éd. Refondue par F. H. Geffcken. Leipzig, 1866. 3 v. O.

Tetot, A. **Repertoire des traités de paix.** Paris, Amyot, 1866-73. 2 v. O.

Bluntschli, J. K. **Das moderne Völkerrecht der Civilisirten Staaten als Rechtsbuch dargestellt.** 3d ed. Nördlingen, C. H. Beck, 1878. 12+541 p. O.

—— *Same.* **Le droit international codifié.** Tr. par C. Lardy, et précéde d'une préface par E: Laboulaye. 3me ed. aug. Paris, Guillaumin, 1881. 8+590 p. O.

Ghillany, F. W., *ed.* **Diplomatisches Handbuch.** Nördlingen, C. H. Beck, 1855-68. 3 v. O.

Heffter, A. W. **Das Europäische Völkerrecht der Gegenwart auf den bisherigen Grundlagen.** 6te aufl. 12+523 p. O. Berlin, 1873.

—— *Same.* **Le droit international public de l'Europe.** Tr. par J. Bergson. Berlin, 1866. 12+507 p. O.

Holtzendorff, FRANZ v. **Handbuch des Völkerrechts.** Hamburg, J. F. Richter. 1886-7. 3 v. 523, 671, 797 p. 68 marks.
A valuable contribution to the literature of international jurisprudence.

Kamarowsky, L., *Count.* **Le tribunal international.** Tr. par Serge de Westman et précédé d'une introd. par J. Lacointa. Bibliothèque internationale et diplomatique, no. 21. Paris, G. Pedone-Lauriel, 1887. 4+34+528 p. O.

Grotius, HUGO. **De Jure Belli et Pacis.** Lond. and N. Y., Macmillan, 1875. 3 v. O. $3.50.
With the notes of Barbeyrac and others; accompanied by an abridged translation of the text by W: Whewell, D.D. The translation separate, 1 v., $1.75. Grotius is the father of the science of international law, but his work is now referred to rather than read.

The State Department, Washington, published in 1881 a catalogue of the works in its library relating to the law of nations and diplomacy.

The Assoc. for the Reform and the Codification of the Law of Nations, 33 Chancery Lane, London, publishes an annual report (no. 1, 1873).

In the interests of peace and international arbitration are issued the *Peacemaker*, Universal Peace Union, 125 N. 4th St., Philadelphia, monthly, $1 per year ; and the *American Advocate of Peace and Arbitration*, Am. Peace Society, 1 Somerset St., Boston, bi-monthly, $1 per year.

In the same interests are published *The Arbitrator*, International Arbitration League, 23 Bedford St., Strand, London, monthly, 1s. 6d. per year ; and *Concord*, International Arbitration and Peace Association, 40 Outer Temple, Strand, London, bi weekly, 2s. 6d. per year.

The Peace Society of London issues many tracts and pamphlets, a catalogue of which may be had from Dyer Bros., 31 Paternoster Square, London.

L'Institut de Droit International of Brussels (C. Muquardt, Brussels) publishes an annual report (no. 1, 1874).

Commercial Diplomacy is treated by J. E. Thorold Rogers in his " Cobden and Modern Political Opinion," 1873, 302-42 p.

D: Dudley Field, in "Speeches, Arguments, and Miscellaneous Papers" (N. Y., Appleton, 1884, 3 v.), treats of an International Code, v. 1, p. 384-475.

International Law, by Prof. T. W. Dwight, is in preparation for the series in Systematic Political Science, by the Univ. Faculty of Pol. Science, Columbia College, N. Y.

STATISTICS AND STATISTICAL SCIENCE.

Dewey, D. R. Elementary Notes on Graphic Statistics. Bost., 1888. 12 p. O.

Dewey, D. R. The Study of Statistics. Baltimore, Am. Economic Assoc., 1889. 18 p. O. pap. 75 c.
> One of three papers in no. 5, v. 4, Assoc.'s series.

Pidgin, C. F. Practical Statistics: a handbook for the use of the statistician at work, students in colleges and academies, census enumerators and others. Boston, W. E. Smythe Co., 1888. 201 p. O. $1.50.
> A practical treatise by the chief clerk of the Massachusetts Bureau of Statistics of Labor well worthy the perusal of every student of political economy. It shows the limits of statistical inquiry, and how within those limits information can be best gathered and digested.

Smith, RICHMOND MAYO. Statistics and Economics. Baltimore, American Economic Assoc., 1888. 127 p. O. pap. 75 c.
> An outline of statistical science, with special reference to the use of statistics in political economy and social science.

Wright, CARROLL D. Statistics in Colleges. Baltimore, Am. Economic Assoc., 1888. 28 p. O. pap. 75 c.
> One of three papers in no. 1, v. 3, Assoc.'s series.

Farr, W: Vital Statistics. Lond., Sanitary Institute, 1885. 30s.

Newsholme, ARTHUR, *M.D.* Elements of Vital Statistics. Lond., Swan Sonnenschein, 1889. 326 p. D.
> A sterling digest of English vital statistics, their methods and interpretation.

Block, MAURICE. Traité theorique et pratique de statistique. 2me ed. Paris, Guillaumin, 1886. 8+577 p. O.

Levasseur, E. La population française. Paris, 1890.

Frankenstein, KUNO. Zur Organisation der amtlichen Lohnstatistik im Deutschen Reiche. Leipzig, Duncker & Humblot, 1889. 90 p. O.

Haushofer, MAX. Lehr- und Handbuch der Statistik. 2d ed. Vienna, Braumüller, 1882. 520 p. O.

Mayr, GEORG. Die Gesetzmässigkeit im Gesellschaftsleben; statistische Studien. Munich, R. Oldenbourg, 1877.

Meitzen, F. E. A. Geschichte, Theorie und Technik der Statistik. Berlin, W: Hertz, 1886. 214 p. O.

—— *Same*, in two v., with an introd. by Dr. Roland P. Falkner. V. 1, History of Statistics. Phila., Am. Academy of Pol. and Social Science, 1891. 90 p. O. $1.25. V. 2, Theory and Technique of Statistics. Phila., Am. Aademy of Pol. and Social Science, 1891. 125 p. O. $1.50.

Westergaard, H. Theorie der Statistik. Jena, G. Fisher, 1890. 286 p. O.

Gabaglio, ANTONIO. Teoria generale della statistica. 2d ed. Milano, 1888. 2 v. V. 1, Storica. V. 2, Filosofica e tecnica.

References to statistical publications will be found under other headings, as, for example, under Capital and Labor.

The American Statistical Association, Boston, Mass., issues four pamphlets a year treating themes of current statistical interest, and presenting the bibliography of statistical science. Annual subscription, $2. D. R. Dewey, Secretary and Librarian, Institute of Technology, Boston.

The American Almanac, A. R. Spofford, Librarian of Congress, editor, v. 1, 1867, gives a record of facts, statistical, financial, and political, compiled from official sources. N. Y., Am. News Co., cl. $1.50; cheap ed. pap. 25 c.

The *Tribune* Almanac, N. Y., and the *World* Almanac, N. Y., each 25 c., give capital statistical tables, corrected to the date of issue.

Canada's Annual Statistical Abstract and Record, published by the Department of Agriculture, Ottawa, gives a summary of the Constitution and Government of the Dominion, with tables of population, vital statistics, trade, agriculture, mineral and fishery products, Dominion lands, railways, canals, banks, insurance, etc.

The Statistical Society of London issues an annual *Journal*, no. 1, 1839; and published a Jubilee volume, 1886.

The Constitutional Year-Book, issued annually, v. 1, 1885, by the Conservative Central Office, St. Stephen's Chambers, Westminster, S. W., London, gives a summary of parliamentary legislation, of noteworthy political events, with statistics of revenue, taxation, national debt, agriculture, commerce, etc., for Great Britain. 1s.

The Statesman's Year Book is a most valuable statistical and historical annual of the States of the civilized world. [Lond. and N. Y., Macmillan, v. 1, 1864, $3.]

This work is valuable not only for its facts about all countries, but especially for the bibliographies appended for each country, not easily to be found elsewhere. Under the caption "United States" it contains a fairly good list of the more important Government publications.

The Statistical Abstract for the United Kingdom, v. 1, 1852, Lond., Eyre & Spottiswoode, is most important.

Each volume contains statistics summarized for the 15 years then past.

The Statistical Abstract for the Colonial and other Possessions of the United Kingdom, v. 1, 1862, is published by Eyre & Spottiswoode, Lond., 1s.

Whitaker's Almanac contains valuable statistics. Lond., 12 Warwick Lane, Paternoster Row, 1s.

L'Institut International de Statistique issues a bulletin in the principal languages of Europe. V. 1, Rome, 1887.

La Société de Statistique de Paris issues important publications; especially valuable is the volume issued on its 25th anniversary, 1886.

The Almanach de Gotha (no. 1, 1763), German and French editions (Gotha, Saxony, Justus Perthes, $2.30), contains valuable statistics of all countries.

American Labor Statistics. R. M. Smith. *Political Science Quarterly*, March, 1886.

U. S. GOVERNMENT PUBLICATIONS.

The U. S. Government issues numerous valuable statistical and descriptive publications, through its several departments and bureaus. There is a (chronological) Catalogue, Mar., 1881 (46th Cong.), containing 100,000 titles, with poor subject-index, comp. by B: Perley Poore, which is supplemented to 1890 by lists arranged by departments in American Catalogue, 1876-84, 1884-90, and by Hickcox's Monthly List of Government Publications ($5 per year, 906 M St., Washington). Some can be procured *gratis* or at fixed prices from the departments, others through Congressmen; W. H Lowdermilk & Co. and other Washington dealers keep many in stock; they can be consulted at those public libraries which are government depositories.

CONGRESS prints its proceedings in full in the *Congressional Record*, daily; it issues also a useful one-volume Abridgment of President's Message and reports of departments, each session; also, each session, the *Senate Journal*, *Senate* [Executive] *Documents*, *Senate Miscellaneous Documents*, and *Senate Reports* [of Committees], and *House Journal*, *House Executive Documents* (embracing, in about thirty volumes per session department and bureau reports in full), *House Miscellaneous Documents*, and *House Reports of Committees*.

The annual Statistical Abstract (Treas. Dept., Bur. of Statistics), issued since 1878, summarizes statistics of all departments, and is extremely valuable.

The AGRICULTURAL DEPARTMENT, particularly through its *Division of Forestry* and *Division of Statistics*, issues a number of annual and other reports, the Monthly Report of the latter on crops, transportation rates, etc., being especially useful.

The INTERIOR DEPARTMENT issues the Official Register of the U. S. (biennial) in two volumes, giving list of officers in all departments; the Census volumes (to be applied for through Congressmen, to whom certain quantities are allotted); valuable special reports and Circulars of Information on Education, through its *Bureau of Education*; a most valuable annual report on "Mineral Resources of the United States" (for 1883-4, 60 c.; 1885, 40 c.; 1886, 1887 and 1888, 50 c. each), through its *Geological Survey*, and full information as to *Indian Affairs*, *Patents*, and *Pensions*, through *Offices* having them respectively in charge.

The NAVY DEPARTMENT issues valuable maps and charts through the several subdivisions of its *Bureau of Navigation*, particularly the *Hydrographic Office*.

The POST-OFFICE DEPARTMENT issues a statistical annual report, also post-route maps of the whole country.

The STATE DEPARTMENT issues the Statutes at-large of the U. S., in paper for each session, in sheep for each Congress, at prices given in its circular. Also, the U. S. Consular Reports (v. 1, 1880) in monthly numbers, with extra issues numbered as halves, binding in stated volumes, with Indexes to Nos. 1-59 (v. 1-17, 1880-85) and Nos. 60-111 (v. 18-31, 1886-89), for particulars of which see American Catalogue, 1876-84, 1884-90; also, valuable special reports from our Consuls abroad, as on Labor in Foreign Countries.

The TREASURY DEPARTMENT issues the Finance Report (annual), also Reports on Collection of Duties, from the Secretary of the Treasury, Digests of Appropriations (annual), Decisions of the Treasury Department on Tariff, etc. (monthly), and Statements of U. S. Debt (monthly broadside); the official Tariff; Report on Internal Revenue (annual), by the *Commissioner of Internal Revenue;* Report on Foreign Commerce, Immigration, and Tonnage (annual), Report on Internal Commerce (annual), also annual, quarterly, and monthly statements of imports, exports, etc., also special reports or tables on Wool, Sugar, Liquor, Prices, etc., from its *Bureau of Statistics;* also, Report on Production of Precious Metals (annual), by the *Director of the Mint,* and the valuable charts, etc., of the *Coast Survey.*

The WAR DEPARTMENT, besides its annual reports, etc., includes the valuable work of the *Signal Service* and other offices.

The CIVIL SERVICE COMMISSION issues the Civil Service laws, rules and regulations, and an annual report.

The DEPARTMENT OF LABOR prints annual reports [first, 1885], each embodying an exhaustive treatment of a special subject, as in 1887, "Strikes and Lockouts, 1881-86."

The INTERSTATE COMMERCE COMMISSION issues a valuable annual report, the laws, decisions, etc.

The SMITHSONIAN INSTITUTION, including the *U. S. National Museum*, the NATIONAL ACADEMY OF SCIENCES, and other semi-governmental bodies, issue valuable scientific publications.

ADDENDA.

Dunbar, C: F. Chapters on the Theory and History of Banking. N. Y., Putnam, 1891. 6+199 p. D. $1.

Gunton, G: Principles of Social Economics. N. Y., Putnam, 1891. 23+447 p. D. $1.75.

Pt. 1, Principles of Social Progress. 2, Economic Production. 3, Economic Distribution. 4, Practical Statesmanship.

Knox, J: J. The Coinage Act of 1873 and the Silver Question. N. Y., J: J. Knox, Nat. Bank of the Republic, 1891. pap. *gratis.*

An interview before the Committee on Coinage of the House of Representatives, Feb. 20, 1891.

Knox, J: J. Free Silver Coinage. N. Y., J: J. Knox, Nat. Bank of the Republic, 1891. 7 p. D. pap. *gratis.*

An address to the Chamber of Commerce, N. Y., Jan. 12, 1891. With "Three Pecks to a Bushel," from the *Journal of Commerce*, N. Y.

Knox, J: J. **The Surplus and the Public Debt.** N. Y., J: J. Knox, Nat. Bank of the Republic, 1887. pap. *gratis.*
An address before the American Bankers' Assoc., Oct. 12, 1887.

Laws Relating to Elections, the Qualification and Registration of Voters, etc. Bost., Wright & Potter Printing Co., 1890. pap. O.
An official compilation of the Massachusetts election laws. Should be in the hands of every student of the subject.

Northam, H: C. **Manual of Civil Government for Common Schools.** 90th ed. Syracuse, N. Y., C. W. Bardeen, 1891. 213 p. S. 75 c.
A thoroughly practical manual. Beginning with the School District, it gives the names, manner of election, and duties of officers from the school trustee to the President of the United States. Specially descriptive of New York, and extensively used in the public instruction of the State.

Palm, A. J. **Capital Punishment,** with a chapter on War. Questions of the Day series, no. 66. N. Y., Putnam, 1891. 8+241 p. $1.25.

Perry, A. L. **Principles of Political Economy.** N. Y., Scribner, 1891. 15+599 p. D. $2.

Sherman, JOHN. **Coin and Currency.** N. Y., Evening Post Pub. Co., 1891. 45 p. D. 2 c.
Speech on the Silver Question in U. S. Senate, Jan. 13, 1891.

Tyler, LYON G. **Parties and Patronage.** Questions of the Day series, no. 67. N. Y., Putnam, 1891. 160 p. D. $1.
By the President of William and Mary College.

Mackay, T:, *ed*. **Plea for Liberty.** With an introd. by Herbert Spencer. N. Y., Appleton, 1891. 22+414 p. O. $2.25.
Contents: Impracticability of Socialism, E: S. Robertson; Limits of Liberty, W. Donisthorpe; Liberty for Labor, G: Howell; State Socialism in the Antipodes, C: Fairfield; Discontentment of the Working-Classes, E. Vincent; Investment, T: Mackay; Free Education, Rev. B. H. Alford; Housing Working-Classes and Poor, A. Raffalovich; Evils of State Trading as Illustrated by the Post-Office, F. Millar; Free Libraries, M. D. O'Brien; The State and Electrical Distribution, F. W. B. Gordon; True Line of Deliverance, Auberon Herbert.

Brentano, L. **Relation of Labor to the Law of To-Day.** Tr. with an introd. by Porter Sherman. N. Y., Putnam, 1891. 300 p. D. $1.75.

Rabbeno, UGO. **Le societa cooperative di produzione.** Milano, Fratelli Dumolard, 1889. 531 p. O.
The best existing treatise on coöperative production.

The *Economic Journal* (no. 1, March, 1891) is published quarterly by the British Economic Association, London. The Association will also issue monographs and translations, F. Y. Edgeworth, editor and secretary, 5 Mount Vernon, Hampstead, N. W. Annual subscription, 21s.

The *Economic Review* (no. 1, Jan., 1891) is published quarterly for the Oxford University Branch Christian Social Union, Lond., Perceval & Co. No. 1 contains " Progress of Socialism in the United States," by Rev. M. Kaufmann.

C: Gide's " Political Economy," tr. by E. P. Jacobsen, with introd. by James Bonar, will be published May 1, 1891, by D. C. Heath & Co., Boston.

Political Economy in Italy. Ugo Rabbeno. *Political Science Quarterly,* June, 1891.

COURSES OF READING.

ELEMENTARY OR YOUTHS' SERIES.

Nordhoff, C: Politics for Young Americans	$0 75
Macy, Jesse. Our Government	1 00
Johnston, Alex. History of American Politics	80
Sterne, Simon. Constitutional History of the United States	1 25
Bowker, R: R. Economics for the People	75
	$4 55

The 5 vols., $4.00.

INTERMEDIATE OR CITIZENS' SERIES.

Cossa, L. Taxation, annotated by Horace White	$1 00
Jevons, W: S. Money and the Mechanism of Exchange	1 75
Laughlin, J. L. Bimetallism	2 25
Walker, F. A. Political Economy, briefer course	1 20
Wells, D: A. Recent Economic Changes	2 00
	$8 20

The 5 vols., $7.50.

ADVANCED OR STUDENTS' SERIES.

Bryce, James. American Commonwealth	$6 00
Constitutional History of the United States, as seen in the development of Law. Lectures by Hon. T: M. Cooley and others	2 00
Graham, W: Socialism, New and Old	1 75
Mill, J: S. Political Economy, abridged and annotated by J. L. Laughlin	3 50
Walker, F. A. Money	4 00
	$17 25

The 5 vols., $15.50.

These series are for sale by G: P. Putnam's Sons, 27 West 23d Street, New York, agents for the Society. Will be sent to any address in the United States on receipt of price, and may be ordered through booksellers generally.

COURSES IN ECONOMIC AND POLITICAL SCIENCE, AMERICAN COLLEGES AND UNIVERSITIES.

AMHERST COLLEGE, AMHERST, MASS.

Department of History and Political Science, 1890-91, includes:

History.—The first course extends through Junior year. It begins with an introductory outline of ancient history, in which the aim is acquaintance with the contributions of each period and people to general civilization. In the fuller study of mediæval and modern history which follows the same aim is pursued. The political development of England and the United States receives particular attention. The second course extends through the first and second terms of Senior year. Its theme is the political and constitutional history of the United States. In each course the means of instruction are text-books, lectures, regular and frequent examinations, abstracts and essays upon topics assigned each student.

Political Economy.—The course extends through Senior year. The first term is devoted to theoretical political economy; the second to the Labor Question, Socialism, and the relations of the state to transportation; the third to Finance, the Principles of Taxation, Public Credit, and Tariffs.

International Law.—This study is one of the electives of the third term of Senior year. The methods of instruction in political economy and international law are like those in history.

Annual tuition fee, full college course, $110.
No scholarships nor prizes in department above mentioned.

BROWN UNIVERSITY, PROVIDENCE, R. I.

Department of History and Political Science, 1890-91, includes:

(4) *History.*—Political and Constitutional History of European and American States during recent years. 3 hrs., first half-year, Seniors, Prof. JAMESON.
(5) History of International Law during recent years. 3 hrs., second half-year, Seniors, Prof. JAMESON.
And four Honor Courses.
(1) *Political Economy.*—Elementary Course. 3 hrs., first half-year, Seniors, Mr. FISHER.
(2) Advanced Course. 3 hrs., second half-year, Seniors, Mr. FISHER.
And Honor Courses.
Tuition fee, $100.
The University has about one hundred scholarships, details concerning which can be learned from the Registrar.

BRYN MAWR COLLEGE, BRYN MAWR, PA. (For Women.)

Programme for 1891 includes:

POLITICAL SCIENCE: MINOR COURSE.

First Semester.—Political Economy.
Second Semester.—Political Institutions.

MAJOR COURSE.

First Semester.—Advanced Political Economy, Administration.
Second Semester.—International Law, and in alternate years Political Theories.

GRADUATE COURSE INCLUDES:

Modern Theories of Sociology.
FRANKLIN H. GIDDINGS, Associate in Political Science.
Tuition irrespective of number courses attended, $100 a year.
Five fellowships are awarded annually, none, however, in foregoing studies. They entitle the holder to free tuition, a furnished room in the college buildings, and $350 yearly.

COLUMBIA COLLEGE, NEW YORK CITY.

University Faculty of Political Science, 1890-91, includes:

(1) *History.*—Mediæval History. 2 hours a week, 1st session, Prof. DUNNING.
(2) Modern History to 1815. 2 hours a week, 2d session, Prof. GOODNOW.

(3) Modern History since 1815. 2 hours a week, 1st session, Prof. MUNROE SMITH.
(4) Political and Constitutional History of Europe. 4 hours a week, 1st session, Prof. BURGESS.
(5) Political and Constitutional History of England to 1688. 2 hours a week, 1st session, Prof. OSGOOD.
(6) Political and Constitutional History of England since 1688. 2 hours a week, 2d session, Prof. OSGOOD.
(7) Political and Constitutional History of the United States. 4 hours a week, 2d session, Prof. BURGESS.
(8) History of New York State. 2 hours a week, 2d session, Mr. WHITRIDGE.
(9) History of the Relations Between England and Ireland. 1 hour through the year, Prof. DUNNING.
(10) Historical and Political Geography. 1 hour through the year, Prof. GOODNOW.
(11) Seminarium in European History. 2 hours through the year, Prof. OSGOOD.
(12) Seminarium in American History. 2 hours through the year, Prof. BURGESS.

(1) *Political Economy.*—Elements of Political Economy. 2 hours a week, 2d session, Prof. OSGOOD.
(2) Historical and Practical Political Economy. 3 hours per week through the year, Prof. R. M. SMITH.
(3) History of Economic Theories. 2 hours through the year, Prof. SELIGMAN.
(4) Socialism and Communism. 2 hours per week through the year, Prof. R. M. SMITH.
(5) Science of Finance. 2 hours per week through the year, Prof. SELIGMAN.
(6) Financial History of the United States. 2 hours per week through the year, Prof. SELIGMAN.
(7) Tariff History of the United States. 2 hours per week, 2d session, Prof. SELIGMAN.
(8) State and Local Taxation. 1 hour per week through the year, Dr. SPAHR.
(9) Statistics, Methods, and Results. 2 hours per week through the year, Prof. R. M. SMITH.
(10) Railroad Problems. 2 hours per week through the year, Prof. SELIGMAN.
(11) Ethnology. 2 hours per week through the year, Prof. R. M. SMITH.
(12) Seminarium in Political Economy. 2 hours per week through the year, Profs. R. M. SMITH and SELIGMAN.
(13) Seminarium in Finance. 2 hours per week through the year, Prof. SELIGMAN.
(14) Seminarium in Social Science and Statistics. 2 hours per week through the year, Prof. R. M. SMITH.

(1) *Constitutional and Administrative Law.*—Comparative Constitutional Law of Europe and the United States. 3 hours per week, Prof. BURGESS.
(2) Comparative Constitutional Law of the Commonwealths of the United States. 2 hours per week, 2d session, Dr. BERNHEIM.
(3) Administrative Organization and the Civil Service of Europe and the United States. 3 hours per week, 1st session, Prof. GOODNOW.
(4) Administrative Action: Police Power, Education, Public Charity, Transportation, etc. 3 hours a week, 2d session, Prof. GOODNOW.
(5) Local Government. 2 hours a week, 1st session, Prof. GOODNOW.
(6) Municipal Government. 2 hours a week, 2d session, Prof. GOODNOW.
(7) Law of Taxation. 1 hour through the year, Prof. GOODNOW.
(8) City and State Politics. 1 hour per week through the year, Dr. BERNHEIM.
(9) Seminarium in Constitutional Law. 2 hours a week through the year, Prof. BURGESS.
(10) Seminarium in Administrative Law. 2 hours a week through the year, Prof. GOODNOW.

(1) *Diplomacy and International Law.*—General History of Diplomacy. 2 hours per week, 1st session, Prof. BURGESS.
(2) Diplomatic History of the United States. 2 hours per week, 2d session, Dr. BANCROFT.
(3) Principles of International Law. 2 hours per week, 2d session, Prof. BURGESS.
(4) Seminarium in International Law. 2 hours per week through the year, Prof. BURGESS and Dr. BANCROFT.

(1) *Legal History and Comparative Jurisprudence.*—History of European Law to Justinian. 2 hours a week, 1st session, Prof. MUNROE SMITH.
(2) History of European Law from Justinian to the present day. 2 hours a week, 2d session, Prof. MUNROE SMITH.
(3) Comparative Jurisprudence. 2 hours a week through the year, Prof. MUNROE SMITH.
(4) International Private Law. 1 hour per week through the year. Prof. MUNROE SMITH.
(5) Seminarium in Comparative Legislation. 2 hours a week through the year, Prof. MUNROE SMITH.

(1) *Political Philosophy.*—History of Political Theories, Ancient and Mediæval. 3 hours a week, 1st session, Prof. DUNNING.

COURSES IN ECONOMIC AND POLITICAL SCIENCE. 131

(2) History of Modern Political Theories. 3 hours a week, 2d session, Prof. DUNNING.
(3) Seminarium in Political Theories of the 19th Century. 2 hours per week through the year, Prof. DUNNING.
Some of the foregoing courses are given only in alternate years. During 1891-92 several new courses will be offered in History and in Sociology.
The course of study covers three years. The degree of A.B. or Ph.B. is conferred at the end of the first year, A.M. at the end of the second, and Ph.D. at the end of the third.
Tuition fee $150 a year, reducible on application to $100. Tuition fee for special courses, $10 for each one-hour course. Twenty-four University Fellowships of $500 each with free tuition, designed to foster original research, are awarded to advanced students in the University. A proportionate number are allotted to the Faculty of Political Science. Four additional fellowships of $250 each, with free tuition, are awarded annually to advanced students of Political Science. Three prize lectureships of $500 each for three years are awarded to graduates in Political Science.
For further information address the Registrar.

CORNELL UNIVERSITY, ITHACA, N. Y.

Department of History and Political Science, 1890-91, includes:

(4) *History.*—Political and Social History of Europe During the Middle Ages. 1 hr. thrice a week, Asst. Prof. BURR.
(5) Political and Social History of Europe from the Renaissance to the French Revolution. 1 hr. thrice a week, Asst. Prof. BURR.
(6) Political and Social History of England from the Saxon Invasion to the Close of the Napoleonic Wars. 1 hr. thrice a week, Asst. Prof. BURR.
(7) Political, Social, and Constitutional History of Europe from Beginning of French Revolution of 1789 to the Franco-German War of 1870. 1 hr. thrice a week. Several lectures in this course from ex-Pres. WHITE and Pres. ADAMS.
(12) American Constitutional History and American Constitutional Law. 1 hr. thrice a week, Prof. TYLER.
(13) American Historical Seminary for Seniors and Graduates, and for Juniors and Seniors. The original investigation of subjects in American Constitutional History. 2 hrs. a week, Prof. TYLER.
(14) History of Institutions. Fall term: General principles of political organization. Winter term: Growth of the English Constitution. Spring term: Methods of municipal administration. 1 hr. thrice a week, Prof. TUTTLE.
(15) International Law and History of Diplomacy. 1 hr. twice a week, Prof. TUTTLE.
(16) Literature of Political Science. 1 hr. a week, Prof. TUTTLE.
(17) General Seminary. Study, from the sources, of obscure political and historical questions. 2 hrs. a week, Prof. TUTTLE.
(19) *Political Economy.*—Elementary course. Principles of Political Economy. Banking. Financial Legislation of the United States. 1 hr. thrice a week, Prof. LAUGHLIN.
(20) Advanced Course. Discussion of economic writers and systems. Investigation of current economic topics: Bimetallism, Shipping, Railway Transportation. 1 hr. twice a week, Prof. LAUGHLIN.
(21) History of Tariff Legislation of the United States. 1 hr. a week, Prof. LAUGHLIN.
(22) Economic seminary. 1½ hrs. a week, Prof. LAUGHLIN.
(26) *Social Science*, including the History and Management of Charitable and Penal Institutions. 1 hr. a week, Prof. COLLIN.
Tuition fee, $125 a year.
Fellowships, eight in number, yielding $400 for one year, or in cases of remarkable merit for two years, are offered for high proficiency in advanced study, without special reference to foregoing departments.

HARVARD UNIVERSITY, CAMBRIDGE, MASS.

Department of Political Economy, 1890-91, includes:

PRIMARILY FOR UNDERGRADUATES.

(1) *First half-year:* Mill's Principles of Political Economy. *Second half-year:* Division A (Theoretical)—Mill's Principles of Political Economy. Cairnes' Leading Principles of Political Economy. Division B (Descriptive)—Money, Finance, Railroads; Social Questions; Laughlin's History of Bimetallism. Dunbar's Chapters on Banking. Hadley's Railroad Transportation. Lectures. 1 hr. thrice a week, Asst. Prof. TAUSSIG, assisted by Mr. COLE.
All students in Course 1 will have the same work during the first half-year, but will be

required in January to make their election between Divisions A and B for the second half-year. The work in Division A is required for admission to Course 2.

(4) Economic History of Europe and America since the Seven Years' War. Lectures and written work. 1 hr. thrice a week, Prof. DUNBAR, assisted by Mr. COLE.

COURSES FOR GRADUATES AND UNDERGRADUATES.

(2) History of Economic Theory. Examination of Selections from Leading Writers. Socialism. 1 hr. thrice a week, Asst. Prof. TAUSSIG and Mr. BROOKS.

(3) Investigation and Discussion of Practical Economic Questions. 1 hr. twice a week (first half-year), counting as a half course, Mr. BROOKS.

(6) History of Tariff Legislation in the United States. Half course. 1 hr. thrice a week (second half-year). Asst. Prof. TAUSSIG.

(8) History of Financial Legislation in the United States. 1 hr. twice a week (second half-year), counting as a half-course, Prof. DUNBAR.

(7) Public Finance and Banking. Leroy-Beaulieu's Science des Finances. 1 hr. twice a week, Prof. DUNBAR.

(9) Railway Transportation. 1 hr. twice a week (second half-year), counting as a half-course, Asst. Prof. TAUSSIG.

PRIMARILY FOR GRADUATES.

(20) *Courses of Research.*—Advanced Study and Research. Prof. DUNBAR and Asst. Prof. TAUSSIG.

Department of History, 1890–91, includes among Courses for Undergraduates :

(2) Constitutional Government (elementary course). Half course. 1 hr. thrice a week (first half-year), Prof. MACVANE.

(9) Constitutional History of England to the Sixteenth Century. 1 hr. thrice a week, Dr. GROSS.

(13) Constitutional and Political History of the United States (1783-1861). 1 hr. thrice a week, Asst. Prof. HART.

(15) Elements of International Law. History of Treaties. 1 hr. thrice a week, Dr. SNOW.

(22) Constitutional History of England to the Tudor Period, with attention to the sources. Dr. GROSS.

(25) English Constitutional History from the Tudor Period to the Accession of George I. Mr. BENDELARI.

(26) History of American Institutions to 1783. Asst. Prof. CHANNING.

(27) Constitutional Development of the United States. Discussion of Constitutional principles in connection with historical questions. Asst. Prof. HART.

(29) Constitutional History of England since the Accession of George I. Second half-year. Prof. MACVANE and Asst. Prof. CHANNING.

(30) Federal Government: historical and comparative. 1 hr. thrice a week (first half-year). Asst. Prof. HART.

(31) Leading Principles of Constitutional Law : selected cases, American and English. 1 hr. thrice a week (second half-year), Prof. MACVANE.

(32) The Historical Development of International Law. Dr. SNOW.

And among Courses of Research :

(20*b*) The History of Local Government During the Middle Ages, especially in Great Britain: Seminary. Dr. GROSS.

(20*c*) English History in the Period of the Long Parliament: Seminary. Mr. BENDELARI.

The full annual tuition fee of a graduate student is $150. If a student has a degree in Arts, Letters, or Science, he enters the Graduate School, and finds any Courses in Political Science open to him which there is *prima facie* reason to suppose him prepared to take. If he has no degree he must apply for admission as a Special Student. Good cases are always favorably acted upon. The tuition fees of special students are: For any full elective course, $45; for a half course, $25 a year.

Among Fellowships are : One having income $450, for the study of Political Economy; another, income $500, for the study of Social Science ; another, income $450, for the study of Ethics in its relation to Jurisprudence or to Sociology ; another, income $450, assigned to students of Constitutional or International Law.

JOHNS HOPKINS UNIVERSITY, BALTIMORE, MD.

Department of History and Politics, 1890-91, includes:

GRADUATE AND ADVANCED COURSES.

(1) The Seminary of History and Politics for original investigation in American Institutional, educational, economic, and social history. Two hours weekly through the year, Dr. HERBERT B. ADAMS.

(2) Early History of Institutions and Greek Politics. Two hours weekly, first half year, Dr. HERBERT B. ADAMS.

(3) History of Prussia, devoting particular attention to the economic, administrative, and educational reforms instituted by Baron vom Stein. HERBERT B. ADAMS.

(4) Lectures on Historical and Comparative Jurisprudence. Two hours weekly, through the year, Mr. EMMOTT.

(5) Finance and Taxation, giving special attention to taxation in American states and cities, and reviewing the tariff legislation of the United States. Two hours weekly, through the year, Dr. R: T. ELY.

(6) Economic Conference. Three out of four of these treat Adam Smith and his English and Scotch predecessors. The fourth is devoted to recent economic periodical literature. One evening each week, Dr. R: T. ELY.

(7) Dr. WOODROW WILSON gives twenty-five lectures upon Administration, beginning a new three-year series. The lectures of 1891 cover general questions of Public Law as connected with Administration, and examine the question of a professional civil service.

(8) Mr. J. M. VINCENT lectures on courses of history and science of historical investigation.

(9) Dr. C. L. SMITH lectures on social science.

UNDERGRADUATE COURSES.

(1) Greek and Roman History. Three hours weekly, from January until June.

(2) Outlines of European History (substitute for Course 1). Three hours weekly, from January until June, with Dr. C. L. SMITH.

(3) History, Minor course: Herodotus and Thucydides, in translation. Weekly through the year, with a classical instructor.

(4) History, Minor course: Livy and Tacitus, in the original. Four times weekly, with classical instructors.

(5) History, Major course: Church History; Mediæval and Modern Europe. Daily through the year, with Dr. ADAMS and Dr. C. L. SMITH.

(6) Political Science, Minor course: Introduction to Political Economy. Daily through the year, with Dr. ELY.

(7) Political Science, Major course: International Law and Diplomatic History; English and American Constitutional History. Daily, with Dr. ADAMS and Mr. EMMOTT.

Fee for tuition, Full University Course, $125 a year. Special students, not candidates for a degree, can follow certain courses, not exceeding five lectures weekly (of which a list may be seen in Treasurer's office), on payment of $50 a year.

Twenty Fellowships, each yielding $500, but not exempting holder from charges for tuition, are annually awarded in the University. These are bestowed almost exclusively on young men desirous of becoming teachers of science and literature, or who propose to devote their lives to special branches of learning. There are also twenty scholarships of $200 each annually; and in addition, scholarships for candidates from Maryland, Virginia, North Carolina, and the District of Columbia, details concerning which are given in the University Register.

INDIANA UNIVERSITY, BLOOMINGTON, IND.

Department of History, Economics and Social Science, 1890-91, includes:

HISTORY.—PROF. EARL BARNES.

English Constitution and its History. 1st and 2d terms, daily.
History of the Constitution of the United States, 1774-1789. 1st term, daily.
American Political History, 1789-1890. Politics and Administration. 2d term, daily.

ECONOMICS AND SOCIAL SCIENCE.—PROF. J. W. JENKS.

Political Economy. 3 times a week, 1st and 2d terms.
Politics, elementary. Twice a week, 1st and 2d terms.
History of Political Economy. 5 times a week, 3d term.
Introduction to Sociology. 3 times a week, 1st term.

134 *COURSES IN ECONOMIC AND POLITICAL SCIENCE.*

Introductory Course in Statistics. Twice a week, 1st term.
Social Problems. 5 times a week, 2d term.
History of Political Ideas. 5 times a week, 3d term.
Comparative Politics. Daily, 1st term.
Finance. 3 times a week, 2d and 3d terms.
Economic Seminary, for advanced students. Once a week, two-hour sessions.
Tuition free. A silver medal is offered annually by the Cobden Club, London, for the best work in Political Economy, Senior Class.

UNIVERSITY OF MICHIGAN, ANN ARBOR.

Departments of Political Economy, International Law, History, and Philosophy, 1890–91, includes :

POLITICAL ECONOMY.—*First Semester.*

(1) Principles of Political Economy. 1 hr. thrice a week, Prof. ADAMS.
(3) Principles of the Science of Finance. 1 hr. twice a week, Prof. ADAMS.
(5) History of Economic Thought. 1 hr. a week, Prof. ADAMS.
(9) Seminary in Economics. 2 hrs. a week, Prof. ADAMS.
(11) Foreign Relations of the United States. 1 hr. twice a week, Mr. HICKS.

Second Semester.

(2) Unsettled Questions in Political Economy. 1 hr. thrice a week, Prof. ADAMS.
(4) Social and Industrial Reforms. 1 hr. twice a week, Prof. ADAMS.
(6) Tariff Legislation in the United States. 1 hr. a week, Mr. HICKS.
(10) Seminary in Economics. 2 hrs. a week, Prof. ADAMS.
(12) Foreign Relations of the United States. 2 hrs. a week, Mr. HICKS.

INTERNATIONAL LAW.—*First Semester.*

(1) Lectures on International Law. 1 hr. twice a week, Pres. ANGELL.

Second Semester.

(2) History of Treaties. 1 hr. twice a week, Pres. ANGELL.

HISTORY.—*First Semester.*

(3) Constitutional History of the United States. 1 hr. twice a week, Asst. Prof. LAUGHLIN.
(5) Constitutional Law of the United States. 1 hr. twice a week, Asst. Prof. LAUGHLIN.
(11) Seminary. Constitutional History of the United States. 2 hrs. a week, Asst. Prof. LAUGHLIN.
(12) Comparative Constitutional Law. 3 hrs. a week, Prof. HUDSON.

Second Semester.

(1) Political and Constitutional History of England. 1 hr. thrice a week, Mr. MCPHERSON.
(4) Constitutional History of the United States. 1 hr. twice a week, Asst. Prof. LAUGHLIN.

PHILOSOPHY.—*Second Semester.*

(13) Seminary. Studies in the History of Political Philosophy. Prof. DEWEY.

The fees are : matriculation, for citizens of Michigan, $10 ; for others, $25. Annual fee in the Department of Literature, Science, and the Arts, in which foregoing studies are included, $20 for citizens of Michigan, $30 for others.
No scholarships. The one fellowship is for proficiency in Greek and Latin.

UNIVERSITY OF NEBRASKA, LINCOLN.

Department of Economic and Political Science, 1890–91, includes :

(1) Political Economy : General study of the subject, with the use of some text as Walker, Ely, or Andrews. Lectures on the character and history of the science, and on specific application of its principles to practical affairs. Topical reports from students required, and exercises assigned in the use of statistics. Junior or Senior Year : First and second terms, three hours.

(2) Taxation ; text and lectures. Junior or Senior Year : Third term, three hours.

(3) International Law : Outline study of the subject, with text. Third term, three hours.

COURSES IN ECONOMIC AND POLITICAL SCIENCE. 135

(4) Municipal Administration: Comparative study of the City Governments of the present time, with especial reference to American practice in the administrative branches. First and second terms, two hours.

(5) Constitutional Law: A study of Cooley's text-book, and lectures on the industrial bearings of the complex limitations imposed by our State and local constitutions. Third term, three hours.

(6) Private Corporations: First term, a comparative and historical view of corporation law in its economic aspects; second term, Railroad Problems; third term, Special reports on assigned topics involving original research. Whole year, two hours.

(7) Charities and Corrections: Lectures, study of reports of the State Boards and of the National Conference of Charities and Corrections, and visits to the charitable and penal institutions of the vicinity; third term, three hours.

(8) Methods of Legislating: A comparative view of the rules and practice of modern legislative assemblies, with special reference to the machinery of congressional and legislative action in the United States; first term, one hour.

All the above are taught by Associate Professor WARNER. In the other departments Professor KINGSLEY offers a course in Anthropology, and many of the courses in History deal with the historical aspects of economic and industrial problems, and with the History of Institutions.

The terms of the year are respectively 14, 11, and 11 weeks. No scholarships. No fees.

COLLEGE OF NEW JERSEY, PRINCETON, N. J.

Departments of History and Political Science, and Jurisprudence and Political Economy, 1890-91, include:

HISTORY AND POLITICAL SCIENCE.—PROF. SLOANE.

(7) Constitutional and Political History of England since 1688. 2 hrs. a week, 1st term. Open to Juniors and Seniors.

(8) American Political History. 2 hrs. a week, 2d term. Open to Juniors and Seniors.

(9) Comparative Politics. Origin and Theory of the State. 2 hrs. a week, 1st term. Open to Seniors.

(10) History of Political Theories. 2 hrs. a week, 2d term. Open to Seniors.

(11) Contrasts between Parliamentary and Congressional Governments. 2 hrs. a week, 1st or 2d term. Open to Graduate Students.

JURISPRUDENCE AND POLITICAL ECONOMY.—PROF. WOODROW WILSON.

(1) In Public Law, its evidence as to the nature of the state and as to the character and scope of political sovereignty. 2 hrs. a week, 1st term, alternate years. Junior and Senior elective.

(3) American Constitutional Law, state and federal. 2 hrs. a week, 2d term, alternate years. Junior and Senior elective.

(5) Administration. 2 hrs. a week, 2d term, alternate years. Senior elective, and open to Graduate Students.

(7) Political Economy: Elementary course. Walker's Elementary Political Economy, and lectures. 2 hrs. a week, 2d term. Required of Juniors.

(8) Political Economy: Advanced course. 2 hrs. a week, 1st term. Senior elective.

Academic tuition fee, $100 per an.

Admission to special courses on terms detailed in College Catalogue, p. 26.

A fellowship of $500 annually is offered in Social Science. Several fellowships in other departments of the academic course are also offered.

Among prizes are: Annual interest on $1000 for best examination, Senior class, Political Science; same, Political Economy; $50, American Political History; annual interest on $1000, best debater, American Politics.

UNIVERSITY OF PENNSYLVANIA, PHILADELPHIA, PA.

Wharton School of Finance and Economy, 1890-91, includes:

(3) *History.*—Constitution of the United States. 2 hrs. each week, Prof. THOMPSON.
(4) Political and Social History of Europe since 1760. 3 hrs., Mr. CHEYNEY.
(6) Economic and Social History of Europe since 1789. 2 hrs., Mr. CHEYNEY.
(7) American Political and Social History, Colonial. 3 hrs., 1st term, Prof. McMASTER.
(8) Church and State in America. 2 hrs., 1st term, Prof. THOMPSON.
(9) American Political and Social History (Washington to Jackson). 3 hrs., 2d term, Prof. McMASTER.
(10) Economic History of the United States. 2 hrs., 2d term, Prof. THOMPSON.

136 COURSES IN ECONOMIC AND POLITICAL SCIENCE.

(13) American Political and Social History (1825-1889). 4 hrs., 1st term, Prof. McMaster.
(14) American Constitutional History (1776-1889). 3 hrs., 2d term, Prof. McMaster.
(1) *Economics and Social Science.*—Political Economy, elementary. 3 hrs., 1st term, Prof. Patten.
(2) Currency and Banking. 3 hrs., 2d term, Prof. Patten.
(3) Social Science. 2 hrs., Prof. Thompson.
(4) Social Science, advanced. 3 hrs., 1st term, Prof. Thompson.
(5) Political Economy, advanced. 3 hrs., 1st term, Prof. Patten.
(6) Political Economy, History of. 3 hrs., 2d term, Prof. Patten.
(7) Revenue System in the United States and leading foreign countries. 2 hrs., 1st term, Prof. James.
(8) History and Theories of Public Finance, especially of Taxation. 2 hrs., 2d term, Prof. James.
(9) Statistics. 2 hrs., 2d term, Dr. Falkner.
(1) *Public Law and Politics.*—Constitution of the United States. 3 hrs., 1st term, Prof. James.
(2) State Constitutional Law. 2 hrs., 2d term, Dr. Thorpe.
(3) History and Theory of the State. 1 hr., 2d term, Prof. James.
(4) Constitutions of leading foreign countries. 2 hrs., 2d term, Prof. James.
(5) Public Administration in the United States. 2 hrs., 1st term, Prof. James.
(6) Public Administration in leading foreign countries. 2 hrs., 2d term, Prof. James.
(1) *Seminaries.*—In Political Science. Prof. James.
(2) In Political Economy. Prof. Patten.

Fees, $150 a year for undergraduate work, and the same for graduate work without the fee for examination for advanced degree.

Five honorary scholarships are granted to graduates of any reputable American college; these make free all instruction in the graduate work of the University relating to subjects studied in the Wharton School.

The Wharton School is a unique endeavor to introduce a business course into the body of advanced college work, to make the college mean at least as much to the business man as to the professional classes.

SMITH COLLEGE, NORTHAMPTON, MASS. (For Women.)

Course for 1890-91 includes :

POLITICAL ECONOMY, POLITICAL SCIENCE, ETC.—PROF. J. B. CLARK.

Political Economy, Lectures, with use of Laughlin's Political Economy and Clark's Philosophy of Wealth. Senior year, fall term.
Political Economy and Political Science, with special readings. Winter term.
Political History of the United States, and Political Economy, Lectures. Summer term.
Tuition fee for all students, regular, special and graduate, $100 a year.
Annual scholarships of $50 and $100 each have been established to assist meritorious students.

VASSAR COLLEGE, POUGHKEEPSIE, N. Y. (For Women.)

The Department of History and Economics, 1890-91, includes :

In the Senior year an advanced course is offered for the critical study of the origin and development of the English and American constitutions and a comparative study of the existing political institutions of the two countries.
In American history the work includes the study of the government of the individual colonies, the different attempts to form a union, and the adoption of the present constitution.
(1) Principles of Economics. Recitations from Walker's Political Economy and Jevons' Money and the Mechanism of Exchange. First semester, elect for Seniors. Associate Professor Mills.
(2) Advanced Course. Special topics. Lectures and investigation. Second semester, elective for Seniors who have had Course 1. Associate Professor Mills.
Tuition, day students, $115 a year.
Several scholarships are offered, particulars of which are given in Calendar.

WELLESLEY COLLEGE, WELLESLEY, MASS. (For Women).

The Department of History, Political Science, and Political Economy, 1889-90, includes :

(1) *History.*—Political History of England and the United States: England, first semester; United States, second semester.

COURSES IN ECONOMIC AND POLITICAL SCIENCE. 137

(4) Constitutional History of England and United States: England, first semester, Coman's Outlines; United States, second semester. Hart's Outlines.

(6) Political Science: lectures on Grecian and Roman methods of government, twice a week, first semester; lectures on the history of political institutions, twice a week, second semester.

(1) *Political Economy.*—Economic Science, first semester. Authorities, Mill, Marshall, Walker.

(2) Economic and Social Problems, second semester. Lectures and special topics.

No text-books are used. Each class is provided with printed outlines, and adequate references to the best authorities. Lectures are given where guidance is needed, but the student is made responsible for a large amount of independent library work.

Tuition, $150 a year.

There are more than twenty scholarships, details of which are given in calendar.

WILLIAMS COLLEGE, WILLIAMSTOWN, MASS.

Department of Political Economy and Political Science, 1890-91, includes:

Political Economy is a prescribed study, running through the 2d and 3d terms (23 weeks). 3 times a week, Prof. A. L. PERRY.

Political Science is an elective study, running through all the terms beginning with the 1st of Junior Year. The basis of instruction is the text of the Constitution, interpreted in the light of decisions of the Supreme Court. Prof. A. L. PERRY.

In 3d term of Senior Year two hours a week are given to Sociology. Prof. J. BASCOM.

History includes principles and methods of historical study as applied to the politics and institutions of Europe.

Fee for tuition, per year, $105.

PERRY prizes, $50 and $25 respectively, are awarded in History and Political Science.

The Cobden Club, of London, offers a silver medal annually for the highest proficiency in Political Economy.

YALE UNIVERSITY, NEW HAVEN, CONN.

Departments of Political Science and Law and History, 1890-91, include:

(10) *Political Economy.*—Political Economy, its elements, recent financial history of the United States, with lectures on elementary principles. 2 hrs., both terms, Prof. SUMNER.

(11) Political Economy. A one-year course planned to give a comprehensive knowledge of essentials to those whose chief interest lies in other departments of study. 3 hrs., both terms (Seniors), Prof. SUMNER.

(Courses 12 to 15 are open only to those who have taken Course 10.)

(12) Advanced Political Economy. 2 hrs., both terms (Seniors), Prof. SUMNER.

(13) Finance. 1 hr., both terms (Seniors), Prof. SUMNER.

(14) School of Political Economy, for those who make this their chief study during the year. Prof. SUMNER and Dr. SCHWAB.

(15) Social Science, an elementary course. 1 hr., both terms (Seniors), Prof. SUMNER.

(16) Industrial History of the United States since 1850. Open only to those who have already studied Political Economy. 2 hrs., first term (Seniors), Prof. HADLEY.

(17) Modern Economic Theories. 2 hrs., 2d term (Seniors), Prof. HADLEY.

(18) *Law.*—Includes constitutional and international law. Open only to those who take Course 19. 2 hrs., 2d term (Seniors), Prof. PHELPS.

(19) Jurisprudence. Includes law in its relation to the origin, development and government of political society, nature and origin of legal rights, and principles of the law governing rights in land. 2 hrs., 1st term (Seniors), Prof. ROBINSON.

(20) *History.*—History of Europe since 1789, mainly political. 2 hrs., both terms (Seniors), Prof. WHEELER.

(21) English History, political and constitutional. 3 hrs., both terms (Seniors), Prof. WHEELER.

(22) American History. In the national period special attention is given to the rise and progress of political parties. 2 hrs., both terms (Juniors), Prof. C. H. SMITH.

(23) American History. Study of the Constitution and Supreme Court interpretations. 2 hrs., both terms (Seniors), Prof. C. H. SMITH.

(24) Europe from 1520 to 1789. With special attention to political history. 2 hrs., both terms, Prof. ADAMS.

The foregoing are among the elective courses. Juniors select nine hours per week, and Seniors select fifteen. The no. of hrs. specified means hrs. per week.

The fee for graduate instruction is generally $100 per annum, but may be more or less according to the course pursued. A variety of fellowships and prizes are offered, none, however, specifically in foregoing courses.

INDEX.

Abel, Mary H. Practical cooking, 88.
About, Edmond. Handbook of social economy, 14, 28.
Ackerbaues, National-ökonomik des. W: Roscher. 23.
Acre-ocracy of England. J: Bateman. 20.
Accidents, Railroad. C: F. Adams, Jr. 47.
Acworth, W. M. Railways of England, 50.
Ackland, A. H. D., *and* Jones, B. Workingmen coöperators, 33.
Adams, C: F., Jr. Railroad accidents, 47. Railroads, their origin and problems, 47.
— *and others*. Taxation of railroads and railroad securities, 66.
— *and* H. Chapters of Erie, 47.
Adams, C: K. Manual historical literature, 2d note, 96.
Adams, Sir F. O., *and* Cunningham, C. Swiss confederation, 106.
Adams, G: H. Tariff of 1890, 54.
Adams, H. B. Notes on literature of charities, 87.
Adams, H: C. Outlines of lectures on political economy, 5. Public debts, 72. Relations state to industrial action, 99. Surplus financiering (*see under* Shaw), 67. Taxation in U. S., 1789-1816, 66.
Addenda, 126.
Adler, G: Karl Marx's Grundlagen, 79.
Administration, Government, 107.
Adulteration, Food. J. P. Battershall. 88.
Agrarian agitation, Canadian chapter in. G: Iles. 23.
Agricultural department, Publications, 125.
Agriculture and prices in England, History of. J. E. Thorold Rogers. 19.
— and the single tax. Horace White, 72.
— Probabilities of. C. W. Davis. 23.
— Tenth census (2d note), 82.
Alaska, Tenth census (2d note), 82. Eleventh census (3d note), 82.
Alden, J. Science of government, 97.
Alexander, E. P. Railway practice, 47.
Alford, *Rev.* B. H. Free education (*see under* T: Mackay), 127.
Allen, C: C. Electoral reform legislation, 109.
Allessio, G. Sistema tributario in Italia, 71.
A'liance News (3d note), 93.
Allinson, F. P., *and* Penrose, Boies. Ground rents in Philadelphia, 18. Philadelphia, 1681-1887. 118.
Almanac, American, 124. de Gotha, 125. *Tribune*, 124. Whittaker, 125. *World*, 124.
Alton, E. Among the lawmakers, 97.

Amé, M. Étude sur les tarifs de commerce, 64.
American academy political and social science (note), 17.
— almanac (3d note), 124.
— citizen's manual. W. C. Ford. 97.
— civil policy. J: W. Draper. 99.
— commonwealth. James Bryce. 99. J: W. Burgess. 101.
— economic assoc. (note) 17, (1st note), 71.
— government, 96.
— institutions. A. De Tocqueville. 100.
— republics, Bureau of (1st note), 65.
— social science assoc. (note), 17.
— statistical assoc. (note), 17.
Amherst College, Courses in pol. and econ. science, 129.
Amos, Sheldon. Fifty years English Constitution, 103. Primer English Constitution, 103. Political and legal remedies for war, 121.
Amusements of the people. W: S. Jevons. 74.
Anarchism, 76. A. R. Parsons, 76.
— Scientific. H. L. Osgood. 81.
Anarchistic Essays. Prince Kropotkin. 78.
Anarchists, Chicago. D. D. Lum. 76.
Anarchy, C. L. James, 76. The coming, Prince Kropotkin, 81.
Andrews, E: B. Economic law of monopoly, 53. An honest dollar, 35. Institutes of Economics, 9. Trusts according to official investigations, 53.
Andrews, G: H. Twelve letters on future of New York, 66.
Anson, Sir W: R. Law and custom constitution, 103.
Appropriations, Digests of. *See* Treasury Dept. 126.
Arbitration. 34.
— Am. republics. *See* International Am. Conference. 120.
— and conciliation (4 titles). J. D. Weeks, 34. C. D. Wright, 34.
— between capital and labor. Dan. J. Ryan. 34.
Arbitrations, International. 119.
Arbitrator, International League (2d note), 123.
Arbor day planting (*see under* Reports Forestry div.), 113.
Argyll, Duke of, *and* George, H: Property in land, 20.
Army regulations, U. S. (2 titles), 113.

INDEX.

Arnold, Arthur. Free land, 20.
Articles of confederation. *See* under Constitution. 97.
Aschrott, P. F. Englisches Armenwesen, English poor law system. 86. Strafensystem und Gefängnisswesen in England, 90.
Ashley, D. D. Anti-railway legislation, 48.
Ashley, W. J. Introduction to English economic history and theory, 7.
Ashworth, H. Cobden and Anti-Corn Law League, 62.
Association, Exposition doctrine of. A. Brisbane. 29.
— of Capital with labor. J: B. A. Godin. 34.
Atkinson, E: Bimetallism in Europe, 38. Common sense of tariff question, 64. Distribution of products (2 titles) 31. Industrial progress of nation, 31. Labor and capital allies, not enemies, 25. Margin of profits, 25. Our national domain, 24. Railway, farmer and public, 48. Single tax, 72. What is a bank? 40.
Atkinson, W. P. Study of politics, 93.
Aucoc, J: L. Conferences sur l'administration, 107.

BADEN-POWELL, G. Protection and bad times, 63.
Bad times. A. R Wallace. 44.
Bagehot, W. Depreciation of silver, 38. Economic studies, 7. English constitution, 103. International coinage, 37. Lombard street, 41. Physics and politics, 94. Postulates of English political economy, 11.
Baird, H: C. On some economic questions, 58. Rights of American producers, 58.
Baker, C: W. Monopolies and the people, 52.
Baker, G. H. Sources and literature political science (note), 95.
Baker, T. B. L. War with crime, 90.
Ballot in England. E. Goadby *and* H. H. Asquith. 109.
— — Massachusetts (*see* Laws), 127.
— — N. Y. A. C. Bernheim. 109.
— system, Australian. J: H. Wigmore. 108.
Bancroft, G: Formation U. S. constitution, 101. Plea for constitution of U. S., 35.
Bank, National, Act, and its judicial meaning. A. S. Bolles. 40.
— notes. J. B. Martin. 43.
— of the United States, History of. M. St. C. Clarke *and* D. A. Hall, 40.
— — U. S, Andrew Jackson and. W: L. Royall. 41.
— — England. C. Tennant. 42.
— — First nine years of. J. E. T. Rogers. 42.
History, 1694-1844. J: Francis. 41. Note issue, Reform of. E. Seyd. 42.
— What is a? E: Atkinson. Distrib. of products. 31, 40.
Banker, Country. G: Rae. 42.
Banking. 40.
— J. W. Gilbart. 41.

Banking and banker's commonplace book. A. S. Bolles. 40.
— Currency and. Bonamy Price. 42.
— — and the exchanges. A. Crump. 41.
— Elements of. H. D. Macleod. 41.
— English. A. Crump. 41.
— History of. W: J. Lawson. 41.
— in U. S., Future of. Horace White. 43.
— law, Treatise on. J. T. Morse. 41.
— in Scotland, History of. A: W. Kerr. 41.
— National. M. L. Scudder, jr. 41.
— — laws. W. A. Richardson. 36.
— Principles of. T. Hankey. 41.
— reform. A. J. Wilson. 42.
— system of N. Y. J. Cleaveland. 40.
— Theory and practice of. H. D. Macleod. 42.
— — — history. C: F. Dunbar. 127.
Banks and banking, 1771-1888. P. P. Hotchkiss. 41.
— History of prominent. T: H. Goddard. 40.
— National. H. W. Richardson. 41.
— Scotch. R. Somers. 42.
Barbour, D. Theory of bimetallism. 38.
Barnard, C: Co-operation as a business. 32.
Barnreither, J. M. English assocs. workingmen. 30.
Barnet, Rev. *and Mrs.* S. A. Practicable socialism, 77.
Barns, W. E. Labor problem, 25.
Bascom, J: Sociology, 73.
Bastable. C. F. Theory of international trade, 63.
Bastiat, M. F. Essays on political economy, 17. Sophisms of protection, 64. Also *see* E. R. Pearce-Edgcumbe, 63.
Batbie, A. P. Traité de droit public et administratif, 107.
Bateman, J. Acre-ocracy of England, 20.
Bates, W. G. Water storage in the West, 115.
Battershall, J. P. Food adulteration, 88.
Bax, E. B. Ethics of socialism, Religion of socialism, 77.
Baxter, R. Panic of 1866, 44.
Baxter, R. D. National debts, 73. Taxation United kingdom, 68.
Bayles, J. C. Shop council, 34.
Beach, C. F., jr. Facts about trusts, 53.
Bebel, A. Woman in the past, present, and future. 79.
Beer, Effects of (2d note) 93.
Bellamy, E: First steps toward nationalism, 81. Looking backward, 76. What nationalism means. 81.
Bemis, E. W. Municipal ownership gasworks (4th note), 119. Plan of tariff reduction (2d line), 68.
Benton, T: H. Thirty years' view, 101.
Berlin, Municipal administration. A. D. White (1st note), 119.
Bernard, G: S. Civil service *vs.* Spoils system, 110.
Bernays, A. J. Food. 88.
Bernhardi, T. Versuch einer Kritik der

Gründe die für grosses und kleines Grundeigenthum angeführt werden, 23.
Bernheim, A. C. Ballot in N. Y., 109.
Bibliography of money. S. D. Horton. 35.
— Political economy. 5.
Biddle, G: W. Influence of Chief Justice Taney, 101.
Bigelow, E. B. Tariff question, 58.
Bilgram, Hugo. Involuntary idleness, 25.
Billings, Dr. J: S. Municipal government and public health, 118.
Bimetallic controversy. H. Gibbs and others, 39.
Bimetallism, 38.
— Hugh McCulloch. 38.
— W: G. Sumner (4th note), 40.
— bibliographies (3d note), 40.
— in 1886. E. Seyd. 39.
— in Europe. E: Atkinson. 38.
— in U. S. J. L. Laughlin. 38.
— Theory of. D. Barbour. 38.
Birch, W. de G. Historical charters London, 118.
Birkbeck, W. Lloyd. Historical sketch of distribution of land in England, 20.
Bismarck and state socialism. W. H. Dawson, 77.
Black and white. T. T. Fortune. 85.
— In plain, and white. H: W. Grady. 85.
Blackley, Rev. W. L. Thrift and independence, 74.
Blaine, J. G. Free trade and protection, 60.
Blair, L. H. Prosperity of South, 84.
Blanc, L. Organisation du travail, 73.
Blanqui, J. A. History of political economy in Europe, 8.
Block, M. Dictionnaire de l'administration française, 107. Progres de la science économique depuis Adam Smith, 8. Traité de statisque, 123.
— *and* Pontlich, H. de. Administration de Paris, 119.
Bluntschli, J. K. Droit international codifié, 122. Geschichte des allgemeinen Staatsrechts, 96. Das moderne Völkerrecht, 122. Politik als Wissenschaft, 95. Theory of the state, 95.
Bodio, Luigi. Emigrazione Italiana, 83.
Böhm-Bawerk, E. v. Capital and interest, 25.
Böhmert, V. Gewinn-betheiligung, 34.
Bohn's political cyclopædia, 6.
Bolles, A. S. Chapters in political economy, 16. Financial history of the U. S., 66. National bank act, and its judicial meaning, 40. Practical banking and bankers' commonplace book, 40.
Bonaparte, C: J. Civil service reform as a moral question, 110.
Bonar, J. Malthus and his work, 81.
Bonner, J. Present stage irrigation question, 115.
Bonnet, V. La question des impôts, 69.
Booth, A. J. Memoir of R. Owen, 77.
Booth, C: Life and labor in East London, 74.

Booth, Gen. W: In darkest England, 86.
Boppe, L. Traité de sylviculture, 114.
Borain, J. Enormités du libre echange Anglais, 59.
Borgeaud, C. Histoire du plébiscité, 109.
Bornhak, C. Preussisches Staatsrecht, 107.
Bossism, Fall of. G. Vickers, 116.
Boston, City government. J. M. Bugbee. 118.
— Report of Com. citizens of, 61.
Bourne, E. G. Surplus revenue of 1837, 66.
Bourinot, J: G. Canada and the U. S., 106. Constutional history Canada, 105. Federal government in Canada, 105.
Boutmy, E. Developpement constitution et société en Angleterre, 105.
Bowen, Francis. American political economy, 9.
Bowers, Ed. Present condition forests on public lands (3d note), 115.
Bowker, R: R. Civil service examinations, 110. Economic fact-book, 60. Economics for the people, 9. Electoral reform, 108. Free trade the best protection, 60. Primer for political education, 97. Workingmen's homes, 89.
Boycott, Conspiracy and, cases. E. P. Cheyney. 53.
Boycotts, 52.
Brace, C: L. Dangerous classes of N. Y., 86. Free trade promoting peace and good-will, 60.
Brackett, J. R: Negro in Maryland (two titles), 84.
Brassey, T: Foreign work and English wages, 31. On work and wages, 32.
Brayer, F. Manuel de police. 119.
Bread-winners abroad. R. P. Porter. 86.
Breckinridge, W: C. P. Free trade and protection, 60.
Brentano, L. History and development guilds, 30. Relation of labor to law of to-day, 127. Zur Geschichte der englischen Gewerkvereine, 31. Zur Kritik der englischen Gewerkvereine, 31.
Brewers', U. S., assoc. (2d note), 93.
Bright, J: Speeches, 63.
Brisbane, A. Exposition doctrine association, 29.
Brisbin, J. S. Trees and tree-planting, 113.
Bristed, J. Resources of U. S., 45.
British Economic Assoc. (1st note), 127.
Broderick, G: C. English land and English landlords, 20.
Bromwell, W: J. History immigration U. S., 83.
Brown, E., *and* Strauss, A. Dictionary Am. politics, 115.
Brown University. Courses pol. and ec. sci., 129.
Brown, W. A. State control of industry in 4th century, 81.
Brown, Willard. Civil service reform in N. Y. custom house, 110.
Bruce, P. A. Plantation negro as freeman, 85.
Bryce, James. American commonwealth, 99. A word as to speakership, 116.

INDEX.

Bryn Mawr College. Courses pol. and ec. sci., 129.
Buchanan, D: Taxation and commercial policy of Great Britain, 68.
Buck, Dr. A. H. Hygiene and public health, 88.
Buckalew, C. R. Proportional representation, 109.
Bugbee, J. M. City government Boston, 118. Selection of laborers, 110.
Building and Loan Assocs., Manual for. H. S. Rosenthal, 33.
— assocs. *See* under Dexter, Seymour. 32.
— — Co-operative (1st note), 33.
— stones. Tenth census (2d note), 82.
Bullion and foreign exchanges. E. Seyd. 39.
— Report on high price of, 39.
Bullitt Bill, 116.
Bureau of American republics (1st note), 65.
Burgess, J: W. American commonwealth, 101. Political science and comparative constitutional law, 93.
Burroughs, W. H. Law of taxation, 66.
Butts, I: Protection and free trade, 60.
Buxton, E. N. A B C of free trade, 63.
Byles, Sir J. B. Sophisms of free trade, 59.

CABET, M. Voyage en Icarie, 78.
Cable, G: W. Negro question, 85. Silent South, Freedman's case in equity, Convict-lease system, 85. Southern elections, *see* Year of Republicanism, 115.
Caine, W. S., *and* Hoyle, W: Local option, 92.
Caird, James. Prairie farming in America, 20.
Cairnes, J. E. Character and logical method of political economy, 11. Colonization, colonial govt. (note), 83. Essays on political economy, 16. Political essays, 94. Some leading principles in political economy, 11.
Calhoun, J: C. Works, 98.
Campaign text-books (last note), 57.
Campbell, D. W. Decisions irrigation cases, 115.
Campbell, *Sir* G: Property in land, 23.
Canada and the U. S. J: G: Bourinot. 106.
— Canals of (2d and 3d notes), 52.
— Can we coerce? Erastus Wiman. 65.
— Capture of. Erastus Wiman. 65.
— Commerce with U. S. (4th note), 57.
— Constitution. J. E. C. Munro. 106.
— — and government, 105.
— Constitutional history. J: G: Bourinot. 105.
— Federal government. J: G: Bourinot. 105.
— Parliamentary government in. C: C. Colby. 105.
— Perplexities she would bring. A. R. Carman. 65.
— Political destiny. Goldwin Smith. 106.
— Statistics (5th note), 124.
— tariff, trade, and navigation (2d and 3d notes), 58.
— Trusts in, *see* Report select com., 53.
Canal and railway. E. J. James. 52.

Canal Commissioner, N. Y. report (2d note), 52.
— Erie, traffic (3d note), 52.
— laws of N. Y. G: W. Chapman. 52
— statistics, U. S. (1st note), 52.
Canals, 52.
— and their economic relation to transportation. L. M. Haupt. 52.
— of Canada (2d and 3d notes), 52.
Canfield, J. H. Taxation, 66. Western farmer and tariff (*see* under Shaw), 67.
Capital. Karl Marx. 25. Note, 80.
— and interest. E. v. Bohm-Bawerk. 25.
— — its earnings. J: B. Clark. 24.
— — labor, 24.
— — — Conflicts of. G. Howell. 27.
— — — Relations. C. Morrison, 27. (1st note), 89.
— currency, and banking. Jas. Wilson. 37.
— Growth of. R. Giffen. 24.
— punishment. A. J. Palm. 127.
— Theory of. F. H. Giddings. 25.
Carey, H: C. Financial crises, 43. Harmony of interests, 58. C. H. Levermore, 60. Manual of social science, 9. The past, the present, and the future, 16. Principles of social science, 9.
Carlier, A. Droit public des états unis, 107.
Carpenter, E: England's ideal, 77.
Carr, E. S. Patrons of husbandry, 29.
Cassagnac, A. G. de. Histoire des classes ouvrières et des classes bourgeoises, 28.
Catholic Univ. and its constitutions, 117.
Caucus, 116.
Census, 81.
Century of dishonor. Helen H. Jackson, 85
Cernuschi, H. Nomisma; or, "legal-tender," 39.
Chalmers, M. D. Local government, 104.
Chamberlain, D. H. State judiciary, 101.
Chamberlain, Mellen. Josiah Quincy (3d note), 119.
Chamberlain, *Rev.* N. H. Our tariff and its taxes, 60.
Chamberlin, E. M. Sovereigns of Industry, 29.
Chandler, Sen. W. E. National control of elections, 109.
Changes, Recent economic. D: A. Wells. 7.
Chapin, A. L. First principles political economy, 9.
Chapin, H. D. Preventable causes of poverty, 76.
Chapman, G: W. N. Y. canal laws, 52.
Charities, 87.
— and Corrections, Nat. conference of (1st note), 87.
— directory, N. Y., 87.
— Literature of. H. B. Adams. 87.
— register and digest, 87.
— State Aid Assoc. (2d note), 87.
Charity Organization, 87.
— — C. S. Loch. 87.
— — handbook. Rev. S. H. Gurteen. 87.
— — societies (3 last notes), 87.
— organizations, English. D. R. Randall (note under H. B. Adams), 87.

INDEX.

Charity, Private, Public relief and. Josephine S. Lowell. 87.
Chaumont, F. de. Habitation and health, 88.
Cherbuliez, A. E. Précis de la science économique, 14.
Chevalier, E. Les salaires au XIXme siècle, 32.
Chevalier, M. Cours d'économie politique, 14. Examen du système protecteur, 64. La monnaie, 38. Probable fall in value of gold, 39. Sur l'organisation du travail, 28.
Cheyney, E. P. Anti-rent agitation in State of N. Y., 18. Conspiracy and Boycott cases, 53.
Child-Labor. W. F. Willoughby and Miss C. de Graffenried. 26.
Child-saving institutions. E. C. Wines. 90.
Chinese, Exclusion of, immigration of, legislation against, 84.
— — *Sir* C: Dilke (4th note), 84.
Chisholm, J. C. Handbook commercial geography, 55.
Christian economics. W. Richmond. 10.
Chubb, Percival. Socialism in England, 81.
Church and State, 116.
— — in Mexico (1st note), 117.
Circulation, State of, 1793-1837. T: Tooke *and* W. Newmarch. 47.
Citizenship, Mass. Soc. for Promoting Good (3d note), 119.
City Reform Club, N. Y. (3d note), 109.
Civics for young Americans. W. M. Giffen. 97.
Civil government in the U. S. J: Fiske. 97.
— — for common schools. H: C. Northam. 127.
— liberty and self-government. F. Lieber. 93.
— service and its reform, 110.
— — Commission, Massachusetts (2d note), 111.
— — — N. Y. (3d note), 111.
— — — 126. U. S. (1st note), 111, 126.
— — in Great Britain. D. B. Eaton. 111.
— — — U. S. J. M. Comstock. 110.
— — law. W. H. Clarke. 110.
— — Our revenue system and. A. L. Earle. 60.
— — question-book, 110.
— — reform. W: G. Sumner (3d note), 103.
— — — Assoc., N. Y. (5th note), 111.
— — assocs. (last note), 111.
— — league, National (4th note), 111.
C'ark, J: B. Capital and its earnings, 24. Certainties of tariff question (*see under* Shaw), 67. Ethics of land tenure, 23. Law of wages and interest. 32. Modern distributive process, 52. Philosophy of wealth, 10. Profits under modern conditions, 25.
Clarke, F. W. Weights, measures, and money of all nations, 35.
Clarke, St. C., *and* Hall, D. A. History of Bank of the United States, 40.
Clarke, W: Influence of socialism upon English politics, 81.
Clarke, W. H. Civil service law, 110.

Cleaveland, J: Banking system of N. Y., 40.
Clement, R. E. Civil gov't in U. S., 97.
Cleveland, *Pres.* Grover. Message, 1887, 61.
Clubs for working-girls. Maude Stanley, 75.
Coast survey charts, *see* Treasury Dept., 126.
Cobden and Anti-Corn Law League. H. Ashworth. 62.
— Club (7th note), 64.
— R:, Life of. J: Morley. 63.
— Political writings, 63.
Cocker, W. J. Government of the U. S., 97.
Codman, J: Free ships, 60. Shipping bounties and subsidies, 60.
Cohn, Gustav. Englische Eisenbahnpolitik, 1873-83, 51. Finanzwissenschaft, 70. Income and property taxes in Switzerland, 72. System der national Oekonomie, 14. Untersuchungen über die englische Eisenbahnpolitik, 51.
Coin and currency. J: Sherman. 127.
Coinage, International. W. Bagehot. 37.
— law of 1878. W. C. Ford, 38.
— State of. T. Tooke (note 38), 47.
Coke. Tenth census (2d note), 82.
Colange, Leo de, *ed.* Dictionary of commerce, manufacture, etc.. 5.
Colby, C: C. Parliamentary government in Canada, 105.
Colleges, Am., courses political and economic science, 128.
Colonies, 82.
— and dependencies. J. S. Cotton *and* E: J. Payne, 82.
— History European. E: J. Payne. 83.
Colonization, 82.
— and colonies. H. Merivale. 82.
— English. *See* G. Baden-Powell. 63.
— Recent experiments in. A. White. 83.
Columbia College. Political science courses, 129.
Combinations, their uses and abuses. S. C. T. Dodd. 52.
Commerce and commercial navigation, J: R. McCulloch's dictionary of, 6.
— Ancient. J. W. Gilbart. 45.
— and shipping, Ancient. W. S. Lindsay. 45.
— — trade, 45.
— British, History of. Leone Levi. 45.
— Foreign (1st note), 57.
— from 1500 to 1789. J: Yeats. 46.
— — 1789 to 1872. J: Yeats. 46.
— manufacture, etc., Dictionary of. Leo de Colange, *ed.* 5.
— of the United Kingdom (4th note), 46.
— — U. S. (2d note), 46.
— — — Statistical view. T. Pitkin. 45.
— Technical history of. J: Yeats. 46.
— with Canada (4th note), 57.
— with Central America, Mexico, South America, West Indies (5th note), 57.
— with foreign countries (6th and 7th notes), 57.
Commercial and financial legislation. J. Macgregor. 45.
— crises, 1847-8, and 1857-8. D. M. Evans. 44.

Commercial geography. J. C. Chisholm. 55.
— union, 65, and 3d note, 65. A. D. Morse (*see under* Shaw,, 67.
— — Handbook of. 65.
Commune, Histoire de la. A. Lepage. 79.
Communism, 76.
— and socialism. T. D. Woolsey. 77.
— Protection and. W. Rathbone. 63.
Communistic societies of the U. S. C: Nordhoff. 76.
Communist party, Manifesto. K. Marx and F: Engels. 80.
Competition, 52.
— and the trusts. G: Iles. 53.
Compromise. J: Morley. 94.
Compulsory voting. F. W. Holls. 109.
Comstock, J. M. Civil service in U. S., 110.
Comte, A. Positive philosophy, 78. Positive polity, 78.
Comte, F. C. L. De la propriété, 24.
Conciliation, 34.
— Industrial. H. Crompton. 34.
— — and social reform, 34.
Congrès monetaire international, 39.
Congress, Proceedings, 125.
Congressional government. W. Wilson. 100.
Conrad, J., Elster, L., Lexis, W., Loening, Edgar, *eds.* Handwörterbuch der Staatswissenschaft, 7.
Conspiracy and boycott cases. E. P. Cheyney. 53.
Constitution, Commentaries on. Joseph Story. 99.
— English. W. Bagehot. 103. E. S. Creasy. 104. E: A. Freeman. 104. Hannis Taylor. 103.
— — Fifty years of. Sheldon Amos. 103.
— — Law and custom. *Sir* W: R. Anson. 103.
— — of. A. V. Dicey. 104.
— — Primer. Sheldon Amos. 103.
— — History. R. Gneist. 105.
— — Implied powers of. G: T. Curtis. 101.
— U. S., 97. Joseph Story. 98.
— — — Exposition of. H: Flanders. 97.
— — — Formation of. G: Bancroft. 101.
— — — History. G: T. Curtis. 101.
— — — in civil war and reconstruction. W: A. Dunning. 103.
— — — Plea for. G: Bancroft. 35.
— — — References to. W: E. Foster. 101.
— — — Unwritten. C. G. Tiedemann. 99.
Constitutional and political history, U. S. H. E. Von Holst. 103.
— conventions. J. A. Jameson. 102.
— history, American, 101.
— — England. *Sir* T. E. May. 104. H: Hallam. 104. T. P. Taswell-Langmead. 104. W: Stubbs. 104.
— — U. S. Simon Sterne. 103.
— — — as developed in Am. law, 101.
— law, American. J. I. C. Hare. 102. Comparative, Am. commonwealths. F. W. Whitridge (note), 99.
— limitations. T: M. Cooley. 98.
— Local. history, U. S. G: E. Howard. 102.
— view late war. A. H. Stephens. 103.

Constitutional year-book (6th note), 124.
Constitutions, American. Horace Davis 101.
— — State. H. Hitchcock. 102.
Consular reports, *see* State Dept., 126.
Consumption, Economy of. R. S. Moffatt. 44.
Conventions, Constitutional. J. A. Jameson. 102.
Convict labor in U. S. (1st note), 29.
— lease system. G: W. Cable. 85.
Cook, W. W. Trusts. 52.
Cooking, Practical. Mary H. Abel. 88.
Cooley, T: M. Constitutional limitations. 98. Federal supreme court, 101. Law of taxation and local assessments. 66. Traffic pooling. 48.
Cooper, J. F. History U. S. Navy, 112.
Cooper, T. V., *and* Fenton, H. T. American politics, 101.
Co-operation, 32.
— as a business. C: Barnard. 32.
— Distributive, Manual of. C. D. Wright. 33.
— History of, in U. S., 33.
— in England, History of. G: J. Holyoake. 33.
— Manual of. G: J. Holyoake. 33.
— Productive (*see* U. Rabbeno), 127.
Coöperative building assocs, (1st note), 33.
— commonwealth. L. Gronlund. 76.
— distribution in Great Britain and elsewhere. C. D. Wright. 33.
— production in France and England. E: Cummings. 33.
— savings and loan assocs. Seymour Dexter. 32.
Coöperators, Manual for. T: Hughes *and* E. V. Neale. 33.
— Workingmen. A. H. D. Ackland *and* B. Jones. 33.
Coquelin, C., *and* Guillaumin, U. G., *eds.* Dictionnaire de l'économie politique, 7.
Corn laws, Catechism of. Perronet Thompson. 63.
Cornell Univ. courses economic and political science, 131.
Corporations, Nature, significance, growth of, future of. R: T. Ely. 46.
Corrupt practices acts (*see* Electoral Reform Legislation). C: C. Allen. 109.
Cossa, L. Guide to study political economy, 7. Primi elementi di scienza delle finanze. Taxation, 71.
Cotton production. Tenth census (2d note), 82.
— textiles in foreign countries (10th note), 57.
— trade of world (11th note), 57.
Cotton, J. S., *and* Payne, E: J. Colonies and dependencies, 82.
Courcelle-Seneuil, J. G. Etudes sur la science sociale, 75. Operation de banque, 42. Traité théorique et pratique, 14.
Cournot, M. Principes de la théorie des richesses, 14.
Courses of reading, 128.

Courses in political and economic science, Am colleges, 129.
Courtois, A., *fils*. Anarchisme théoretique et collectivisme pratique, 78. Histoire des banques en France, 42.
Couturier, R. Organisation politique de France, 107.
Cox, S S. Free land and free trade, 18, 60.
Coxe. Bishop A. C. Government by aliens, 84.
Craik, H. The state and education, 104.
Crane, W., *and* Moses, B. Politics, 93.
Crawford. J. B. Credit mobilier, 48.
Creasy, E. S. English constitution, 104.
Credit, 40.
— in England, Organization of. C. Tennant. 42.
— mobilier. J. B Crawford. 48.
— Theory of. H D. McLeod. 42.
Crime. 90.
— S. M. Green. 90.
— and prison system. W. D. Morrison. 90.
— Causes and remedy. L. G. Rylands. 90.
— in England. L. O. Pike. 90.
— — — and Wales. W. Hoyle. 90.
— Punishment and prevention. *Sir* E. F. Du Cane. 90.
— Science and. A. Wilson. 90.
— War with. T. B. L. Baker. 90.
Criminal. The. H. Ellis. 90.
Criminals and Christianity. W: M. F. Round. 90
Crises. 43
— Commercial. Horace White (last note), 44.
Crocker, G G. Double taxation personal property, Massachusetts. 66.
Crompton. H. Industrial conciliation, 34.
Cronsel, A. Coalitions et grèves 30.
Crown of wild olive. J: Ruskin. 74.
Crump, A. Banking, currency, and the exchanges, 41. English manual of banking, 41 Fall in prices and demonetization of silver, 39. Theory stock speculation, 44.
Cullom, Sen. S. M. Protection and the farmer, 60.
Cumming, A. N. Value of political economy to mankind, 6.
Cummings, E: Coöperative production in France and England, 33.
Cunningham, W. English industry and commerce, middle ages, 45. Politics and economics, 104.
Currencies, Regulation of. J. Fullarton. 37.
Currency. 35.
— American, History. W: G. Sumner. 36.
— and banking. Bonamy Price. 42. C. Raguet. 36.
— — Principles. Bonamy Price. 39.
— — — System, U. S. A. Gallatin. 35.
— — finance. W: S. Jevons. 37.
— — — U. S. laws of. C: F. Dunbar. 35.
— Metallic, and paper. Lord Overstone. 37.
— Report to Congress on. Alex. Hamilton (*see under* Goddard, T: H.). 41.
Curtis, G: T. History U. S. constitution, 101. Implied powers constitution 101.

Curtis, G: W: Address to voters, U. S., 110. Addresses (4th note), 111.
Curtis, W. E. Trade and transp. between the U. S. and Latin America, 65.
Cushing, L. S. Law and practice legislative assemblies. Manual parliamentary practice, 116.
Custom House, N. Y., Spoils system in. D. B. Eaton. 111.
Customs revenue in England. H. Hall. 55.
— tariff, U. S. R. F. Downing. 54.
Cusumano, V. La teoria del commercio dei grani in Italia, 55.
Cyclopædia, Bohn's political, 6.
— of commerce, Homans', 45.
— — political science. J: J. Lalor, ed. 6.

Dabney, W: D. Public regulation of railways, 48.
Dacus, J. A. Annals great strikes, U. S., 1877, 29.
Danby, J. Grèves ouvrieres, 30.
Dangerous classes of N. Y. C: L. Brace. 86.
— tendencies in American life. J. B. Harrison. 73.
Davies, J. T. System taxation State of N. Y., 66.
Davis, C. W. Exhaustion of arable lands, 23. Probabilities of agriculture, 23. When farmer will be prosperous, 23. Why farmer is not prosperous, 23.
Davis, G. B. International law, 120.
Davis, Horace. American constitutions. 101.
Dawes, Anna L. How we are governed, 97.
Dawson, W. H. Bismarck and state socialism, 77. German socialism and Lassalle, 77.
Debate, Questions for, in politics and economics, 6.
Debt, Public, of U. S. W. A. Richardson, 36.
— National, taxes and Rates. A. J. Wilson, 69.
Declaration of Independence. *See under* Constitution, 97.
Decay of our ocean mercantile marine. D: A. Wells. 62.
Decisions, Public lands. 24.
Defective, dependent, and delinquent classes. Tenth census (2d note), 82.
De Flaix, E. F. L'impôt, 63.
De Franqueville, Comte. Gouvernement et parlement Britanniques. 105.
De la Chavanne, C. D. Histoire des classes agricoles en France, 28.
Delaire, A. La reforme sociale, 75.
Democracy in America. A. De Tocqueville, 100.
— in Europe. Sir T: E. May. 96.
Democratic campaign text-book (last note), 57.
Demombynes, G. Constitutions Européennes, 106.
Demontzey, P. Traité de reboisement, 114.
Denslow, Van Buren. Principles of economic philosophy. 10.
De Parieu, F. E. Histoire des impôts généraux, 69. Traité des impôts, 70.

Depression in trade, 1885. E: Goadby *and* W. Watt. 44.
Destiny, Our. L. Gronlund. 76.
De Tocqueville, A. American institutions, Democracy in America, 100.
Deutsch-Amerikaner, Auskunft und Rath für. E. Stürenburg *und* E. Steiger. 98.
Deutsches Staatsrecht. H. Schultze. 106.
Dewey, D. R. Graphic statistics, Study of statistics, 123.
Dexter, Seymour. Coöperative savings and loan assocs., 32.
Dicey, A. V. Law of [English] constitution, 104.
Dictionary of political economy. H: A. Macleod. 6. R. H. Inglis Palgrave. 6.
Dictionnaire de l'économie politique. Coquelin *and* Guillaumin, *eds.* 7.
— nouveau. de l'économie politique. Say *and* Chailley, *eds.* 7.
Dilke, *Mrs.* A., *and* Woodall, W. Woman suffrage, 108.
Dilke, Sir C: Chinese, Exclusion of (4th note), 84. Immigration (4th note), 84. Problems of Greater Britain, 82.
Diplomacy, 119.
— American. E. Schuyler. 120.
— Commercial. J. E. T. Rogers (5th note), 123.
— of the revolution. W. H. Trescot. 120.
— — U. S. Theo. Lyman. 120.
Diplomatic agents, U. S., Personal instructions, 120.
Discount, Rate of, and prices. R. Giffen (2d note). 43.
Disestablishment. H. Richard *and* J. C. Williams. 117.
Disinfection (3d note), 89.
Distribution of products. E: Atkinson (*see* 2 titles). 31.
Distributive, Modern, process. J: B. Clark *and* F. H. Giddings. 52.
Divorce, Marriage and (1st note), 29.
Dixwell. G: B. Progress and poverty, 19.
Dodd, S. C. T. Combinations, their uses and abuses, 52.
Dolge, Alf. Just distribution of earnings. 33.
Dollar, An honest. E. B. Andrews. 35.
— Standard. H. W. Richardson. 38.
Domain. Our national. E: Atkinson. 24.
— Public. T. Donaldson. 24.
Donaldson. T. Public domain. 24.
Donisthorpe, W. Individualism, 77. Limits of liberty (*see under* T: Mackay), 127.
Dos Passos, J. R. Interstate commerce act, 48.
Doubleday, T: True law of population, 81.
Dougherty, J. H Constitutions of N. Y., 103.
Dowell, S. Taxation in England, 68.
Downing. R. F. U. S. customs tariff, 54.
Draper, J: W. American civil policy, 90.
Drinking, Art of. G. G. Gervinus (2d note), 93.
Droit au travail, 30.

Droit international, L'institut de. Brussels (4th note), 123.
Du Cane, Sir E. F. Punishment and prevention crime, 90.
Dugdale, R: L. The Jukes, 90.
Dühring, E. Kritische Geschichte der Nationalökonomie und des Socialismus, 8.
Dunbar, C: F. Direct tax of 1861, 72. Laws of currency and finance, U. S., 35. Some precedents followed by Alex. Hamilton, 73. Theory and history banking, 126.
Dunn, J. P. Mortgage evil, 23.
Dunning, W: A. Constitution, U. S., in civil war and reconstruction, 103. History political theories (1st note), 96.
Dutcher, Salem. Minority or proportional representation, 109.
Duties, Collection of, report (2d last note), 56.
— Comparative. J. Nimmo, Jr. (10th note), 56.
Dwellings for laboring classes. A. T. White, 89.
— Healthy. D. Galton. 89.
Dwight, T. W. International law (7th note), 123. Legality of trusts, 53.

EARLE, A. L. Our revenue system and the civil service, 60.
Early history of institutions. Sir H. J. Sumner Maine. 21.
Earnings, Just distribution of. Alf. Dolge. 33.
Eaton, Dorman B. Civil service in Great Britain, 111. Secret sessions Senate, 99. Spoil system and civil service reform in Custom House and P. O , N. Y., 111. Term and tenure of office, 111.
Economic philosophy principles. H: D. Macleod. 12.
— Assoc., American (note), 17.
— changes, Recent. David A. Wells. 7.
— fact-book. R: R. Bowker. 60.
— interpretation of [English] history. J. E. Thorold Rogers. 8.
— *Journal* (1st note), 127.
— philosophy, Principles of. Van Buren Denslow. 10.
— *Review* (2d note), 127.
— studies. Walter Bagehot. 7.
Economics. J. M. Sturtevant. 11.
— Elements of. H: Dunning Macleod. 12.
— for beginners. H: D. Macleod. 12.
— for the people. R: R. Bowker. 9.
— Institutes of. E. B. Andrews 9.
— of industry. Alfred *and* Mary P. Marshall. 12.
— Principles of. Alfred Marshall. 12.
Economie sociale (3d note), 75.
Economist, American, 59.
— *The* (3d note), 18.
Eden, Sir F: M. State of the poor, 86.
Education, Bureau of. *See* Interior Department. 125.
— Eleventh census (3d note), 82.
— Free. *Rev.* B. H. Alford (*see under* T: Mackay), 127.

INDEX. 147

Education, The state and. H. Craik. 104.
Edwards, Rev. W. W. Poor law experiment at Elberfeld, 86.
Egleston, Melville. Land system of the New England Colonies, 19.
Egleston, N. H. Home and its surroundings, 73.
Eheberg, K. T. Agrarische Zustände in Italien, 23.
Eight-hours' law agitation. F. A. Walker. 32.
Eisenhart, H. Geschichte der Nationalökonomie, 8.
Elder, W. Conversations on political economy, 16. Questions of the day, economic and social, 16.
Election laws, Massachusetts, 127.
— system, 108.
Elections, National control of. Sen. W. E. Chandler. 109.
— Theory and practice, and Presidential. W: G. Sumner (2d note), 103.
Elective franchise, U. S. D. C. McMillan. 108.
Electoral reform, 108.
— — R: R, Bowker. 108.
— — legislation. C. C. Allen. 109.
— system, U. S. D. A. McKnight, 108. C. A. O'Neil. 108.
Electorate and legislature. S Walpole. 108.
Electrical distribution, The State and. F. W. B. Gordon (see under T: Mackay), 127.
Ellero, P. La questione sociale, 75.
Elliot, Arthur. State and church, 117.
Elliot, Jonathan. Funding systems, 72.
Elliott, J. R. American farms, 19.
Elliott, T. J. Land question, 20.
Ellis, H. The criminal., 90.
Elmes. W. Executive departments, U. S., 107.
Ely, R: T. Corporations, nature, significance. growth of. future of. 46. German and French socialism, 76. Introduction to political economy, 10. Labor movement in America, 25 Labor problem (see under Barns, W. E.) 25. Past and present of political economy, 7. Problems of to-day, 60. Railways. Three articles on, 51. Recent American socialism, 76. Social objects of Christianity, 73. Tariff and trusts (see under Shaw). 67.
— and Finley, J. H. Taxation in American states and cities, 67
Emigration and immigration. R. M. Smith. 83.
— Commissioners' report (3d note), 84.
— Theory of. R. M. Smith. 84.
Employers' liability. C. G. Fall. 26.
Engel, E. v. Eisenbahn-reform. 51.
Engels, F: Condition of the working-class in England. 1844, 29.
England and her colonies, 82.
England's ideal. E: Carpenter. 77.
English constitution and government, 103.
— history, Dictionary. S. J. Low and F. S. Pulling. 104.
— industry and commerce, middle ages. W. Cunningham. 45.

English land and English landlords. G: C. Broderick. 20.
— local government bill. F. J. Goodnow. 105.
Ensley, Enoch. Tax question, 67.
Ethics, Board of trade. (See under Trumbull, M. M.) 26.
— of socialism. F. H. Giddings. 81.
— — land tenure. J. B. Clark. 23.
— Political. F. Lieber. 93.
European schools of history and politics. A. D. White. 94.
Evans, C. H. Imports—duties, 1867-83. 54.
Evans, D. M. Commercial crises, 1847 8, and 1857-8. Speculative notes, 44.
Exchange, 40.
Exchanges, Foreign, Bullion and. E. Seyd. 39.
— Theory of foreign. G: J. Goschen. 41.
Excise Reform Assoc. (1st note), 93.
Executive departments, U. S. W. Elmes, 107. A. Guggenheimer (2d note), 108.

FABIAN ESSAYS IN SOCIALISM. G. B. Shaw. 78.
Fackler, D. P. Life insurance table, 53.
Factory system. C. D. Wright. 26.
— — Introduction to history of. E. W. C. Taylor. 27.
Falkner, R. P. Arbeit in den Gefängnissen, 91. Prison statistics, 90.
Fall, C. G. Employers' liability, 26.
Fair trade. (1st note). 60.
— — free trade, vs. T: H. Farrer. 63.
— — unmasked. G: W. Medley. 63.
Fairfield, C: State socia'ism at the Antipodes (see under T: Mackay), 127.
Fano, Enrico. Della carita preventiva, 86.
Farm for nothing, A good. C: C. Nott. 19.
— mortgages and the small farmer. W. F. Mappin. 23.
Farmer, Protection and the. Sen. S. M. Cullom. 60.
— Western, and tariff. J. H. Canfield (see under Shaw), 67.
— What protection does for the. J. S. Leadam. 63.
— when will be prosperous. C. W. Davis. 23.
— why not prosperous. C. W. Davis. 23.
Farmers, Friendly letters to Am. J. S. Moore. 61.
Farmers' movement in the U. S.. 31.
Farming in America. Prairie. J. Caird. 20.
— Pioneers and progress of English. R. E. Prothero. 21.
Farms, American. J. R. Elliot. 19.
Farr, W: Vital statistics, 123.
Farrer, Sir T: H. Free trade vs. fair trade, 63. State in relation to trade, 104.
Fawcett, H. Economic position of British laborer, 32. Free trade and protection, 63. Indian finance. 68. Manual of political economy, 11. Pauperism, 86.
Fawcett, Mrs. M. G. Political economy for beginners, 12. Tales in political economy, 12. Why women require franchise (1st note), 109.

Fawcett, W. L. Gold and debt, 38.
Federal election bill. H: C. Lodge *and* T. V. Powderly. 109.
— governments. A. B. Hart. 106.
— restraints on State action. C. S. Patterson. 98.
Federalist, The. 101.
Fernald, J. C. Economics of prohibition. 91.
Fernow, B. E. Governmental control forests U. S. (2d note), 115. Need of forest administration, U. S., 113. Our forestry problem. 113.
Ferraris, C. F. Moneta e corso forzoso, 42.
Ferriss, W. M. Obstacles to civil service reform, 112.
Field, D: Dudley. On international code. (6th note), 123. Outlines of an international code, 120. Representation of minorities, 110.
Firth, J: B. Municipal London. 118.
Flanders, H: Exposition of constitution U. S., 97.
Flint, H. M. Railroads of U. S., 49.
Finance, A B C of. S. Newcomb. 36.
— Alphabet in. G. McAdam. 36.
— and taxation. I: Sherman. 68.
— Historical and comparative science of. E. R. A. Seligman (note), 11.
— Public, 66.
— statistics Am. commonwealths. E. R. A. Seligman. 67.
Finances, Report on U. S. (2d note), 40.
Financial condition of counties. Eleventh census. (3d note), 82.
Finch, J: B. People *vs.* liquor traffic, 91.
Fink, Albert. Railroad problem (8 titles), 48.
Fire underwriters' text-book. J. Griswold. 53.
Fiscal legislation. J. Noble. 55.
Fisher, J. History land holding in England. 20.
Fiske, J: American political ideas, 101. Civil government in the U. S., 97.
Folwell, W. W. Protective tariffs (*see under* Shaw), 67.
Food. A. J. Bernays. 88.
— question. E: Atkinson. Industrial progress, 31.
Foods, Healthy. (3d note), 89.
Ford, W. C. American citizen's manual, 97. Silver or legal-tender notes, 40. Standard silver dollar and coinage law of 1878, 38.
Forest commissions, Reports (2d note), 114.
— *Leaves* (3d note), 115.
— policy abroad. Gifford Pinchot. (3d note), 115.
— trees of N. A. Tenth census (2d note), 82.
Forestry, 113.
— American association (1st note), 115.
— division, Reports, 113.
— in Europe, 113.
Fortune, T. T. Black and white, 85.
Foster, W: E. References to history presidential administrations, 102. References to political economic topics, 6. References to U. S. constitution, 101.

Fougerousse. A. Patrons et ouvriers de Paris, 28.
Fouillé, A. La science sociale, 78. La science sociale contemporaine. 75.
Foulkes, W: D. Civil service reform, later aspects, 111.
Fourier, C: Œuvres, 78.
— oville, A. de. Le Morcellement, 22. Transformation des moyens de transport, 50.
Fowler, W: Appreciation of gold, 39.
Fowle, *Rev.* T. W. English poor law, 86.
Foxwell, H. S. Development of monopolies, 53.
France, Constitutional history. H. C. Lockwood, 106.
— Constitutions de la. M. F. Hélie. 106.
— Travels in. Arthur Young. 22.
Francis, J. History Bank of England, 1694-1844, 41. History English railway, 50.
Francisco, M. J. Review of argument for limited post and telegraph 112.
Frankenstein, K. Lohnstatistik im Deutschen Reiche 124.
Franklin, B. Essay on political economy. 16.
Freedman's case in equity. G: W. Cable. 85.
Free land and free trade. S. S. Cox. 18.
Freeman, E. A. Comparative politics, 94. English constitution, 104.
Free trade, 60.
— — A B C. E. N. Buxton. 63.
— — as promoting peace and good-will. C: L. Brace. 60.
— — and protection. H: Fawcett. 63. W. E. Gladstone, J. G. Blaine, R. Q. Mills, Sen. Morrill, W: C. P. Breckinridge, 60.
— — bubbles. E: Sullivan. 59.
— — club, N. Y. (4th note), 64.
— — Creed of. D: A. Wells. 62.
— — folly. R. P. Porter. 60.
— — Free land and. S. S. Cox. 18, 60.
— — isolated. E: Sullivan *and* Duke of Manchester. 60.
— — League, Am. (4th note), 64.
— — Refutation. E C. Seaman. 59.
— — Sophisms of. *Sir* J. B. Byles. 59.
— — struggle in England, Am. lesson of. M. M. Trumbull. 62.
— — the best protection. R: R. Bowker. 60.
— — *vs.* fair trade. T: H. Farrer. 63.
— traders and revenue reformers, National conf., 61.
French works, Political economy. 14.
Friendly society movement. *Rev.* J. F. Wilkinson. 75.
Fullarton, J. Regulation of currencies, 37.
Fuller, A. S. Practical forestry, 113.
Funding systems. Jonathan Elliott. 72.
Furber, W. H., *ed.* Which? protection, free trade or revenue reform, 54.
Furey, F. T. Explanation constitution U. S., 97.
Fur-seal islands. Tenth census (2d note), 82.

GABAGLIO, A. Teoria della statistica, 124.
Gage, L. J. Ethics board of trade (*see* Trumbull, M. M.), 26.

INDEX.

Gallatin, A. Currency and banking system, U. S., 35.
Gallaudet, E. M. International law, 120.
Galton, D. Healthy dwellings, 89.
Garden and Forest (4th note), 115.
Garden, G., Comte de. Traités de paix, 121.
Garnier, J. Principe du population, 82.
Gas supply, Municipal. E. J. James. 113.
— works, Municipal ownership. E. W. Bemis (4th note). 119.
Gayer, K. Die Forstbenutzung. Der Waldbau, 114.
Geffcken, F. H. Church and state. Staat und Kirche. 117.
Geography, Commercial. J. C. Chisholm. 55.
George, H: Irish land question, 19. Labor movement (*see* McNeill, G. E.), 26. Land question, 19. Progress and poverty, 19 Protection or free trade, 61. Single tax, 72. Social problems. 73. And Argyll, Duke of. Property in land. 20.
Gerhard, W: P. Sanitary house inspection, 88.
German works, Political economy, 14.
Germany, Federal constitution. E. J. James. 106.
Ghillany, F. W. Diplomatisches Handbuch, 122.
Gibb, H. H., *and others*. Bimetallic controversy. 39.
Gibbons, Cardinal John. Denominational schools. 116.
Gibson, G. R. Stock exchanges of London, Paris and New York, 43.
Giddings, F. H. Ethics of socialism, 81. Modern distributive process, 52. Natural rate of wages, 32. Province of sociology, 76. Theory of capital, 25.
Gide, C: Principes d'économie politique, 14. (3d note), 127.
Giffen, R. American silver bubble, 40. Gold supply, Rate of discount and prices (2d note), 43. Growth of capital, 24. Index numbers, 47. Progress of working classes in last half century, 27. Trade depression and low prices (last note), 44. Stock exchange securities, 44.
Giffin, W. M. Civics for young Americans, 97.
Gilbart, J. W. Ancient commerce, 45. Banking, 4¹.
Gilman, N: P. Profit sharing, 33
Giornale degli economisti (6th note), 18.
Gladden, Rev. W. Working-people and their employers. 26.
Gladstone, W: E. Financial statements, 68. Free trade and protection, 60. Vatican decrees, 117.
Glasgow, A municipal study. Albert Shaw, 119.
Gleed, J. W. Western mortgages, 23.
Gneist, R. Englisches Parlament, English Parliament, 105. Englisches Verwaltungsrecht, 105; 2 titles, 107. History English constitution, 105. Self-government in England, 105.

Goadby, E., *and* Asquith, H. H. Ballot in England, 109.
— *and* Watt, W. Depression in trade, 1885, 44.
Goddard, T: H. History prominent banks, 41.
Godin, J: B. A. Association of capital with labor, 34. Social solutions, 78.
Godkin, E. L. Danger of an office-holding aristocracy, 111. Republican party and negro, 85.
Godwin, W: Power of increase in mankind, 81.
Gold, 38.
— and debt. W. L. Fawcett. 38.
— — silver commission, 39.
— Appreciation of. W: Fowler, 39.
— coinage. J. B. Martin. 40.
— Probable fall in value of. M. Chevalier. 39.
— supply. R. Giffen (2d note), 43.
Gomme, G. L. The village community, 20.
Goodloe, D. R. Western farm mortgages, 23.
Goodnow, F. J. Comparative administrative law and science (1st note), 108. Local government, England (2 titles), 105. Local government, Prussia, 106.
Goodwin, T. S. The Grange, 29.
Gordon, F. W. B. State and electrical distribution (*see under* T: Mackay), 127.
Goschen, G: J. Local taxation, 68. Theory of foreign exchanges, 41.
Gouge, W: M. Fiscal history Texas, 67. Paper money and banking in U. S., 35.
Gough, J: B. Temperance lectures, 91.
Government administration, 107.
— American, 96.
— publications, 125.
— by aliens. Bishop A. C. Coxe. 84.
— Civil, in U. S. R. E. Clement. 97.
— Congressional. W. Wilson. 100.
— Democratic. A. Stickney. 100.
— Local. M. D. Chalmers. 104.
— — England and Wales. R. S. Wright *and* H: Hobhouse. 69.
— of people, U. S. F. N. Thorpe. 98.
— the U. S. W. J. Cocker. 97.
— Our. Jesse Macy. 98.
— Popular. Sir H: J: S. Maine. 94.
— Representative. J: S. Mill. 94.
— — History origin. F. P: G. Guizot. 96.
— Science of. J. Alden. 97.
— Self, in England. R. Gneist. 105.
— Studies in civil. W. A. Mowry. 98.
— Thoughts upon. A. Helps. 94.
Governments and constitutions, Foreign (other than Canadian), 106.
— State and federal, U. S. W. Woodrow Wilson. 99.
Grady, H: W. In plain black and white 85.
Graham, Robert. Tracts (3d note), 92.
Graham, W. Social problem, 77. Socialism, new and old, 77.
Grange movement, History of. E. W. Martin. 29.
— National, Patrons of Husbandry, 30.

Grange, The. T. S. Goodwin. 29.
Greeley, Horace. Essays on political economy, 10.
Green, G: Walton. Repudiation, 73.
Green, S M. Crime, 90.
Greene, T. L. Changes in form railway capital, 51.
Greg, W. R. Political problems, 94.
Gregory, J. M. New political economy, 10.
Grierson, J. Railway rates, English and foreign, 50.
Griswold, J. Fire underwriters' text-book, 53.
Gronlund, L. Coöperative commonwealth, Our destiny. Socialism vs. tax reform, 76.
Grosvenor, W. M. Does protection protect? 61. Trades-unions, 29. Unlimited silver coinage (see Year of republicanism), 115.
Grotius, Hugo. De jure belli et pacis. Of war and peace, 122.
Guer, E. G. de. Manuel électoral, 109.
Guggenheimer, A. Development executive departments (2d note), 108.
Guide to study political economy. L. Cossa. 7.
Guilds, History and development. L. Brentano. 30.
— Mediæval, of England. E. R. A. Seligman. 30.
— Trade, of Europe, 30.
Guyot, Yves. L'impôt sur le revenu, 70.
Gunton, G: Economic and social aspects of trusts, 53. Social economics, 126. Wealth and progress, 31.
Guizot, F. P: G. History origin representative government, 96.
Gurteen, Rev. S. H. Handbook charity organization, 87.
Gustafson, A. Foundation of death, 91.

HADLEY, A. T. Prohibition railway pools, 51. Railroad business under interstate com. act, 51. Railroad transportation, 49. Steamship subsidies (see under Shaw), 67. Workings interstate commerce law, 51.
Hall, C. H. Patriotism and national defence, 99.
Hall, H: American navigation, 58.
Hall, Hubert. Customs revenue in England, 55.
Hall, W: H. Irrigation development. Irrigation in [Southern] California, 115.
Hallam, H: Constitutional history England, 104.
Halleck, H. W. International law, 120.
Hamilton, Adelbert. Interstate commerce law, 49.
Hamilton, Alex., Life of. W: G. Sumner, 68. Report on manufactures, 58. Report to Congress on currency (see under Goddard, T: H.), 41. Some precedents followed by. C: F. Dunbar. 73.
Hamilton, Dr. J: B. Report on immigration (2d note), 84.
Hamilton, R. Money and value, 37.
Hamilton, R. S. Present status of social science, 73.

Hammerstein, L. v. De ecclesia et statu, 117.
Hampton Institute (1st note), 85.
Handbook for hospitals, 87.
— for visitors among poor, 87.
— — visitors to poorhouse, 87.
Handwörterbuch der Staatswissenschaft. J. E. Conrad and others, eds. 7.
Hankey, T. Principles of banking, 41.
Hare, J. I. C. American constitutional law, 102.
Hare, T: Election of representatives, 110.
Harper, J. C. Law of interstate commerce, 49.
Harris, W. T. Right of property and ownership of land, 19.
Harrison, F: The new trades-unionism, 31. Order and progress, 94.
Harrison, J. B. Dangerous tendencies in American life, 73. Indian reservations, 85.
Hart, A. B. Disposition of our public lands, 24. Do the people wish civil service reform? 112. Federal governments, 106.
Hartley, W. N. Water, air, and disinfectants, 88.
Hartshorn, E. A. Wages, Living, and the tariff, 58.
Harvard Univ. courses ec. and pol. sci., 131.
Hasbach, W: Englisches Arbeiterversicherungswesen, 29.
Haupt, L. M. Canals and their economic relation to transportation, 52.
Haushofer, M. Lehr- und Handbuch der Statistik, 124.
Hawaiian reciprocity treaty (2d note), 65.
Hayes, J. L. Wool and woolen tariff of 1883, 58.
Health and occupation. Dr. B: W. Richardson. 88.
— Boards of (2d note), 89.
— Care of. Dr. E. A. Parkes, 88.
— Dangers to. T. P. Teale. 89.
— Habitation and. F. de Chaumont. 88.
— Household. Dr. B: W. Richardson. 88.
— Public. Dr. A. H. Buck. 88.
— Public, Am. Assoc. (3d note), 89.
Healthy homes (3d note), 89.
— houses. Fleeming Jenkin. 88.
Hecker, Very Rev. I. T. The church and the age, 116.
Heffter, A. W. Droit international public de l'Europe, Europäisches Völkerrecht, 122.
Held, Ad. Die Einkommensteuer, 70. Sociale Geschichte Englands, 79. Socialismus, Socialdemokratie und Socialpolitik, 80.
Held, O. Die preussische Polizei-verwaltung, 119.
Hélie, M. F. Constitutions de la France, 106.
Helps, Sir Arthur. Social pressure, 74. Thoughts upon government, 94.
Herbert, Auberon. True line of deliverance (see under T: Mackay), 127.
Hermann, F. B. W. v. Staatswirthschaftliche Untersuchungen, 15.
Hertzka, H. Wahrung und Handel, 38.
Hess, R: Der Forstschutz, 114.
Heyl, L. U. S. duties, 54.

INDEX. 151

Hildebrand, Bruno. Die Nationalökonomie der Gegenwart und Zukunft. 15.
Hildebrand, R. Theorie des Geldes, 38.
High license (1st and 2d notes), 93.
Hill, G. B. Life of Sir Rowland Hill, and history penny postage, 112.
Hill, Octavia. Homes of London poor, 89. Our common land, 20.
Hilliard, Fcs. Law of taxation, 67.
Hine, C. C. Fire insurance, 53.
Hinton, R. J. Irrigation in U. S., 115.
Histoire de l'économie politique. J. P. A. de Villeneuve-Bargemont. 8.
Historical literature, Manual of. C: K. Adams (2d note), 96.
History, Financial, of U. S. A. S. Bolles, 66.
— political economy, 7. J: K. Ingram. 7.
— — theories. W: A. Dunning (1st note), 96.
— Studies in ancient. J. F. McLennan. 95.
Hitchcock, H. American state constitutions, 102. Influence of Chief Justice Marshall, 101.
Hoadley, G: Constitutional guarantees of right of property, 25.
Hock, C. F. v. Die öffentlichen Abgaben und Schulden, 70.
Hodder, F. H. References on municipal govt., U. S., 116.
Holls, F. W: Compulsory voting. 109.
Horr, N. T., and Bemis, A. A. Municipal police ordinances, 119.
Holtzendorff, F. v. Handbuch der Völkerrechts, 122. and Jagemann, E. v. Handbuch des Gefängnisswesens, 91.
Holyoake, G: J. History of coöperation in England, Manual of coöperation, 33.
Homans' cyclopædia of commerce, 45.
Home and its surroundings. N. H. Egleston. 73.
Homes of London poor. Octavia Hill. 89.
Hopkins, Johns, Univ. Courses pol. and ec. sci., 133.
Horn, J. E. Liberté des banques, 42.
Horton, S. D. Partial list publications on money, 35. Silver in Europe, 38.
Hosack, J. Law of nations, 121.
Hospitals, Handbook for. 87.
Hutchkiss, Philo P. Banks and banking, 1771-1888, 41.
Hough, F. B. Elements forestry, 113.
Houghton, W. R. History political parties. 102.
Housing poor Am. cities (2d note), 89.
— working classes. Report, 89. A. Raffalovich (see under T: Mackay), 127.
Howard, G: E. Local constitutional history U. S., 102.
How the other half lives. J. A. Riis. 73.
— we are governed. Anna L. Dawes. 97.
Howe, W. W. City government, New Orleans, 118.
Howell, G. Conflicts of capital and labor, 27. Liberty for labor (see under T: Mackay), 127.
Hoyle, W. Crime in England and Wales, 90.

Hoyt, C: S. Causes of pauperism, 86.
Hoyt, H. M. Protection vs. free trade, 58.
Hubert-Valleroux, P. Corporations d'arts et métiers, 30.
Hübner, O. Die Banken, 42.
Hudson, J. F. Railways and republic, 49.
Huff, L. J. F. Lassalle, 81.
Humboldt, Baron W: v. Sphere and duties of government, 95.
Hungary, Railroad passenger fares in. Jane J. Wetherell. 51.
Hughes, T:, and Neale, E. V. Manual for coöperators, 33.
Huskisson, W. Depreciation of our currency, 39.
Hygeia, a city of health. Dr. B: W. Richardson. 88.
Hygiene. Dr. A. H. Buck. 88.
— Practical. Dr. E. A. Parkes. 88.
Hyndman, H. M. Socialism in England, 77.
— and Morris, W: Principles of socialism, 77.

ICARIA. A. Shaw. 76.
Ice industry. Tenth census (2d note), 82.
Idleness, involuntary. Hugo Bilgram. 25.
Iles, G: Canadian chapter in agrarian agitation, 23. Competition and the trusts, 53. Liquor question in politics, 91.
Immigration, 83.
— Sir C: Dilke (4th note), 84.
— and crime. W. M. F. Round. 84.
— Emigration and. R. M. Smith. 83.
— Italian. Eugene Schuyler. 84.
— Laws of (1st note). 84.
— into U. S., History. W: J. Bromwell. 83.
— Report Committee on, 83. (See also Testimony, 83.)
— Report on. Dr. J: B. Hamilton (2d note), 84.
— State N. Y. F. Kapp. 83.
— Statistics of (note), 83.
— Tables of, and Prices, 46.
Imperial federation. See England and her colonies. 82.
Imports—Duties, 1867-83. C. H. Evans. 54.
Income and property taxes in Switzerland. G. Cohn. 72.
In darkest England. Gen. W: Booth. 86.
Indebtedness of States. Eleventh census (3d note), 82.
— of U. S., and of States (1st note), 73.
Independent in politics. J. R. Lowell. 99.
Index numbers. R. Giffen. 47.
Indian, The, 85.
— affairs, Commissioner's report (1st note), 85.
— [British] finance. H: Fawcett. 68.
— reservations. J. B. Harrison. 85.
— Rights Assoc. (2d note), 85.
— wards, Our. G. W. Manypenny. 85.
Indiana Univ. courses in ec. and pol. science, 133.
Indians, Ten years' work for. Helen W. Ludlow. 85.
Individualism. W. Donisthorpe. 77.
Industrial depressions (1st note), 29.

Industrial peace. L. L. F. R. Price. 34.
— progress of nation. E. Atkinson. 31.
— remuneration conference, 32.
— revolution in England. A. Toynbee. 27.
— situation and wages question. J. Schoenhof. 31.
— village of the future. Prince Kropotkin. 81.
Inebriety. Dr. N. Kerr. 91.
— and crime (2d note), 93.
Ingersoll, L. D. History War Department, 112.
Ingram, J: K. History of political economy, 7. Present position and prospects of political economy. 8.
Insurance, Commissioners of, Reports (note, life ins.), 53.
— Fire and life, 53.
— Life. N. Willey. Tables. D. P. Fackler. 53.
— National. *See* note under Blackley. 74.
— Workmen's, in Germany. F. W. Taussig. 53.
Intemperance. Dr. Bowditch (2d note), 93.
— Disease and (2d note), 93
— Effects of (2d note), 93
Intercontinental railway (2 titles), 49.
Interest, 25.
— and value money. J. Locke (note under J. R. McCulloch's 2d title), 12.
— Capital and. E. v. Bohm-Bawerk. 25.
— Law of wages and. J: B. Clark. 32.
— Rate of. Sidney Webb. 25.
Interior Department, Publications, 125.
Internal revenue report (*see* Treasury Dept.), 126.
— — Shall it be retained? R. M. Smith. (*see under* Shaw), 67.
International American conference (3 titles), 65; (2 titles), 120
— History of the. H. Villetard. 79.
— law, 119.
Interstate commerce act. J. R. Dos Passos. 48. Amendment, 47. Railroad business under. A. T. Hadley. 51.
— — Commission, 126. Reports, 49 (2d note), 51.
— — Law. Adelbert Hamilton. J. C. Harper. 49. Railway tariffs and. E. R. A. Seligman. 49. Workings of. A. T. Hadley. 51.
Introduction to English economic history and theory. W. J. Ashley. 7.
Invasion of pauper foreigners. Arnold White. 84.
Investment. T. Mackay (*see under* Plea for liberty), 127.
Irrigation, 115.
— cases, Decisions. D. W. Campbell. 115.
Italien, Agrarische Zustände in. K. T. Eheberg, 23.
Ivins. W. M. Machine politics and money in elections in N. Y. City, 116. Municipal finance, 119. Municipal government. 119.

Jackson, Helen H. Century of dishonor, 85.
Jacob, W. Historical inquiry production and consumption precious metals, 39.

Jahrbücher für Gesetzgebung, Verwaltung und Volkswirthschaft. H. Schmoller (5th note), 18.
— für Nationalökonomie und Statistik (5th note). 18.
James, C. L. Anarchy, 76.
James, E. J. Canal and railway, 52. Federal constitution Germany, 106. Federal constitution Switzerland, 106. Federal regulation of railways (*see* railway question), 49. Labor movement (*see* McNeill, G. E.), 26. Municipality and gas supply. 118.
Jameson, J. A. Constitutional conventions, 102.
Janet, Paul. La science politique et la morale, 95.
Jannet, C. Le socialisme d'état et le reforme sociale, 78. L'organization du travail, 28.
Janssen, J. Kirche und Staat, 117.
Jay, John. Denominational schools, 116.
Jeans, J. S. Railway problems, 50. Waterways, 52.
Jefferson, T: Parliamentary practice, 116.
Jellinek, G: Gesetz und Verordnung. 105.
Jenkin, Fleeming. Healthy houses, 88.
Jenkins, Rev. T: J. Am. Christian state schools, 117.
Jenks, J. W. Mich. Salt Assoc. Whiskey trust, 53.
Jevons, W: S. Investigations in currency and finance, 37. Methods of social reform, 74. Money and mechanism of exchange, 37. Primer political economy. 12. State in relation to labor, 104. Theory of political economy, 12.
Jews, Vital statistics. Eleventh census (3d note), 82.
Johnson, J: Rudimentary society among boys, 73.
Johnston, A. History American politics, 102. Political science (1st note), 103.
Jones, W: H. Federal taxes and State expenses, 67.
Journal des économistes (4th note), 18.
— *of economics, Quarterly* (1st note), 18.
Judeich, F: Die Forsteinrichtung, 114.
Judiciary, State. D. H. Chamberlain, 101.
Juglar, C. Crises commerciales, 44.
Jukes, The. R: L. Dugdale, 90.

Kaizl, J. Die Lehre von der Ueberwälzung der Steuern, 70.
Kamaroasky, Count L. Le tribunal international, 122.
Kapital, Das. Karl Marx, 25.
Kapp, F: Immigration, State N. Y.. 83.
Kasson, J: A. Municipal government Vienna (2d note), 119.
Kaufmann, Rev. M. Christian socialism, 77. Socialism in U. S. (3d note), 127.
Kautz, Julius. Geschichtliche Entwickelung der Nationalökonomie und ihrer Literatur, 8. Nationalökonomie als Wissenschaft, 15.
Kay, Jos. Free trade in land, 20. Social condition and education of England, 1848, 27.

INDEX.

Keane, Bishop. Denominational schools, 116.
Kearny, J. Sketch of Am. finance, 1789-1835, 67.
Keeler, B. C. Public control of the telegraph, 112.
Kelly, J. B. Summary of history and law of usury, 25.
Kelley, J. D. J. Question of ships, 61.
Kelley, W. D. Industrial and financial questions, 58.
Kempner, M. Common-sense socialism, 77.
Kent, C. A. Supreme court decisions since 1865. 101.
Kent, James. Commentary on international law, 120.
Kerr, A: W. History of banking in Scotland, 41.
Kerr, Dr. N. Inebriety, 91.
Ketteler, Bp. v. Arbeiterfrage und das Christenthum, 29.
Keyes, E. W. Savings banks in U. S., 43.
King, Clarence. Statistics production precious metals, U. S., 35.
Kinnear, J. B. Principles of property in land, 20.
Kirchenheim, A. v. Einführing in das Verwaltungsrecht, 107.
Kirkup, T: Inquiry into socialism, 77.
Kleinwachter, J. F. Die Kartelle, 53.
Knies, Karl. Geld und Credit, 39. Politische Oekonomie vom Standpunkte der geschichtlichen Methode, 15.
Knight, G. N. Management federal land grants, 24.
Knownothingism, old and new. E: McGlynn, D.D. 117.
Knox, J. Jay. Coinage act of 1873 and Silver question, 126. Free silver coinage, 126. The surplus and the public debt, 127. U. S. notes, 36.
König, B. E. Geschichte der deutschen Post, 112.
Kropotkin, Prince Pierre. The coming anarchy. Industrial village of the future, 81. Paroles d'un revolté, 79. War, law and authority, expropriation, 78.
Kupka, P. F. Die Verkehrsmittel in den Vereinigten Staaten, 51.

Laband, P. Das Staatsrecht des deutschen Reichs. 107.
Labor a hundred years ago. Talcott Williams. 26.
— and capital allies, not enemies. E: Atkinson. 25.
— Bureau, Missouri. History railway strike, 1886, 30.
— Bureaus of statistics of (3d note), 29.
— Capital and, 24.
— Commissioner of, Reports (1st note), 29.
— Convict, in U. S. (1st note), 29.
— Department of, 126.
— differences and their settlement. J. D. Weeks. 34.
— Growth and purposes of bureaus of statistics of. C. D. Wright. 26.

Labor, hand, in prisons. Carroll D. Wright. 90.
— History and relations to capital, 25.
— Honest money and. C. Schurz. 36.
— in Europe and America. E. Young. 27.
— Knights of. C. D. Wright. 30.
— Land and law. W. A. Phillips. 19.
— Liberty for. G: Howell (see under T: Mackay), 127.
— movement. G. E. McNeill and others, 26.
— — in America. R: T. Ely. 25.
— On. W. T. Thornton. 27.
— Politics of. Phillips Thompson. 26.
— problem. W. E. Barns. 25.
— question. M. M. Trumbull. [Wheelbarrow.] 26.
— — Plain man's talk on. Simon Newcomb. 26.
— — Relation of political economy to. C. D. Wright. 26.
— — — to law of to-day. L. Brentano. 127.
— Reports on (2d and 3d notes), 29.
— State in relation to W: S. Jevons. 104.
— statistics, Am. R. M. Smith. 125.
— Taxation of. C. B. Spahr. 72.
— Uniform hours of. C. D. Wright. 27.
— value fallacy. M. L. Scudder, jr. 31.
Laborer, British, Economic position of. H: Fawcett. 32.
Laborers, Selection of. J. M. Bugbee. 110.
Laboulaye, E. Histoire du droit de propriété fonciere en occident, 22.
Lalor, J: J., ed. Cyclopædia of political science, etc., 6.
Lamphere, G: N. U. S. Government, organization, 107.
Land and its rent. F. A. Walker. 20.
— — labor in the U. S. W: G. Moody. 19.
— — landlords, English. G: C: Broderick. 20.
— — rent, 18.
— Commissioners' report (note), 24.
— Essay on the right of property in. J: Ogilby. 21.
— Free. Arthur Arnold. 20.
— Free trade in. Joseph Kay. 20.
— holding among the Germans, Early history of. Denman W. Ross. 19.
— — in England, History of. Joseph Fisher. 20.
— — — Historical sketch of distribution of. W. L. Birkbeck. 20.
— laws. F. Pollock. 21.
— — Irish. A. G. Richey. 22.
— nationalization. F. L. Soper. 23. A. R. Wallace, 22.
— Our common. Octavia Hill. 20.
— Ownership of, and right of property. W. T. Harris. 19.
— Principles of property in. J. B. Kinnear. 20.
— Property in. Duke of Argyll and. H: George, 20. Sir G: Campbell, 23. H. Winn, 20.
— question. T. J Elliott, 20. H: George, 19. J. Macdonell, 21.
— — in the U. S., History of. Shosuke Sato. 20.

INDEX.

Labor question, Irish. H: George. 19.
— — Symposium on. J. H. Levy, *ed*. 21.
— — United Kingdom (2d note), 23.
— system of the New England colonies. M. Egleston. 19.
— systems. T. E. Cliffe Leslie. 21.
— tenure, Ethics of. J. B. Clark. 23.
— — in Ireland, History of. W. E. Montgomery. 21.
— — in various countries. J. W. Probyn, *ed*. 21.
— tenures and land classes of Ireland, History of. G. Sigurson. 22.
— Transfer of, by registration. Sir Robert Torrens. 22.
— — reform. D. H. Olmstead. 19.
Landed property and economy of estates. D: Low. 21.
Lands, Disposition of our public. A. B. Hart. 24.
— Exhaustion of arable. C. W. Davis. 23.
— Public, Decisions. 24.
— Railroad indemnity. F. P. Powers. 24.
Lange, F. A. Arbeiterfrage. 29.
Lassalle, F. L. J. Huff, 81. Workingman's programme, 80.
Laughlin, J. L. Bimetallism in U. S., 38. Elements political economy, 10. Study political economy, 6. Wages and tariff (2d line), 68.
Laurent, E. Pauperisme et les associations de prevoyance, 86.
Laveleye, E. de. Elements political economy, 14. Le marché monetaire et ses crises, 44. New tendencies of political economy, 8. Primitive property, Propriété et de ses formes primitives, 22. Socialisme contemporain. Socialism of to-day, 79.
Lavergne, L. de. Economie rurale de la France, 22, 28. Rural economy of England, Scotland and Ireland, 22.
Law of nations, Assoc. for reform and codification (last note), 122.
Lawmakers, Among the. E. Alton. 97.
Lawson, W: J. History of banking. 41.
Laws relating to survey and disposition public domain. 24.
Lawton, G. W. American caucus system, 116.
Lea, H: C. Keynotes from Rome, 117.
Leadam, J. S. What protection does for the farmer, 63.
Leaden images, True story of. D: A. Wells (*see* Practical economics), 62.
Lee, J. Anti-Chinese legislation (two titles), 84.
Lees, F. R. Text-book temperance, 92.
Lefèvre, F. Consulat français, 121.
Legality of trusts. T. W. Dwight, 53.
Legal rights, Methods of assisting working classes in enforcement, 87.
— tender. H. Cernuschi, 39.
— — act. F. A. Walker *and* H. Adams (*see* Adams, C: F., jr., Chapters in Erie), 47.
— — — History. E. G. Spaulding. 36.

Legal tender decision, 36. *Also* under Knox, J. J. 36.
Legislation, Defective and corrupt. Simon Sterne. 100.
— Experimental. W: S. Jevons. 74.
Legislative assemblies, Law and practice. L. S. Cushing. 116.
Leib, H. The protective tariff, what it does for us, 61.
Lepage, A. Histoire de la commune, 79.
Le Play, P. G. F. L'organisation du travail. Organization of labor, 28. Les ouvriers Européens, 28. La reforme sociale, 75, 79.
Le Roy-Beaulieu, Paul. Le collectivisme, 79. De la colonisation, 83. De l'état moral et intellectuel des populations ouvrieres, 28. L'état moderne et ses fonctions, 95. La question ouvriere au XIXme siècle, 28. Répartition des richesses, 75, 79. Le travail des femmes au XIXme siècle, 28. Traité des science des finances, 70.
Leslie, T. E. Cliffe. Essays in political and moral philosophy, 16. Land systems, 21.
Levasseur, E. Histoire des classes ouvrieres en France, 28. La population française, 123.
Levermore, C: H. H: C. Carey. 60.
Levi, Leone. History of British Commerce, 45. International law, 121. Wages and earnings, 1883-84, 32. Work and pay, 30.
Levy, J. H., *ed*. Symposium on land question, 21.
Lewins, W. Her Majesty's mails, 112. Savings banks Great Britain and Ireland, 43.
Liberty. J: S. Mill. 94.
— and liberalism. Bruce Smith, 95.
— equality, and fraternity. Fitz James Stephen. 95.
— Plea for. H. Spencer *and others* (*see* T: Mackay), 127.
Libraries, Public. W: S. Jevons. 74. M. D. O'Brien (*see under* T: Mackay), 127.
Lieber, F. Civil liberty and self-government. Political ethics, 93.
Life and labor in East London. C: Booth, 74.
Lilienfeld, P. Sociale Wissenschaft der Zukunst, 80.
Linderman, H. R. Money and legal tender in U. S., 36.
Lindsay, W. S. Ancient shipping and commerce, 45.
Liquor laws of U. S. (2d note), 93.
— question, 91.
— — in politics. G: Iles. 91.
— traffic, People *vs*. J: B. Finch. 91.
Liquors, Malt, Alleged adulterations (2d note), 93.
List, F. National system of political economy, 15.
Literature of political economy. J: R. McCulloch. 6.
Lloyd, H: D. Strike of millionaires against miners, 29.
Local government and taxation. Cobden Club essays, 69.

INDEX. 155

Local government in England. F. J. Goodnow. 105.
— option. W. S Caine and W. Hoyle. 92.
— taxation. J: Noble. 69.
Loch, C. S Charity organization, 87.
Locke, J. Interest and value money (note *under* J. R. McCulloch's 2d title), 12.
Lockwood, H. C. Abolition of the presidency, 99. Constitutional history France, 106.
Lodge, H: C. Why patronage in offices is un-American, 112.
— and Powderly, T. V. Federal election bill, 109.
Lombard street. W. Bagehot. 41.
Lombroso, C. L'uomo delinquente, 91.
London, Historical charters. W. G. Birch. 118.
— how governed. Albert Shaw. 119.
— Municipal. J: F. B. Firth. 118.
Looking backward. E: Bellamy. 76.
Loria, Achille. La rendita fondiaria, 23.
Low, D. Landed property and economy estates, 21.
Low, S. J., *and* Pulling, F. S. Dictionary English history, 104.
Low, Seth. Problem city government, 118.
Lowell, J. R. The independent in politics, 99.
Lowell, Josephine S. Public relief and private charity, 87.
Lubbock, *Sir* J: Origin of civilization. Prehistoric times, 95. Representation, 108.
Ludlow, Helen W. Ten years' work for Indians, 83.
Ludlow, J. M., *and* Jones, Lloyd. Progress of the working-classes. 1832–67, 27.
Lum, D. D. Chicago anarchists, 76.
Lunt, E. Clark. Present position of political economy, 16.
Lyman, Theo. Diplomacy of U. S., 120.

McAdam, G. Alphabet in finance, 36.
McCullagh, W. T. Industrial history of free nations, 45.
McCulloch, Hugh. Bi-metallism, 38.
McCulloch, J: R. Dictionary commerce and commercial navigation. Literature of political economy, 6. Principles of political economy, 12. Taxation and funding system, 69.
Macdonell, J. Land question. 21.
McDonnell, W. D. History and criticism wages theories, 32.
McGlynn, E., *D.D.* Old Knownothingism and new, 117.
Macgregor, J. Commercial and financial legislation, 45.
Machine, 116.
Mackay, T:, *ed* Plea for liberty. Investment (*thereunder*), 127.
McKee, T. H., *ed.* Protection echoes from the Capitol. 58.
McKinley bill (9th note), 56.
McKnight, D. A. Electoral system, U. S., 108.
McLennan. J. F. Patriarchal theory, 96. Studies in ancient history, 95.

Macleod, H: D. Dictionary political economy, 6. Economics for beginners, 12. Elements banking, 41. Elements economics, 12. Principles economical philosophy 12. Theory and practice of banking, 42. Theory credit, 42.
McMillan, D. C. Elective franchise, U. S., 108.
McNeill. G. E., *and others*. Labor movement, 26.
McPherson, E: Political history, U. S. (3 titles), 102.
McQuaid, Bishop. Religious teaching in schools, 117.
Macvane, S. M. Working principles, political economy. 10.
Macy, Jesse. Our government, 98. Theory and practice of protection, (*see under* Shaw), 67.
Magliani, Ag. La questione monetaria, 38.
Maine, *Sir* H. J. Sumner. Early history institutions, 21. International law, 121. Popular government. 94. Village communities in the east and west, 21.
Maistre, J. M., *Comte de.* Du Pape, 117.
Mallock, W. H. Property and progress, 21.
Malthus, T: R. Population, 81. Principles of political economy, 12.
— *and* his work. J. Bonar. 81.
Manchester, Duke of. Free trade isolated, 60.
Manufactories, Injury and death in (3d note), 89.
Manufactures, Power and machinery. Tenth census (2d note) 82.
— Report on. Alex. Hamilton. 58.
— Tenth census (2d note), 82.
Manypenny. G. W. Our Indian wards, 85.
Mappin, W. F. Farm mortgages and the small farmer, 23.
Marlo, Karl. Organization der Arbeit, 80.
Marriage and divorce (1st note), 29.
Marshall, A. Present position economics, 8. Principles of economics, 12.
— *and* Mary P. Economics of industry, 12.
Marshall, Chief Justice, Influence of. H: Hitchcock. 101.
Martens, G: F. v. Cours diplomatique, 121. Droit des gens modernes de l'Europe. Receuils de traités (6 titles), 122.
Martin, E. W. History Grange movement, 29.
Martin, J. B. Bank notes, 43. Our gold coinage, 40.
Martineau, Harriet. Illustrations political economy, 12.
Marx, Karl. Das Capital. Capital, 25 (note), 80.
— *and* Engels, F: Manifesto communist party, 80.
Maryland, Ground rents in. Louis Mayer. 19.
Marzano, F. Compendio di scienza delle finanze, 71.
Mason, A. B., *and* Lalor, J. J. Primer of political economy, 10.

Mason, D. H. Short tariff history, U. S., 54.
Mason, E. C. The veto power, 99.
Mathews, R. Municipal administration, 118.
May, *Sir* T: E. Constitutional history England, 104. Democracy in Europe, 96.
Mayer, Louis. Ground rents in Maryland, 19.
Mayo, A. D. Third estate of South, 85.
Mayo, G: Gesetzmässigkeit im Gesellschaftsleben, 124.
Mayr, H: Die Waldungen von Nordamerika, 114.
Mazzini, J. Democracy in Europe and duties of man, 80.
Mazzola, U. I dati della finanza pubblica, 71.
Mead, E. D. Denominational schools, 116.
Measures, weights, and money of all nations. F. W. Clarke, 35.
Medley, G: W. Fair trade unmasked, 63. Trade depression, 44.
Meitzen, F. E. A. Geschichte, Theorie und Technik der Statistik. History of statistics. Theory and technique of statistics, 124.
Mendicancy, Bill to promote, 84.
Menier, A. L'impôt sur le capital, 70.
Merchant marine, Our. D: A. Wells. 62.
Merivale, H. Colonization and colonies. 82.
Meriwether, Lee. Tramp at home. Tramp's trip, 26.
Metals, Precious. Tenth census (2d note), 82.
— — Statistics of production in U. S. Clarence King. 35.
Methods of study, political economy, 5.
Messedaglia, A. Teoria della popolazione, 82.
Mexico, Commerce with (5th note), 57.
Meyer, Robert. Principien der gerechten Besteuerung, 70.
Meyer, Rudolph. Emancipationskampf des vierten Standes, 29. Heimstätten und andere Wirthschaftsgesetze, 23.
Michigan, Univ. of. Courses in econ. and pol. science, 134.
Military laws, U. S. R. N. Scott. 113.
Mill, James. Elements of political economy, 12.
Mill, J: S. On liberty, 94. Principles of political economy, unabridged and abridged, 13. Representative government, 94. Socialism, 78.
Millar, F. Evils of State trading by P. O. (*see under* T: Mackay), 127.
Miller, J. Bleecker. Progress and robbery, 19, 30. Trade organizations in politics, 30. Unconstitutionality of protection, 61.
Mills, R. Q. Free trade and protection, 60.
Mills, W. T. Science of politics, 98.
Mineral resources, U. S. (*see* Interior Dept.), 125.
Minority representation, 109.
Minot, W., jr. Taxation in Massachusetts, 67.
Minghetti, M. Economia pubblica e delle sur attinenze colla morale e col diritto. Rapports de l'économie publique avec la morale et le droit, 75.

Mining laws and industries. Tenth census (2d note), 82.
— districts, Land laws of. C: H. Shinn. 24.
Mint, Director of, Report (2d note), 40.
Moffatt, R. S. Economy of consumption, 44.
Mohl, R. v. Staatswissenschaften, 96.
Monetary conferences, International (1st note), 40.
Money, 35.
— F. A. Walker. 37.
— and banks, State tamperings with. H. Spencer (2d note). 43.
— — its laws. H. V. Poor. 36.
— — — substitutes. Horace White. 37.
— — legal tender in U. S. H. R. Linderman. 36.
— — mechanism of exchange. W: S. Jevons. 37.
— — monetary problems. J. S. Nicholson. 37.
— — value. R. Hamilton. 37.
— Honest, and labor. C. Schurz. 36.
— in relations to trade and industry. F. A. Walker. 37.
— Robinson Crusoe's. D: A. Wells. 37.
— weights, and measures of all nations. F. W. Clarke. 35.
Mongredien, A: Free trade and English commerce, 63. History, free trade in England. Pleas for protection examined, 63. Trade depressions, 44.
Monnet, E. Histoire de l'administration en France, 107.
Monnier, A. L'assistance publique, 86.
Monopolies and the people. C: W. Baker. 52.
— Development of. H. S. Foxwell. 53.
Monopoly, 52.
— Economic law of. E. B. Andrews. 53.
Montesquieu, M. de S. Spirit of laws, 95.
Montgomery, W. E. History of land tenure in Ireland, 21.
Moody, W: G. Land and labor in the U. S., 19.
Moore, J. S. Friendly letters to American farmers. Sermons to protectionist manufactures, 61.
Morcellement, Le. A. de Foville. 22.
Morley, J: Life of R: Cobden. 63.
— On compromise, 94.
Morrill, Sen. J. S. Free trade and protection, 60.
Morris, W: Signs of change, 78.
Morrison, C. Relations between capital and labor, 27.
Morrison, W. D. Crime and prison system, 90.
Morrison bill (4th note), 56.
Morse, A. D. Equality in taxation—Commercial union with Canada (*see* under Shaw), 67.
Morse, J. T. Treatise on banking law, 41.
Mortality. Tenth census (2d note), 82.
Mortgage evil. J. P. Dunn. 23.
— statistics (note), 23.
Mortgages in foreign countries (note), 23.

Mortgages, Western. J. W. Gleed. 23.
— — farm. D. R Goodloe. 23.
Morton, O. T. Some popular objections to civil service reform, 112.
Moses, B. Federal government, Switzerland, 106. Municipal government, San Francisco, 118.
Mowry, W. A. Studies in civil government, 98.
Mulford, E. The nation, 100.
Mulhall, M. G. Prices since 1850, 47.
Municipal finance. W: M. Ivins, 119.
— government, 118.
— Reform, selection, appointment officers, 118.
Municipalities and quasi-public works, 118.
Munro, J. E. C. Constitution of Canada, 106.
Murhard, Carl. Theorie des Handels, 46.
Murray, J. B. C. History of usury laws, 25.
Museums, Use and abuse of. W: S. Jevons. 74.

NATION, The. E. Mulford. 100.
Nation's drink bill (2d note), 93.
National Academy Sciences (last note), 126.
— debts. R. D. Baxter, 73.
— History (1st note), 73.
— domain, Our. E: Atkinson. 24.
— Grange, Patrons of Husbandry, 30.
— League for Protection Am. Institutions (2d note), 117.
— loans, U. S (1st note), 73.
Nationalism, First steps toward. What it means. E: Bellamy. 81.
Nations, Relative strength and weakness of. E: Atkinson. Industrial progress, 31.
Navigation, American. H: Hall. 58.
— Commissioner of, Report (2d note), 52.
— interests, causes of decline (2d note), 57.
Navy, 112.
— Department, Laws, 113. Publications, 125.
Nebraska. Univ. of. Courses ec. and pol. science, 134.
Negro, The, 84.
— education. G. R. Stetson. 85.
— Elevation of. L. H. Blair. 84.
— in Maryland. J. R. Brackett. (two titles), 84.
— Plantation, as freeman. P. A. Bruce. 85.
— question. G: W. Cable. 85.
— Republican party and. E. L. Godkin. 85.
Neumann, F. J. Bevölkerung in Deutschland, 82.
Neumann, F. T. Progressive Einkommensteuer, 70.
Neumann-Spallart, F. X. v. Uebersichten der Weltwirthschaft, 46.
New England, Economic and social history. W. B. Weeden 45.
New Jersey, College of. Courses ec. and pol. science, 135.
New Orleans, City government, 118.
New York, Anti-rent agitation in State of. E. P. Cheyney. 18.
— charities directory, 87.

New York City, Machine politics. W. M. Ivins. 116.
— Constitutions of. J. H. Dougherty. 103.
— custom house, Civil service reform in. W. Brown. 110.
— Forest Commission Report, 113.
— Municipal civil service (3d note), 111.
— property tax, History of. J: C. Schwab. 67.
— [State] legislature, Report on management railroads, 49.
— taxation, Reports on. D: A. Wells. 68.
— Twelve lectures on future of. G: H. Andrews. 66.
Newcomb, Simon. A B C of finance, 36. Plain man's talk on labor question, 26. Principles political economy, 10.
Newsholme, Dr. A. Vital statistics, 123.
Newspapers. Tenth census (2d note), 82.
Newton, Rev. R. H. Social studies, 73.
Neymarck, A. Public debts of Europe, 73.
Nicholls, Sir G: History English poor law. History Irish poor law, 86.
Nicholson, J. S Money and monetary problems, 37. Profit sharing, 34. Tenants' gain not landlord's loss, 21.
Noble, J. Fiscal legislation, 55. Local taxation, 69. The Queen's taxes, 69.
Noel, Octave. Chemins de fer en France et à l'étranger, 50.
Nordhoff, C: Communistic societies of the U.S., 76. Politics for young Americans, 98.
Northam, H: C. Civil gov't for common schools, 127.
Northcote, Sir Stafford H. Twenty years of financial policy, 1843-61. 69.
Note circulation. R. H. I. Palgrave. 43.
Notes, U. S. J. Jay Knox. 36.
Nott, C: C. A good farm for nothing, 19.
Noyes, J. H. History of American socialisms, 76.

O'BRIEN, M D. Free libraries (see under T: Mackay), 127.
Ogilby, J: Essay on the right of property in land, 21.
Old South leaflets (note), 98.
Olmstead, Dwight H Land transfer reform, 19.
Olmsted, F. L. Tobacco tax, 1861-90, 72.
O'Neil, C. A. American electoral system. 108.
Order and progress. F. Harrison. 94.
Organization of labor. P G. F. Le Play. 28.
Original package case. C. S. Patterson. 93
Origin of civilization. Sir J: Lubbock. 95.
Osgood, H. L. Rodbertus, 81. Scientific anarchism, 81.
Oswald, Dr. F. L. Poison problem, 92.
Our continent, 65.
— country. Rev. Josiah Strong. 74.
Outdoor relief and tramps. F. Wayland 87.
Ouvry, H. A. Stein and his reforms in Prussia, 21.
Overstone, Lord. Metallic and paper currency, 37.

Owen and Christian socialists. E. R. A. Seligman 76.
Owen, R., Memoir. A. J. Booth. 77.
PALGRAVE, R. H. I. Dictionary political economy, 6. Local taxation, Great Britain and Ireland, 69. Note circulation, 43.
Palm, A. J. Capital punishment, 127.
Panic of 1837 (last note), 44.
— of 1866. R. Baxter. 44.
Panics, 43.
Pantaleone, M. Teoria della translazione dei tributi. 71.
Papacy and civil power. R. W. Thompson. 117.
Paper money and banking in U. S. W: M. Gouge. 35.
— currency, Historical sketches of. H. Phillips, jr. 36.
— money inflation in France. A. D. White. 37.
Paris Comte de. Associations ouvrières en Angleterre. Trades-unions in England, 30.
Parkes, Dr. E. A. Care of health, 88. Practical hygiene, 88.
Parliament, English. R. Gneist, 105. Short history. B. C. Skottowe. 104.
Parliamentary government British colonies. A. Todd. 104.
— — England. A. Todd. 104.
— practice. 116.
— — T: Jefferson. 116.
Parsons, A. R. Anarchism. 76.
Parties, 115.
— and patronage L. G. Tyler. 127.
Parton, James. Beginnings of spoils system national government, 111.
Party history, 115.
Past and present of political economy. R: T. Ely. 7.
Patents, Publications. See Interior Department, 125.
Patten. S. N. Economic basis protection, 58. Premises political economy, 16. Stability of prices, 46.
Patterson, C. S. Federal restraints on State action, 98. Original package case, 93.
Patriarchal theory. J. F. McLennan. 96.
Patriotism and national defence. C. H. Hall. 99.
Patrons of Husbandry. E. S. Carr. 29.
Patton, J. H. Democratic party, History. 115.
Pauperism, 86.
— H: Fawcett. 86.
— Causes of. C: S. Hoyt. 86.
Pauper-labor argument. D: A. Wells. 62.
Payne, E: J. History European colonies, 83.
Peace Society, London (3d note), 123.
— and arbitration, Am. Advocate (1st note), 123.
Peacemaker (1st note), 123.
Pearce-Edgcumbe, E. R: Fallacies regarding trade and duties. 63.
Peasant proprietors, Plea for. W. T. Thornton. 22.

Peel's, Sir Robert, Act, 1844. R. Torrens. 42.
Pennsylvania, Finances of. T. K. Worthington. 68.
— Univ. of. Courses ec. and pol. sci., 135.
Penological principles. W. Tallack. 90.
Pensions, Laws of army and navy, 113.
— Publications. See Interior Department, 125.
Pentecost, Hugh O. Single tax question (see under Trumbull, M. M.), 26.
Péreire, I: Constitution des banques et l'organization du credits, 42.
Perplexities that Canada would bring. A. R. Carman. 65.
Perry, A. L. Elements of political economy, 10. Introduction to, 10. Principles political economy, 127.
Peto, Sir S. Morton. Taxation, its levy and expenditure, 69.
Petroleum. Tenth census (2d note), 82.
Philadelphia, (see Bullitt bill), 116 (see Fall of bossism, G. Vickers), 116.
— 1681-1887. E. P. Allinson and B. Penrose. 118.
— Ground rents in. E. P. Allinson and B. Penrose. 18.
Phillimore, Sir R. Commentaries upon international law, 121.
Phillipovich, E. L'. Emigration Européen, 84.
Phillips, H., jr. Historical sketches of paper currency, 36.
Phillips, W. A. Labor, land, and law, 19.
Philosophy of wealth. J: B. Clark. 10.
Philpott, H. J. Tariff chats, 61.
Picard, Alf. Chemins de fer français. Traité des chemins de fer, 50.
Pidgeon, C. Old world questions and new world answers, 27.
Pidgin, C. F. Practical statistics, 123.
Pierce, E: L. Treatise on law of railroads, 49.
Pigeonneau, H. Histoire du commerce de la France, 46.
Pig iron production. Eleventh census (3d note), 82.
Pike, L. O. Crime in England, 90.
Pinchot, Gifford. Forest policy abroad (2d note), 115.
Pitman, R. C. Alcohol and the State, 92.
Pitkin, T. Statistical view commerce, U. S., 45.
Plunkett, Mrs. H. M. Women, plumbers, and doctors, 88.
Police, 119.
Political economy. W. Bagehot. 11. F. Bastiat. 17. (History of), J. A. Blanqui. 8. A. S. Bolles. 16. J. E. Cairnes, (2 titles), 11. (Essays). 16. A. L. Chapin. 9. Emile de Laveleye. 8, 14. R: T. Ely. 10. H: Fawcett. 11. (For beginners), and (Tales in). Mrs. M. G. Fawcett. 12. C. Gide (3d note), 127. Horace Greeley. 10. J. M. Gregory. 10. W: Stanley Jevons (2 titles), 12. J. Lawrence Laughlin. 18. F. List. 15. J: R. McCulloch, (2 titles),

INDEX. 159

12. S. M. Macvane. 10. T: R. Malthus. 12. Harriet Martineau. 12. A. B. Mason *and* J. J. Lalor. 10. James Mill. 12. J: Stuart Mill (2 titles), 13. Simon Newcomb. 10. A. L. Perry (2 titles), 10, 127. Simon N. Patten. 16. D: Ricardo. 13. J. E. Thorold Rogers. 13. W: Roscher. 15. J. B. Say. 14. N. W. Senior. 13. J. L. Shadwell. 13. H: Sidgwick. 13. G: M. Steele. 10. R. E. Thompson. 11. (Progress of, in Europe since the 16th century), Travers Twiss. 8. F. A. Walker (2 titles), 11. F. Wayland (2 titles), 11.
— education, primer. R: R. Bowker. 97.
— essays. J. E. Cairnes. 94.
— ethics. F. Lieber. 93.
— history, American. 101.
— — U. S., 3 titles. E: McPherson. 102.
— ideas, American. J: Fiske. 101.
— — of the Puritans. H: L. Osgood. 101.
— parties, History. W. R. Houghton. 102.
— problem. A. Stickney. 100.
— problems. W. R. Greg. 94.
— record (2d note). 103.
— science. J: W. Burgess. 93. T. D. Woolsey. 94. Cyclopædia of.): J. Lalor, *ed.* 6. General works. 93.
— — History, early institutions, 95.
— — *Quarterly* (last note), 17.
— — sources and literature. G. H. Baker (note), 95.
Politics. W. Crane and B. Moses. 93.
— American. T. V. Cooper and H. T. Fenton. 101.
— and economics. W. Cunningham. 104.
— as duty and career. Moorfield Storey. 100.
— Comparative. E. A. Freeman. 94.
— for young Americans. C: Nordhoff. 98.
— history, American. A. Johnston. 102.
— Introduction to history science of. *Sir* F. Pollock. 96.
— Physics and. W. Bagehot. 94.
— Practical, Essays on. T. Roosevelt. 100.
— Science of. W. T. Mills. 98.
— Study of. W. P. Atkinson. 93.
Pollock, *Sir* F: Introduction to history science of politics, 96. Land laws, 21.
Pomeroy, J. N. International law, 120.
Pooling, Traffic. T: M. Cooley. 48.
Poor, Associated effort on behalf. *Miss* L. L. Schuyler. 87.
— Handbook for visitors among, 87.
Poor, H. V. Manual railroads U. S., 49. Money and its laws, 36. Twenty-two years of protection, 59.
Poorhouse, Handbook visitors to. 87.
Poor law, English. *Rev.* T. W. Fowle. 86. *Sir* G: Nicholls. 86.
— — Experiment at Elberfeld. *Rev.* W. W. Edwards. 86.
— — Irish. *Sir* G: Nicholls. 86.
— — system, English. P. F. Aschrott. 86.
— laws, 86.
— — in foreign countries, 86.

Poor, relief of, in Germany. A. G. Warner, 86.
Population, 81.
— Eleventh census (3d note), 82.
— T: R. Malthus. 81.
— Tenth census (2d note), 82.
— Law of. M. T: Sadler. 81.
— Over-, and its remedy. W: T: Thornton. 81.
— True law of. T: Doubleday. 81.
Porter, R. P. Bread-winners abroad, 26. Free trade folly. Protection and free trade, 59.
Post, Weekly, N. Y. (6th note), 64.
Post-office, 112.
— Evil State-trading by. F: Millar (*see under* T: Mackay), 127.
— Department, Publications, 126.
— N. Y., Spoils system in. D. B. Eaton. 111.
Postal savings banks, 43. British (note), 43.
— telegraph service foreign countries (last note), 112.
Poverty, Preventable causes of. H. D. Chapin, 76.
Powers, F. Perry. Railroad indemnity lands, 74.
Practical economics. D: A. Wells. 16.
Precious metals. W. Jacob. 39.
— — Production, U. S. (2d note), 40.
Prehistoric man. D. Wilson. 96.
— times. *Sir* J: Lubbock. 95.
Present position and prospects political economy. J: K. Ingram. 8.
— — of economics. A. Marshall. 8.
Presidency, Abolition of. H. C. Lockwood. 99.
President's message, 1887 (annot. by R: R. Bowker), 61.
Presidential administrations, References to history. W: E. Foster. 102.
— elections, History. E. Stanwood. 102, 108.
Preventable causes disease (3d note), 89.
Price, Bonamy. Political economy, 16. Currency and banking, 42. Principles currency and banking, 39.
Price, L. L. F. R. Industrial peace, 34.
Prices, 46.
— Changes in (1st note), 47.
— Congested. M. L. Scudder, *jr.*, 43.
— High and low, 1793-1822. T: Tooke. 47.
— History of. T: Tooke *and* W. Newmarch. 47.
— in England, History of agriculture and. J. E. Thorold Rogers. 22.
— of commodities, 46.
— Schedules of (2d and 4th notes), 47.
— since 1850. M. G. Mulhall. 47.
Primer civil service reform, 111.
— tariff reform. D: A. Wells. 62.
Primitive culture. E. B. Tylor. 96.
Principles social science. H: C. Carey. 9.
Prins, A. La democratie et le régime parlementaire, 109.
Prison ethics. Herbert Spencer (4th note), 91.
— Nat., Assoc (1st note) 91.
— science. Eugene Smith. 90.
— statistics. R. P. Falkner. 90.

Prisons, 90.
— E. C. Wines. 90.
Problems of Greater Britain. Sir C: W. Dilke. 82.
— — to-day. R: T. Ely. 60.
Probyn, J. W., *ed.* Systems of land tenure in various countries, 21.
Profit, 25.
Profit-sharing, 33.
— N: P. Gilman. 33. J. S. Nicholson. 34. Sedley Taylor. 34. C. D. Wright. 33.
Profits, Margin of. E: Atkinson. 25.
— under modern conditions. J: B. Clark. 25.
Progres de la science économique depuis Adam Smith. M. Block. 8.
Progress and poverty. H: George. 19.
— — A review. G: B. Dixwell. 19.
— — robbery. J. Bleecker Miller. 19, 30.
Prohibition (1st and 2d notes), 92.
— G. C. Low (2d note), 93.
— Economics of. J. C. Fernald. 91.
Prohibitionists, Mistakes of. J. Mudie (2d note), 93.
Prohibitionists' text-book, 92.
Property and progress. W. H. Mallock. 21.
— Constitutional guarantees of right of. G: Hoadley. 25.
— Primitive. E. de Laveleye. 22.
Propriété, De la. F. C. L. Comte. 24. M. A. Thiers. 24.
— fonciere en occident, Histoire du droit de. E. Laboulaye. 22.
Prothero, R. E. Pioneers and progress of English farming, 21.
Protection, 58.
— and agriculture. F. A. Walker (*see under* Shaw), 67.
— — bad times. G. Baden-Powell. 63.
— — communism. W. Rathbone. 63.
— — free trade. I. Butts. 60. H: George. 61. H. M. Hoyt. 58. R. P. Porter. 59. J. Wharton. 60.
— — the farmer. Sen. S: M. Cullom. 60.
— — protectionists. F. A. Walker. 64.
— Benefits of. J. Roach. 60.
— Does, protect? W. M. Grosvenor. 61.
— echoes from the capitol. T. H. McKee, *ed.* 58.
— Economic basis of. S. N. Patten. 58.
— Facts and fallacies. R. B. Wise. 64.
— History of, U. S. W: G. Sumner. 54.
— Pleas for, examined. A: Mongredien. 63.
— Sophisms of. F: Bastiat. 64.
— Theory and practice of. Jesse Macy (*see under* Shaw), 67.
— to home industry. R. E. Thompson. 59.
— Twenty-two years of. H: V. Poor. 59
— Unconstitutionality of. J. B. Miller. 61.
Protectionism. W: G. Sumner. 62.
Protectionist manufacturers, Friendly sermons to. J. S. Moore. 60.
Protectionists' manual. G. B. Stebbins. 59.
Protective policy defended. R. E. Thompson (*see under* Shaw), 67.
— questions abroad. R. E. Thompson. 60.
— tariff, History. R. W. Thompson. 55.

Protective Tariff League (2d note), 59.
— tariffs as a question of national economy. W. W. Folwell (*see under* Shaw), 67.
Proudhon, P. J. Œuvres, 79. System of economical contradictions, 28.
Prussia, Local government. F. J. Goodnow. 106.
Public debt of U. S. W. A. Richardson. 36, 73 (*see* Treasury Dept.), 126.
— — — Surplus and. J: J. Knox. 127.
Public debts, 72.
— — H: C. Adams. 72.
— — of Europe. A. Neymarck. 73.
— finance, 66.
— health, 88.
— — Municipal government and. Dr. J: S. Billings. 118.
— indebtedness. Tenth census (2d note), 82.
— lands, 24.
Puritans, Political ideas of. H. L. Osgood. 101.

Quarterly Journal of Economics (1st note), 18.
Questions for debate in politics and economics, 6.
Quicksilver mining. Eleventh census (3d note), 82.
Quincy, Josiah. M. Chamberlain (3d note). 119.
Quincy, J. P. Double taxation in Massachusetts, 67. Protection of majorities, 109.

RAE, G: Country banker, 42.
Rae, J: Contemporary socialism, 78. State socialism and popular right, 81.
Rabbeno, Ugo. Political economy in Italy. Le societa coöperative di produzione, 127.
Raffalovich, A. Housing working-classes and poor (*see under* T: Mackay), 127.
Raguet, Condy. Currency and banking, 36. Principles of free trade, 61.
Railroad Commissioners, Argument for. S. Sterne. 50.
— — State, 49.
— indemnity lands. F: P. Powers. 24.
— labor (1st note), 29.
— management and legislation, 47.
— ownership, State, 50.
— passenger fares in Hungary. Jane J. Wetherell. 51.
— problem. Albert Fink (8 titles), 48.
— rates (2d note), 51.
Railroads, Relations to forest supplies (2d last line), 113.
— Report on management, N. Y. [State] legislature, 49.
— Taxation of. C. F. Adams, jr. 66.
— their origin and problems. C: F. Adams, jr. 47.
— transportation. A: T. Hadley. 49.
— Treatise on law. E: L. Pierce. 49.
— U. S. H. M. Flint. 49.
— — — Poor's manual, 49.
Railway, American, 47.

INDEX. 161

Railway and public and private interests. S. Sterne. 50.
— capital, Changes in form of. T. L. Greene. 51.
— farmer, and public. E: Atkinson. Distrib. of products. 31, 48.
— History English. J. Francis. 50.
— Intercontinental (2 titles), 49.
— pools, Prohibition of. A. T. Hadley. 51.
— practice. E. P. Alexander, 47.
— problems. J. S. Jeans. 50.
— question. Am. Ec. Assoc. 49.
— rates, English and foreign. J. Grierson. 50.
— reorganization. Simon Sterne. 51.
— tariffs and Interstate Commerce Law. E. R. A. Seligman. 49.
Railways and republic. J. F. Hudson. 49.
— Federal regulation. E. J. James (see Railway question), 49.
— Metal as substitute for wooden ties (see Reports Forestry Div., 5 titles), 113.
— of England. W. M. Acworth. 50.
— Public regulation of. W: D. Dabney. 48.
— State purchase of. C: Waring. 50.
— Three articles on. R: T. Ely. 51.
Rambaud, A. La France coloniale, 83.
Randall, D. R. English charity organizations (note under H. B. Adams), 87.
Rapid transit in cities. Eleventh census (3d note), 83.
Rathbone, W. Protection and communism, 63.
Rau, K. H. Lehrbuch der politischen Oekonomie, 15.
Reciprocity, 65.
Reed, T: B. "A deliberative body." Reforms needed in the House. Reply to X. M. C. and J: G. Carlisle. Limitations speakership, 116.
Reed's, Speaker, error. X. M. C. 116.
Reform Club, N. Y. (see note, The tariff), 62.
Reforme sociale, La. (3d note), 75.
Regulations, Navy, U. S., 113.
Reinaud, E. Syndicats professionels, 30.
Reitzenstein, F. F. v., and Nasse, E. Agrarische Zustände in Frankreich und England, 23.
Religious freedom. Rev. P. Schaff. 117.
Report on high price bullion, 39.
Representation. Sir J: Lubbock. 108.
Republic, A true. A. Stickney. 100.
Republican campaign text-book (last note), 57.
Republicanism, A year of, 115.
Repudiation. G: W. Green. 73.
Revenue reformers, National conference, 61.
— Reports as Com'r. D: A. Wells. 68.
Revenues, Readjustment of. E. R. A. Seligman (see under Shaw), 67.
Revue d'économie politique (4th note), 18.
Rent, Land and, 18.
Rents, Ground, in Maryland. Louis Mayer. 19.
— — — Philadelphia. E. P. Allinson and B. Penrose. 18.

Ricardo, D: Principles of political economy and taxation, 13.
Ricca-Salerno, G. Teoria generale dei prestiti pubblici, 73.
Richard, H., and Williams, J. C. Disestablishment, 117.
Richardson, Dr. B: W. Household health. Hygeia, a city of health. Health and occupation, 88. Lectures on alcohol. Temperance lesson-book, 92.
Richardson, H. W. National banks, 41. Standard dollar, 38.
Richardson, W. A. Public debt U. S., and national banking laws, 36. Public debt U. S., 73.
Richelot, M. Histoire de la reforme commerciale en Angleterre, 64.
Richey, A. G. Irish land laws, 22.
Richmond, H: A. Workingmen's interest in civil service reform, 111.
Richmond, Wilfrid. Christian economics, 10.
Rights, Legal, Methods of assisting working classes in enforcement, 87.
Riis, Jacob A. How the other half lives, 73.
Ronna, A. Les irrigations, 115.
Roach, J: Benefits of protection, 60.
Roberts, E. H. Government revenue, 59.
Robertson, E. S. Impracticability of socialism (see under T: Mackay), 127.
Rodbertus-Jagetzow, C: Werke, 80. His scientific socialism. H. L. Osgood. 81.
Roesler, C. F. H. Zur Critik der Lehre vom Arbeitslohn. 32.
Rogers, J. E. Thorold. Cobden and modern political opinion, 63. Economic interpretation of [English] history, 63. Free trade (3d note), 64. First nine years Bank of England, 42. History of agriculture and prices in England, 22. Manual of political economy, 13. Six centuries of work and wages. Work and wages, 32. Social economy, 13.
Roosevelt, T. Essays on practical politics, 100. Merit system vs. Patronage system, 112. Object lesson in civil service reform, 112.
Roscher, W: Finanzwissenschaft, 70. Geschichte der Nationalökonomie in Deutschland, 8. Colonien, Colonialpolitik und Auswanderung, 83. Nationalökonomie des Ackerbaues, 23. Nationalökonomie des Handels und Gewerbefleisses, 46. Principles of political economy, 15. Ueber Kornhandel und Theuerungspolitik, 55. Zur Geschichte der englischen Volkswirthschaftslehre, 8.
Rosenthal, H. S. Manual for Building and Loan Assocs., 33.
Ross, Denman W. Early history of landholding among the Germans, 19.
Rossi, P. Cours d'économie politique, 14.
Rota, P. Principii di scienza bancaria, 42.
Rothschild, A. Histoire de la poste aux lettres, 112.
Round, W. M. F. Immigration and crime, 84. Our criminals and Christianity, 90.

INDEX.

Royall, W: L. Andrew Jackson and Bank of U. S., 41.
Rural economy of England, Scotland, and Ireland. L. de Lavergne. 22.
Ruskin, J. Crown of wild olive, 74. Fors clavigera, 27. Munera pulveris, 17. "Unto this last," 17.
Rüttimann, H. Das Nordamerikanische Bundestaatsrecht, 107.
Ryan, Dan. J. Arbitration between capital and labor, 34.
Rylands, L. G. Crime, causes and remedy, 90.

SADLER, M. T: Law of population, 81.
St. Louis, City government. M. S. Snow. 118.
Saint-Simon, H. Œuvres. 79.
Salt, Mich., Assoc. J. W. Jenks. 53.
Sanborn, F. B. Three-fold aspect of social science in America, 76.
San Francisco, Municipal govt. B. Moses. 118.
Sanitary drainage. G: E. Waring, jr. 88.
— house inspection. W: P. Gerhard. 88.
Sanitation, 88; 3 notes, 89.
Sargent, C: S. Silva of North America, 114.
Sarwey, O. v. Allgemeines Verwaltungsrecht, 108.
Sato, Shosuke. History of the land question in the U. S, 20.
Savings banks, 43.
— — in U. S. E. W. Keyes. J. P. Townsend. 43.
— — in Great Britain and Ireland. W: Lewin. 43.
— — school. J. H. Thiry. 43.
Say, J. B. Treatise on political economy, 14.
Say, Leon. Dictionnaire des finances, 70. Le socialisme d'état, 79. Solutions democratique de la question des impôts, 70.
— and Chailley, Jos., eds. Nouveau dictionnaire de l'économie politique, 7.
Scalabrini, G. B. Emigrazione Italiana, 83.
Schaeffle, A. E. F. Capitalismus und Socilismus, 80. Gesammelte Aufsätze, 17. Gesellschaftliches System der menschlichen Wirthschaft, 15 Grundsätze der Steuerpolitik, 70. Quintessenz des Socialismus, Quintessence of socialism, 80. Socialdemokratie, 80.
Schaff, Rev. P. Church and State, U. S. 116. Progress religious freedom, 117.
Schanz, G. Die Steuern der Schweiz, 70.
Scheel, H. v. Theorie der socialen Frage, 80.
Schlich, W. Manual of forestry, 114.
Schmoller, H. Grundfragen des Rechts und der Volkswirthschaft, 80. Jahrbücher für Gesetzgebung, Verwaltung und Volkswirthschaft (5th note), 18.
Schoenberg, Gustav, ed. Handbuch der politischen Oekonomie, 7.
Schoenhof, J. Destructive influence of tariff, 61. Industrial situation and wages question, 31. On protection (ad note), 64. Wages and trade, America and Europe, 61.

Schoettle, G. Der Telegraph, 112.
School life, Sanitary needs (3d note), 89.
Schools, Am. Christian State. Rev. T: J. Jenkins. 117.
— Denominational, 116.
— Public, and ecclesiastical control (2d note), 117.
— Religious teaching in. Bishop McQuaid, 117.
Schultze, H. Lehrbuch des deutschen Staatsrechts, 106.
Schultze-Delitsch, H. Volksbanken, 42.
Schurz, Carl. Honest money and labor, 36. Need of rational forest policy, 114.
Schuyler, E. American diplomacy, 120. Italian immigration 84.
Schuyler, Miss I.. L. Associated effort in behalf poor, 87.
Schwab, J: C. History N. Y. property tax, 67.
Science of wealth. Amasa Walker. 11.
Scope and method economic science. H: Sidgwick. 6.
Scotch banks and system issue. R: Somers. 42.
Scotland, History of banking in. A: W. Kerr. 41.
Scott, R. N. Digest military laws, U. S., 113.
Scudder, M. L., jr. Congested prices. 43. Labor-value fallacy, 31. National banking, 41.
Seaman, E. C. Refutation free trade, 59.
Seebohm, F. English village community, 22 (and 3d note), 96.
Seeley, J: R. Expansion of England, 83.
Seligman, E. R. A. Finance statistics of the Am. commonwealths. General property tax, 67. Historical and comparative science finance (note), 11. Mediæval guilds of England, 30. Owen and Christian socialists, 76. Railway tariffs and Interstate Commerce law, 49. Readjustment of the revenues (see under Shaw), 67. Taxation of corporations, 67.
Semler, H, Tropische und nordamerikanische Waldwirthschaft und Holzkunde, 114.
Senate, secret sessions. Dorman B. Eaton. 99.
Senior, Nassau W. Lectures on political economy, 13.
Seyd, E. Bimetallism in 1886. Bullion and foreign exchanges, 39. Reform of Bank of England note-issue, 42.
Shadwell, J. L. System of political economy, 13.
Shaw, Albert. Glasgow, a municipal study. How London is governed, 119. Icaria, 76. Municipal govt. in Great Britain, 119. Municipal govt. in England, 118. National revenues, 67.
Shaw, G. B. Fabian essays in socialism, 78.
Shearman, T: G. Distribution of wealth, 61.
Shepard, E: M. Competitive tests, and civil service of States and cities, 111.
Sherman, I. Exclusive taxation real estate, 68.

Sherman, J: Coin and currency (Silver question), 127. On finance and taxation. 68.
Shinn, C: H. Land laws of mining districts, 24.
Ship-building, tenth census (2d note). 82.
Shipping bounties and subsidies. J: Codman. 60.
Ships, Free. J: Codman. 60.
— Question of. J. D. J. Kelley. 61.
Shop council. J. C. Bayles. 34.
Shriver, E. J. How customs duties work, 64.
Sidgwick, H. Economic socialism, 80. Political economy, 13. Scope and method economic science, 6.
Signal Service reports (see War Dept.), 126.
Signs of change. W: Morris. 78.
Sigurson, G. History of land tenures and land classes of Ireland, 22.
Silva of North America, C: S. Sargent. 114.
Silver, 38.
— act, How it will work. F. W. Taussig. 40.
— bubble, American. R. Giffen. 40.
— coinage, Unlimited. Sen. W. M. Stewart and W. M. Grosvenor (see Year of Republicanism), 115. J: J. Knox (2 titles), 127.
— Commission Reports (1st note), 40.
— demonetization, and fall in prices. A. Crump. 39.
— Depreciation of. W. Bagehot. 38.
— dollar, Standard. W. C. Ford. 38.
— in Europe. S. D. Horton. 38.
— or legal-tender notes. W. C. Ford. 40.
— question. D: A. Wells. 38. J: J. Knox, J: Sherman. 127.
— — in U. S. F. W. Taussig. 40.
— situation. Horace White. 40.
Simon, Jules. L'ouvrière, 28.
Single tax. H: George and E: Atkinson. 72.
— — Agriculture and the. Horace White. 72.
— — debate, 72.
— — on land. E: Atkinson. Industrial progress, 31.
— — question (see under Trumbull, M. M.), 26.
Sismondi, J. C. L. de. Nouveaux principes d'économie politique, 14.
Skottowe, B. C. Short history Parliament. 104.
Slate mining, eleventh census (3d note), 82.
Slow-burning construction. E: Atkinson. Industrial progress, 31.
Smith, Adam. Wealth of nations, 13.
Smith, Bruce. Liberty and liberalism, 95.
Smith College, courses in ec. and pol. sci., 136.
Smith, Eugene. Prison science, 90.
Smith, Goldwin. False hopes, 76. Political destiny of Canada, 106.
Smith, H. L. Economic aspects state socialism, 78.
— and Nash, V. Dockers' strike, 30.
Smith, L. Coalitions et grèves, 30.
Smith, Richmond Mayo. American labor statistics, 125. Emigration and immigration, 83. Historical and practical political economy (note), 11. Shall internal revenue be retained? (see under Shaw), 67. Statistics and economics, 123. Theory of emigration, 84.
Smithsonian Institution, 126.
Snow, M. S. City government St. Louis, 118.
Social aspects of Christianity. R: T. Ely. 73.
— classes, What they owe to each other. W: G. Sumner. 74
— Economics, Principles of. G. Gunton. 127.
— economy. J. E. Thorold Rogers. 13. Handbook. E. About. 14, 28.
— pressure. Sir Arthur Helps. 74.
— problem. W. Graham. 77.
— problems. H: George. 73.
— reform, Methods of. W: S. Jevons. 74.
— solutions. M. Godin. 78.
— statics. H. Spencer. 74, 95.
— — of cities. Tenth census (2d note), 82.
— studies. Rev. R. H. Newton. 73.
— science and sociology, 73.
— — Assoc., American (note 17, 1st note). 75.
— — in America. Three-fold aspect of. F. B. Sanborn. 76.
— — Manual of. H: C. Carey. 9.
— — Method of study in. W: T. Harris. 75.
— — National Assoc. (2d note), 75.
— — Popular instruction in. C. D. Wright. 74.
— — Present status of. R S. Hamilton. 73.
Sociale Frage, Rede über die. Ad. Wagner. 17.
Socialism, 76.
— J: S. Mill. 78.
— Christian. Rev. M. Kaufmann, Rev. P. W. Sprague. 77.
— Common-sense. M. Kempner. 77.
— Contemporary. J: Rae. 78.
— Economic. H. Sidgwick. 80.
— Ethics of. E. B. Bax. 77.
— Fabian essays in. G. B. Shaw. 78.
— French and German. R: T. Ely. 76.
— German, and Lassalle. W. H. Dawson. 77.
— in England. Percival Chubb. 81. H. M. Hyndman. 77. Sydney Webb. 78.
— in U. S. M. Kaufmann (3d note), 127.
— Impracticability of. E. S. Robertson (see under Mackay), 127.
— Influence of, on English politics. W: Clarke. 81.
— Inquiry into. T: Kirkup. 77.
— New and old. W. Graham. 77.
— Practicable. Rev. and Mrs. S. A. Barnet. 77.
— Principles of. H. M. Hyndman and W: Morris. 77.
— Quintessence of. A. E. F. Schaeffle. 80.
— Recent American. R: T. Ely. 76.
— Religion of. E. B. Bax. 77.
— State, at the Antipodes. C: Fairfield (see under T: Mackay), 127.
— — Economic aspects of. H. L. Smith. 78.

Socialism vs. tax-reform. L. Gronlund. 76.
Socialisms, History of American. J. H. Noyes. 76.
Socialists, Christian. Owen and. E. R. A. Seligman. 76.
Societies, Trades. Tenth census (2d note), 82.
Society, Rudimentary, among boys. J: Johnson. 73.
Sociology. J: Bascom. 73. W: G. Sumner (4th note), 75.
— Descriptive. H. Spencer. 75.
— Dynamic. L. F. Ward. 74.
— Principles of. H. Spencer. 74.
— Province of. F. H. Giddings. 76.
— Study of. H. Spencer. 74.
Soetbeer, A. On precious metals (*see note under* E: Atkinson), 38, 40.
Solly, *Rev.* H: Rehousing industrial classes, 89.
Somers, R: Scotch banks and system of issue, 42.
Soper, F. L. Nationalization of land, 23.
South, Third estate of. A. D. Mayo. 85.
— The silent. G: W. Cable. 85.
— Kingstown town meetings (2d note), 72.
Southern elections. A. W. Tourgee *and* G: W. Cable (*see* Year of Republican), 115.
Sovereigns of Industry. E. M. Chamberlin. 29.
Spahr, C. B. Taxation of labor, 72.
Spaulding, E. G. History legal-tender act, 36.
Speakership, Limitations. T: B. Reed *and* J: G. Carlisle. 116.
— A word as to. J. Bryce. 116.
Speculation, 43.
— Stock Exchange. A. Crump. 44.
Speculative notes. D. M. Evans. 44.
Spencer, Herbert. Descriptive sociology. 75. The man vs. the State, 74. Plea for liberty (*see* T: Mackay), 127. Principles of sociology, 74. Prison ethics (4th note), 91. Railway morals and policies (1st note), 51. Social statics, 74, 95. State tamperings with money and banks (2d note), 43. Study of sociology, 74.
Spirit of laws. M. de S. Montesquieu. 95.
Spofford, A. R. Am. almanac (3d note), 124.
Sprague, *Rev.* P. W. Christian socialism. 77.
Staatswissenschaft, Handwörterbuch der. J. E. Conrad *and others, eds.* 7.
Standard, The (*note under* H: George), 19.
Stanley, Maude. Clubs for working-girls, 75.
Stanton, Elizabeth Cady. Woman suffrage, 108.
Stanwood, E. History presidential elections, 102, 108.
State, The. Woodrow Wilson, 94.
— — man vs. the. H. Spencer. 74.
— Alcohol and the. R. C. Pitman? 92.
— banking in U. S. (1st note), 43.
— control of industry 4th century. W. A. Brown. 81.
— department publications, 126.
— railroad ownership, 50.
— — Commissioner's reports (2d note), 51.

State railroad commissions, 49.
— Relations of, to industrial action. H. C. Adams. 99.
— socialism and popular right. J: Rae. 81.
— tamperings with money and banks. H. Spencer (2d note), 43.
— Theory of the. J. K. Bluntschli. 95.
Statesman's year-book (7th note), 124.
Statistical abstract British possessions (1st note). 125. Canada's (5th note), 124. United Kingdom (last note), 124. U. S., 125.
— Assoc., American, note 17 (2d note), 124.
— science, 123.
— Society, London (1st note), 125.
Statistics, 123.
— Finance. Am. commonwealth. E. R. A. Seligman. 67.
— of wages. J. D. Weeks. 31.
— production precious metals, U. S. Clarence King. 35.
— Vital. Tenth census (2d note), 82.
Statistique, L'institut international de (3d note), 125.
— Société de. de Paris (4th note), 125.
Statutes-at-large, U. S. (*see* State Dept.), 126
Stebbins, G. B Protectionists' manual, 59.
Steel production. Eleventh census (3d note), 82.
Steele, G: M. Outline study of political economy, 10.
Stein and his reforms in Prussia. H. A. Ouvry. 21.
Stein, L. v. Finanzwissenschaft, 71. Handbuch der Verwaltungslehre, 108. Lehrbuch der Nationalökonomie, 15. Socialismus und Communismus des heutigen Frankreichs, 80.
Stephen, Fitzjames. Liberty, equality and fraternity, 95.
Stephens, A. H. Constitutional view late war, 103.
Stetson, G. R. Negro education, 85.
Sterne, Simon. Argument for railroad commissioners, 50. Closing arguments on railroads, 50. Constitutional history, U. S., 103. Defective and corrupt legislation, 100. Railway and public and private interests, 50. Railway reorganization, 51. Representative government and personal representation, 110. Suffrage in cities, 108.
Stewart, Sen. W. M. Unlimited silver coinage (*see* Year of Republicanism), 115.
Stickney, A. Democratic government. Political problem, 100. True republic, 100.
Stock Exchange securities. R. Giffen. 44.
— Exchanges of London, Paris and New York. G. R. Gibson. 43.
Storey, Moorfield. Politics as duty and career, 100.
Story, Joseph. Commentaries on the constitution, 99. Exposition of constitution, 98.
Strike, Dockers'. H. L. Smith *and* V. Nash. 30.
— of millionaires against miners. H: D. Lloyd. 29.

INDEX.

Strike on Southwestern R'y system, 1886, 30.
Strikes, 29.
— and lockouts (1st note), 29. Report Commissioner of Labor, 30.
— in U. S., 1877, Annals of. J. A. Dacus. 29.
Strong, Josiah, *D.D.* Our country, 74.
Stubbs, *Rev* C: W. Village politics, 27
Stubbs, W: Constitutional history England, 104.
Studnitz, A. v. Nordamericanische Arbeiterverhältnisse, 31.
Stürenburg, E., *and* Steiger, E. Auskunft und Rath für Deutsch-Amerikaner, 98.
Sturtevant, J. M. Economics, 11.
Subsidies, Shipping. J: Codman. 60.
— Steamships, as a means reducing surplus. A. T. Hadley (*see under* Shaw), 67.
Sudre, A. Histoire du communisme, 79.
Suffrage, 108.
Sugar and molasses (9th note), 57.
— — the tariff. D: A. Wells. 62.
Sullivan, E: Free trade bubbles, 59. Free trade isolated, 60.
Sumner, W: G. Bimetallism (4th note), 40. Civil service reform. Elections (3d note), 103. Essays political and social science, 16. History American currency. 36. History protection, U. S., 54. Life Alex. Hamilton, 68. Problems political economy, 6. Protectionism, 62. Sociology (4th note), 75. Wages (2d note), 32. What social classes owe to each other, 74.
Supreme Court decisions (*see* Foster's references to constitution, *and* C. A. Kent), 101.
— — Federal. T: H. Cooley. 101.
Surplus and public debt. J: J. Knox. 127.
— financiering. H. C. Adams (*see under* Shaw), 67.
— revenue of 1837. E. G. Bourne. 66.
— What shall we do with it? 68.
Swiss confederation. *Sir* F. O. Adams *and* C. Cunningham (2 titles), 106.
Switzerland, Federal constitution. E. J. James. 106.
— — government. B. Moses. 106.
— Income and property taxes in. G. Cohn. 72.

Tait, W. C. Arbeiter-Schutzgesetzgebung in den Vereinigten Staaten, 29.
Talbott, H., *ed.* Tariff from the White House, 55.
Tallack, W. Penological and preventive principles, 90.
Taney, Chief Justice, Influence of. G: W. Biddle. 101.
Tariff, The, 62.
— act, First (1st note), 56.
— and its taxes. *Rev.* N. H. Chamberlain. 60.
— and trusts. R. T. Ely (*see under* Shaw), 67.
— Bibliography (4th note). 58.
— Canadian (2d note), 58.
— chats. H. J. Philpott. 61.
— Commission, 1882 (2d note), 56.

Tariff decisions (11th note), 56.
— Destructive influence of. J. Schoenhof. 61.
— English (1st note), 58.
— from the White House. H. Talbott, *ed.* 55.
— history, U. S. F. W. Taussig. 55. D. H. Mason. 54.
— laws. U. S. C. F. Williams. 55.
— legislation. Report on. E. Young. 55.
— — Scientific basis. C. D. Wright. 55. (3d line), 68.
— U. S. (2d last note), 57.
— of 1883, 55.
— — 1890. O: H. Adams. 54.
— Official U. S. (*see* Treasury Dept.), 126.
— question. E. B. Bigelow. 58. Horace White. 62.
— — Certainties of. J: B. Clark (*see under* Shaw), 67.
— Common sense of. E: Atkinson. 64.
— reduction, Plan of. E. W. Bemis (2d line), 63.
— reform, 60.
— — (Journal) (6th note), 64.
— — Primer of. D: A. Wells. 62.
— Reform Club, N. Y. (*see* note, The tariff), 62.
— Relation of. to wages. D: A. Wells. 62.
— returns (12th note), 57.
— revenue. A. Yager (1st line), 68.
— revision (5th note), 56.
— Speeches on (last note), 56.
Tariffs and foreign commerce, 54.
— Foreign (3d and 11th notes), 57.
— old and new, indexed (3d note), 56.
Taswell-Langmead, T. P. English constitutional history, 104.
Taussig, F. W. Silver question in U. S., 40. Tariff History, U. S., 55. Workmen's insurance in Germany, 53.
Tax, Direct, of 1861. C: F. Dunbar. 72.
— General property. E. R. A. Seligman. 67.
— State, Commissions (2d note), 71.
Taxation. J. H. Canfield. 66.
— Tenth census (2d note), 82.
— and appropriation. Woodrow Wilson (*see under* Shaw), 67.
— — the funding system. J. R. McCulloch. 69.
— — local assessments, Law of. T: M. Cooley. 66.
— as it is and ought to be. C: Tennant. 69.
— Bases of. F. A. Walker. 72.
— Consular reports on. 67.
— distilled spirits. D: A. Wells (1st note), 72.
— Double, in Massachusetts. G: G. Crocker, 66. J. P. Quincy. 67.
— Equality in. A. D. Morse (*see under* Shaw), 67.
— in Am. States and cities. R: T. Ely *and* J. H. Finley. 67.
— — England. S. Dowell. 68.
— — Massachusetts. W. Minot, jr. 67.
— — Mexico. D: A. Wells (4th note), 71.
— — the U. S., 1789-1816. H: C. Adams. 66.
— its levy and expenditure. *Sir* S. Morton Peto. 69.

INDEX.

Taxation, Law of. W. H. Burroughs. 66. Fcs. Hilliard. 66.
— Local. G: J. Goschen. 68.
— — England and Wales. R, S. Wright *and* H: Hobhouse. 67.
— — Government and. Cobden Club essays, 69.
— — in Great Britain and Ireland. R. H. I. Palgrave. 69.
— N. Y., Reports on. Wells, D: A. 68.
— of corporations. E. R. A. Seligman. 67.
— labor. C. B. Spahr. 72.
— — railroads. C: F Adams, jr. 66.
— principles, Political economy and. D: Ricardo. 13.
— real estate. I. Sherman. 68.
— Relief of, through distrib. surplus. R. E. Thompson. 68.
— State of N. Y. J. T. Davies. 66.
— United Kingdom. R. D. Baxter. 68.
— Valuation and, real and personal property, U. S. (6th note), 72.
Taxed, What shall be? E: Atkinson, industrial progress, 31.
Taxes, Federal, and State expenses. W: H. Jones. 67.
— The Queen's. J. Noble. 69.
Taylor, E. W. C. Introduction history of factory system, 27.
Taylor, Hannis. English constitution. 103.
Taylor, Sedley. Profit-sharing, 34.
Teale, T. P. Dangers to health, 89.
Telegraph, Public control of. B. C. Keeler. 112.
— service, 112.
Temperance and prohibition, Cyclopedia, 91.
— Church, Society (3d note), 92.
— Congress (2d note), 93.
— lesson-book. *Dr.* B; W. Richardson. 92.
— National, League's annual (3d note), 93.
— — Society (1st note), 92.
— problem (2d note), 93.
— text-book. F. R. Lees. 92.
Tenant's gain not landlord's loss. J. S. Nicholson. 21.
Tenement-house Building Co. (3d note), 89.
Tennant, C: Bank of England and organization credit, 42. People's blue-book. Taxation as it is and ought to be, 69.
Terrill, W. G., *ed.* Appeal to Am. people as jury. 55.
Testut, O. Le livre bleu de l'Internationale, 79.
Tetot, A. Traités de paix, 122.
Texas, Fiscal history. W: M. Gouge. 67.
Thierry, A. L'histoire du tiers état, 28.
Thiers, M. A. De la propriété, 24.
Thirty years' view. T: H. Benton. 101.
Thiry, J. H. School savings-banks, 43.
Thomann, G. Works (2d note), 93.
Thompson, Perronet. Catechism of the corn laws, 63.
Thompson, Phillips. Politics of labor, 26.
Thompson, R. E. Defence of protective policy (*see under* Shaw), 67. Political economy,

11. Protection, 59. Protective questions abroad, 60 Relief of taxation through distrib. surplus, 68.
Thompson, R. W. History protective tariff laws, 55. Papacy and civil power, 117.
Thonissen, J. J. Socialisme depuis l'antiquité, 79.
Thornton, W. T. On labor, 27. Over-population and its remedy, 81. Plea for peasant proprietors, 22.
Thorpe F. N. Government of people U. S. 98.
Thrift and independence. *Rev.* W. L. Blackley. 74.
Tiedemann, C. G. Unwritten constitution U. S., 99.
Timber, Increasing durability of (*see* Reports Forestry Div.), 113
Todd, A. Parliamentary government in British colonies, 104. In England, 104.
Tobacco tax 1861-90. F. L. Olmsted. 72.
Toniolo, G. Sulla distribuzione della richezza, 75.
Tooke, T:, and Newmarch, W. History of prices, 47.
Torrens, R. Production of wealth, 17. Sir Robert Peel's act, 1844, 42. Transfer of land by registration, 22.
Tourgee, A. W. Southern elections (*see* Year of Republicanism), 115.
Townsend, J: P. Savings-banks in the U. S., 43.
Toynbee. Arnold. Industrial revolution in England, 27.
Trade and commerce, 45.
— — navigation, Canadian (3d note), 58.
— depression. G. W. Medley. A. Mongredien. 44.
— — and low prices. R. Griffin (last note), 44.
— — beginning 1873 (last note), 44.
— guilds of Europe, 30.
— International, 54.
— organizations in politics. J. Bleecker Miller. 30.
— State in relation to. *Sir* T: H. Farrer. 104.
Trades organizations, 29.
— societies. Tenth census (2d note), 82.
— unions. W. M. Grosvenor. 29. W. Trant. 30.
— unionism. The new. F. Harrison. 31.
— unions in England. Comte de Paris. 30.
Tramp at home. Lee Meriwether. 26.
Tramp's trip. Lee Meriwether. 26.
Transporation. Tenth census (2d note), 82.
Trant, W. Trades-unions. 30.
Travail, Le droit au, 30.
Treasury Department publications, 126. Report (5th note), 72.
Treaties, 119.
— and conventions, U. S., 120.
Tree-seedlings, Growing (*see* Reports Forestry Div., 2 last titles), 113.
Treitscke, H. v. Die Gesellschaftswissenschaft, 75. Socialismus und seine Gönner, 80.

INDEX. 167

Trescot, W. H. Diplomacy of the Revolution, 120.
Tribune, N. Y. (2d note), 60. (4th note), 124.
Trumbull, M M. Am. lesson of free trade struggle in England, 62. Labor question, 26.
Trust, Whiskey. J. W. Jenks. 53.
Trusts, 52.
— W. W. Cook, 52.
— according to official investigations. E. B. Andrews. 53.
— Canadian govt. investigation (*see* report Select Com.), 53.
— Competition and the. G: Iles. 53.
— Congressional investigation (*see* Proceedings Com. on Mfrs.), 52.
— Economic and social aspects of. G. Gunton. 53.
— Facts about. C. F. Beach, jr. 53.
— Investigation, N. Y. State, 52.
— Tariff and. R: T. Ely (*see under* Shaw), 67.
Tuckett, J. A. History laboring population, 28.
Twiss, *Sir* Travers. Law of nations, 121. Progress political economy in Europe since 16th century. 8.
Tyler, L. G. Parties and patronage, 127.
Tylor, E. B. Primitive culture, 96.

ULRICH, Franz. Das Eisenbahntarifwesen, Traité général des tarifs de chemins de fer. 51.
Unemployed, Experiments on behalf. A. G. Warner. 81.
U. S. Government publications, 125.
— — organization. G: N. Lamphere. 107.
Usury, 25.
— laws, History of. J. B. C. Murray. 25.
— question, 25.
— Summary history and law of. J. B. Kelly. 25.

VALUATION. Tenth census (2d note), 82.
Value, Money and. R. Hamilton. 37.
Vassar College, Courses ec. and pol. sci., 136.
Veto power. E. C. Mason. 99.
Vickers, G. Fall of bossism, 116.
Vienna, Municipal government. J: A. Kasson (2d note), 119.
Vierteljahresschrift für Volkswirthschaft und Culturgeschichte (5th note), 18.
Vignes, E: Traité des impôts en France, 70.
Vignon, L. Les colonies Françaises 38.
Village communities in the east and west. *Sir* H. J. Sumner Maine. 21.
— community. G. L. Gomme. 20.
— — English. F. Seebohm. 22.
— politics. *Rev.* C. W. Stubbs. 27.
Villeneuve-Bargemont, J. P. A., *de*. Histoire de l'économie politique, 8.
Villetard, H. History of the international, 79.
Villey, E. La question des salaires, 32.
Vincent, E. Discontent working-classes (*see under* T: Mackay), 127.

Vine, J. R. S. English municipal institutions, 118.
Vivien, A. F. A. Études administratives, 107.
Vocke, W: Die Abgaben, Auflagen und die Steuer. Geschichte der Steuer des Britischen Reiches, 71.
Von Holst, H. E. Constitutional and political history, U. S. Verfassung und Demokratie der V. S. A., 103.

WAGES, 31.
— W: G. Sumner (2d note), 32.
— and cost of production (1st note), 32.
— — earnings, 1883-84. Leone Levi. 32.
— — interest, Law of. J: B. Clark. 32.
— — prices in Massachusetts. C. D. Wright. 31.
— — tariff. J. L. Laughlin (2d line). 68.
— — trade, America and Europe. J. Schoenhof. 61.
— English, Foreign work and. T: Brassey. 31.
— Living, and the tariff. E. A. Hartshorn. 58.
— Natural rate of. F. H. Giddings. 32.
— question. F. A. Walker. 31.
— — Industrial situation and. J. Schoenhof. 31.
— Relation of tariff to. D: A. Wells. 62.
— Statistics of. J. D. Weeks. 31.
— Tenth census (2d note), 82.
— Theory of. Stuart Wood. 31.
— theories, History and criticism of. W. D. McDonnell. 32.
— What makes rate of. E: Atkinson. Distrib. of products, 31.
Wagner, Ad. Abschaffung des privaten Grundeigenthums, 23. Finanzwissenschaft, 71. Rede über die sociale Frage, 17.
Waitz, T. Grundzüge der Politik, 96.
Walford's cyclopædia insurance (note under Life Ins.), 53.
Walker, Amasa Science of wealth, 11.
Walker, Francis A. Bases of taxation, 72. Eight hours law agitation, 32. First lessons in political economy, 11. Land and its rent, 20, Money, 37. Money in relations to trade and industry. 37. Political economy, 11. Protection and agriculture (*see under* Shaw), 67. Protection and protectionists, 64. Wages question, 31.
— *and* Adams, H. Legal tender act (*see* Adams, C: F., jr., Chapters of Erie), 47.
Wallace, A. R. Bad times, 44. Land nationalization, 22.
Walpole, S. Electorate and legislature, 108.
Waltershausen, A. S. F. v. Sozialismus in den V. S. v. Amerika, 80.
Walras, L. Théorie mathematique du billet de banque, 42.
War, 113 (*see* A. J. Palm), 127.
— Department, 126.
Ward, C. Osborne. History of ancient working people, 26.

Ward, Lester F. Dynamic sociology, 74.
Waring, C: State purchase of railways, 50.
Waring, G: E., jr. Sanitary drainage, 88.
Warner, A. G. Experiments on behalf unemployed, 81. Relief of poor in Germany. 86.
Water, air, and disinfectants. W. N. Hartley. 88.
— power. Tenth census (2d note), 82.
— supply of cities. C: F. Wingate. 89.
— ways. J. S. Jeans. 52.
Waterworth, J. A. Labor problem (*see under* Barns, W. E.), 25.
Wayland, F. Elements political economy, 11.
Wayland, Fcs. Outdoor relief and tramps, 87.
Ways and Means Committees (4th, 6th, 7th, 8th notes), 56.
Wealth and progress. G: Gunton. 31.
— Distribution of. T: G Shearman. 61.
— of nations. Adam Smith. 13.
Webb, Sidney. Rate of interest and laws of distribution, 25. Socialism in England, 78.
Weber, Max v. Nationalität und Eisenbahnpolitik. Privat Staats- und Reichsbahnen, 51. Die Wasserstraassen Nord Europa's, 52.
Weeden, W. B. Economic and social history New England, 45.
Weeks, Joseph D. Arbitration and conciliation (4 titles), 34. Statistics of wages, 31.
Weights, measures and money of all nations. F. W. Clarke. 35.
Wellesley College, Courses in ec. and pol. sci., 136.
Wells, D: A. Creed of free trade. 62. Decay of our ocean mercantile marine, 62. Governmental interference with international commerce (1st note), 64. How Congress and public deal with great revenue and industrial problem, 62. Our merchant marine, 62. Practical economics, 16, 62. Primer of tariff reform, 62. Recent economic changes, 7. Relation of tariff to wages, 62. Relation of government to telegraph, 112. Reports as Com'r Revenue. Reports on taxation, N. Y., 68. Robinson Crusoe's money, 37. Silver question, 38. Sugar and the tariff, 62. Tariffs and tariff legislation (3d note), 64. Taxation distilled spirits. (1st note), 72. Taxation in Mexico (3d note), 71. Trade depression beginning 1873 (last note), 44. Why we trade and how we trade, 62.
Westergaard, H. Theorie der Statistik. 124.
Westlake, J: International law, 121.
Wetherell, Jane J. Passenger fares in Hungary, 51.
Wharton, F. Digest international law, U. S., 121.
Wharton, Joseph. International industrial competition. National self-protection, 59. Protection and free trade, 60.
Wharton School finance and economy, Courses ec. and pol. sci. (*see* Univ. Pa.), 135.
Whateley R: Political economy (2 titles), 14.

Wheaton, H. Droit international. History law nations. International law (2 titles), 121.
"Wheelbarrow" on labor question, 26.
Wheeler, E. J. Prohibition, 92.
Whitaker's Almanac (2d note), 125.
White, A. D. European schools of history and politics, 94. Government Am. cities, 119. Municipal administration Berlin (1st note), 119. Paper money inflation in France, 37.
White, Arn. Invasion of pauper foreigners, 84. Recent experiments in colonization, 83.
White, A. T. Improved dwellings (title and note), 89.
White, Horace. Agriculture and the single tax, 72. Commercial crises (last note). 44. Money and its substitutes, 37. Silver situation, 40. Tariff question, 62.
Whitridge, F. W. Caucus system, 116. Comparative constitutional law Am. commonwealths (note), 99.
Why we trade, and how. D: A. Wells. 62.
Wigmore, J: H. Australian ballot system, 108.
Wilkinson, *Rev.* J. F. Friendly society movement, 75.
Willey, N. Principles and practice life insurance, 53.
Williams, C. F. Tariff laws, U. S., 55.
Williams College, Courses in ec. and pol. sci., 137.
Williams, Talcott. Labor a hundred years ago, 26.
Willoughby, W. F., *and* Graffenried, Miss C. de. Child labor, 26.
Wilson, Andrew. Science and crime, 90.
Wilson, A. J. Banking reform, 42. National budget, 69. Resources of modern countries, 46.
Wilson, D. Prehistoric man, 96.
Wilson, Jas. Capital, currency, and banking, 37.
Wilson, Woodrow. Congressional government, 100. Taxation and appropriation (*see under* Shaw), 67. The State, 94. State and federal governments U. S., 99.
Wiman, Erastus. Can we coerce Canada? Capture of Canada, 65.
Wines, E. C. Prisons and child-saving institutions, 90.
Wingate, C: F. Water supply of cities, 89.
Winn, H. Property in land, 20.
Wirth, Max. Geschichte der Handelskrisen, 44.
Wise, R. B. Facts and fallacies protection, 64.
Wolowski, L. De la monnaie, 38. L'or et l'argent, 39. La question des banques, 42.
Woman suffrage. Mrs. A. Dilke *and* W. Woodall. Eliz. Cady Stanton. 108.
Woman's Journal (2d note), 109.
Women plumbers and doctors. *Mrs.* H. M. Plunkett. 88.
— Working, in large cities (1st note), 29.
Wood, Stuart. Theory of wages, 31.
Woodrow, F. (*see under* Barns, W. E., Labor problem), 25.

Wool and manufactures of (8th note). 57.
— — woolen tariff of 1883. J. L. Hayes. 58.
— *Mfrs.' Bulletin* (3d note). 59
Woolsey, T. D. Communism and socialism. 77. International law, 121. Political science, 94.
Work and pay. Leone Levi. 30.
— — wages. T: Brassey. 32.
— — *also*, Six centuries of. J. E. Thorold Rogers. 32.
Working-class England. F. Engels. 29.
Working-classes, Discontent of. E. Vincent (*see under* T: Mackay). 127.
— — Progress. J. M. Ludlow *and* L. Jones. 27.
— — — 1832-67. J. M. Ludlow *and* Lloyd Jones. 27.
— — — in last half century. R. Giffen. 27.
Working-girls' clubs. Maude Stanley. 75.
— — of Boston. C. D. Wright. 27.
Workingman, Present actual condition. C. D. Wright. 26.
Workingmen, English Assocs. of. J. M. Barnreither. 30.
Workingmen's dwellings, 89.
— homes. R: R. Bowker. 89.
— interest in civil service reform. H. A. Richmond. 111.
Working-people and their employers. *Rev.* W. Gladden. 26.
— — History of ancient. C. O. Ward. 26.
Workmen's insurance in Germany. F. W. Taussig. 53.
Works of reference, Political economy, 5.
World Almanac (4th note), 124.

Worthington, T. K. Finances of Penn., 68.
Wright, Carroll D. Coöperative distribution in Great Britain and elsewhere, 33. Factory system. 26. Growth and purposes Bureau Statistics of Labor. 26. Hand labor in prisons, 30. Industrial conciliation and arbitration, 34. Manual of distributive coöperation. 33. Popular instruction in social science, 74. Present actual condition workingman, 26. Profit sharing. 33. Relation political economy to labor question, 26. Scientific basis tariff legislation, 55 (3d line), 68. Sketch Knights of Labor, 30. Statistics in colleges, 123. Uniform hours of labor, 27. Wages and prices in Massachusetts. 31. Working-girls of Boston, 27.
Wright. R. S., and Hobhouse, H: Local govt. and taxation, England and Wales. 69.

YAGER, A. Revenue tariff (1st line), 66.
Yale Univ., Courses ec. and pol. sci., 137.
Yeats, J. Commerce from 1500 to 1789, from 1789 to 1872. Technical history of commerce, 45.
Young, Arthur. Farmer's tour through east of England. Six weeks' tour through the southern countries of England and Wales. Tour in Ireland. Travels in France, 22.
Young, E. Customs tariff legislation. 55. Labor in Europe and America, 27.

ZELLER, E: Staat und Kirche, 117.
Zorn. Ph. Staatsrecht des deutschen Reichs 108.

COURSES OF READING.

ELEMENTARY OR YOUTHS' SERIES.

NORDHOFF, C: *Politics for Young Americans*	$0 75
MACY, JESSE. *Our Government*	1 00
JOHNSTON, ALEX. *History of American Politics*	80
STERNE, SIMON. *Constitutional History of the United States*	1 25
BOWKER, R: R. *Economics for the People*	75
	$4 55

The 5 vols., $4.00.

INTERMEDIATE OR CITIZENS' SERIES.

COSSA, L. *Taxation*, annotated by Horace White	$1 00
JEVONS, W: S. *Money and the Mechanism of Exchange*	1 75
LAUGHLIN, J. L. *Bimetallism*	2 25
WALKER, F. A. *Political Economy*, briefer course	1 20
WELLS, D: A. *Recent Economic Changes*	2 00
	$8 20

The 5 vols., $7.50.

ADVANCED OR STUDENTS' SERIES.

BRYCE, JAMES. *American Commonwealth*	$6 00
Constitutional History of the United States, as seen in the development of Law. Lectures by Hon. T: M. COOLEY and others	2 00
GRAHAM, W: *Socialism, New and Old*	1 75
MILL, J: S. *Political Economy*, abridged and annotated by J. L. Laughlin	3 50
WALKER, F. A. *Money*	4 00
	$17 25

The 5 vols., $15.50.

These series are for sale by G: P. PUTNAM'S SONS, 27 West 23d Street, New York, agents for the Society; they will be sent to any address in the United States on receipt of price, and may be ordered through booksellers generally.

The Society for Political Education.

(*ORGANIZED* 1880.)

OBJECTS.—The SOCIETY was organized by citizens who believe that the success of our government depends on the active political influence of educated intelligence, and that parties are means, not ends. The growing tendency of government to enlarge its sphere, and the demands constantly made to increase the power and responsibility of the STATE, make political education more than ever a supreme necessity for the just limitation and right guidance of governmental authority. Entirely non-partisan in its organization, the one aim of the Society is the awakening of an intelligent interest in government methods and purposes, that political morality may be promoted, and the abuses of parties restrained.

Among its organizers are numbered Democrats, Republicans, and Independents, who differ among themselves as to which party is best fitted to conduct the government, but who are in the main agreed as to the following propositions:

The right of each citizen to his free voice and vote must be upheld, and every possible safeguard must be employed to assure independence of vote.

Office-holders must not control the suffrage. The office should seek the man, and not the man the office.

Public service, in business positions, should depend solely on fitness and good behavior.

The crimes of bribery and corruption must be relentlessly punished.

Local issues should be independent of national parties.

Coins made unlimited legal-tender must possess their face value as metal in the markets of the world.

Sound currency must have a metal basis, and all paper money must be convertible on demand.

Labor has a right to the highest wages it can earn, unhindered by public or private tyranny.

Trade has a right to the freest scope, unfettered by taxes, except for government expenses.

Corporations must be restricted from abuse of privilege.

Neither the public money nor the people's land must be used to subsidize private enterprise.

A public opinion, wholesome and active, unhampered by machine control, is the true safeguard of popular institutions.

All members of the Society are not, however, required to endorse the above.

The Society's Reader's Guide, Economic Tract No. 27, has been prepared with the aid of competent authorities in special branches of economic, social, and political science. It tells which are the most recent and important books, articles, and reports in these fields, and which of them are the best. Brief courses of reading are recommended in the Guide—elementary, intermediate, and advanced. It is suggested that clubs be formed to take up these courses, and if such clubs wish to inform themselves regarding special topics, as the currency, or protection question, they will find helpful notes available for the purpose under the sub-headings of the Guide.

Questions for Debate, No. 28, may be used with advantage in connection with No. 27.

Hereafter the publications of the Society will be issued, not at stated intervals, but as occasion may offer. See full list of publications on third cover page.

The Society for Political Education.

ECONOMIC TRACTS.

1. ATKINSON (E.). What Is a Bank? (Out of print.)
2. POLITICAL ECONOMY AND POLITICAL SCIENCE. A priced and classified bibliography by Sumner, Wells, Foster, Dugdale, and Putnam. (Out of print.) Superseded by No. 27.
3. PRESENT POLITICAL AND ECONOMIC ISSUES, with suggestions of subjects for debate and for essays. 25 cents. (Out of print.) Superseded by No. 28.
4. THE USURY QUESTION, by Calvin, Bentham, Dana, and Wells, with bibliography. 25 cents.
5. COURTOIS (Alphonse). Political Economy in One Lesson. Translated by W. C. Ford. 10 cents. (Out of print.)
6. WHITE (Horace). Money and Its Substitutes. (Out of print.)
7. WHITE (A. D.). Paper-Money Inflation in France: a History and Its Application. 25 cents.
8. WHITRIDGE (Frederick W.). The Caucus System. 10 cents.
9. CANFIELD (James H.). Taxation. 15 cents.
10. BOWKER (R. R.). Of Work and Wealth: a Summary of Economics. 25 cents.
11. GREEN (George Walton). Repudiation. 20 cents.
12. SHEPARD (E. M.). The Work of a Social Teacher; Memorial of Richard L. Dugdale. 10 cts.
13. FORD (W. C.). The Standard Silver Dollar and the Coinage Law of 1878. 20 cents.
14. SHEPARD (Edwd. M.). The Competitive Test and the Civil Service of States and Cities. 25 cents.
15. RICHARDSON (H. W.). The Standard Dollar. 25 cents.
16. GIFFEN (Robert). The Progress of the Working Classes in the Last Half Century. 25 cents.
17. FOSTER (W. E.). References to the History of Presidential Administrations—1789-1885. 25 cents.
18. HALL (C. H.). Patriotism and National Defence. 15 cents.
19. ATKINSON (E.). The Railway, the Farmer, and the Public. 15 cents.
20. WEEKS (Jos. D.). Labor Differences and Their Settlement. 25 cents.
21. BOWKER (R. R.). Primer for Political Education. 15 cents.
22. BOWKER (R. R.). Civil Service Examinations. 15 cents.
23. BAYLES (J. C.). The Shop Council. 15 cents.
24. WILLIAMS (Talcott). Labor a Hundred Years Ago. 15 cents.
25. Electoral Reform, with the Massachusetts Ballot Reform Act, and New York (Saxton) Bill. 15 cents.
26. ILES (George). The Liquor Question in Politics. 15 cents.
27. BOWKER (R. R.) and ILES (George), editors. Reader's Guide to Economic, Social, and Political Science. A classified bibliography, American, English, French, and German, with descriptive notes, author, title, and subject index, courses of reading, college courses, etc. 170 pp. Paper, 50 cents; cloth, $1.
28. QUESTIONS FOR DEBATE IN POLITICS AND ECONOMICS, with a form of Constitution and By-laws for Debating Clubs. 25 cents.
29. FOSTER (W. E.). References on the Constitution of the United States: Its Sources, Commentaries, and Interpretations. With Decisions of the U. S. Supreme Court on questions of National or State supremacy since 1865. 25 cents.
30. SMITH (Eugene). Prison Science, with Special Reference to Recent New York Legislation. 10 cents.
31. FOULKES W. D.). Civil Service Reform, Its Later Aspects. 10 cents.

G. P. PUTNAM'S SONS, Publishing Agents,

27 WEST 23D STREET, NEW YORK.

www.ingramcontent.com/pod-product-compliance
Lightning Source LLC
Chambersburg PA
CBHW020259170426
43202CB00008B/442